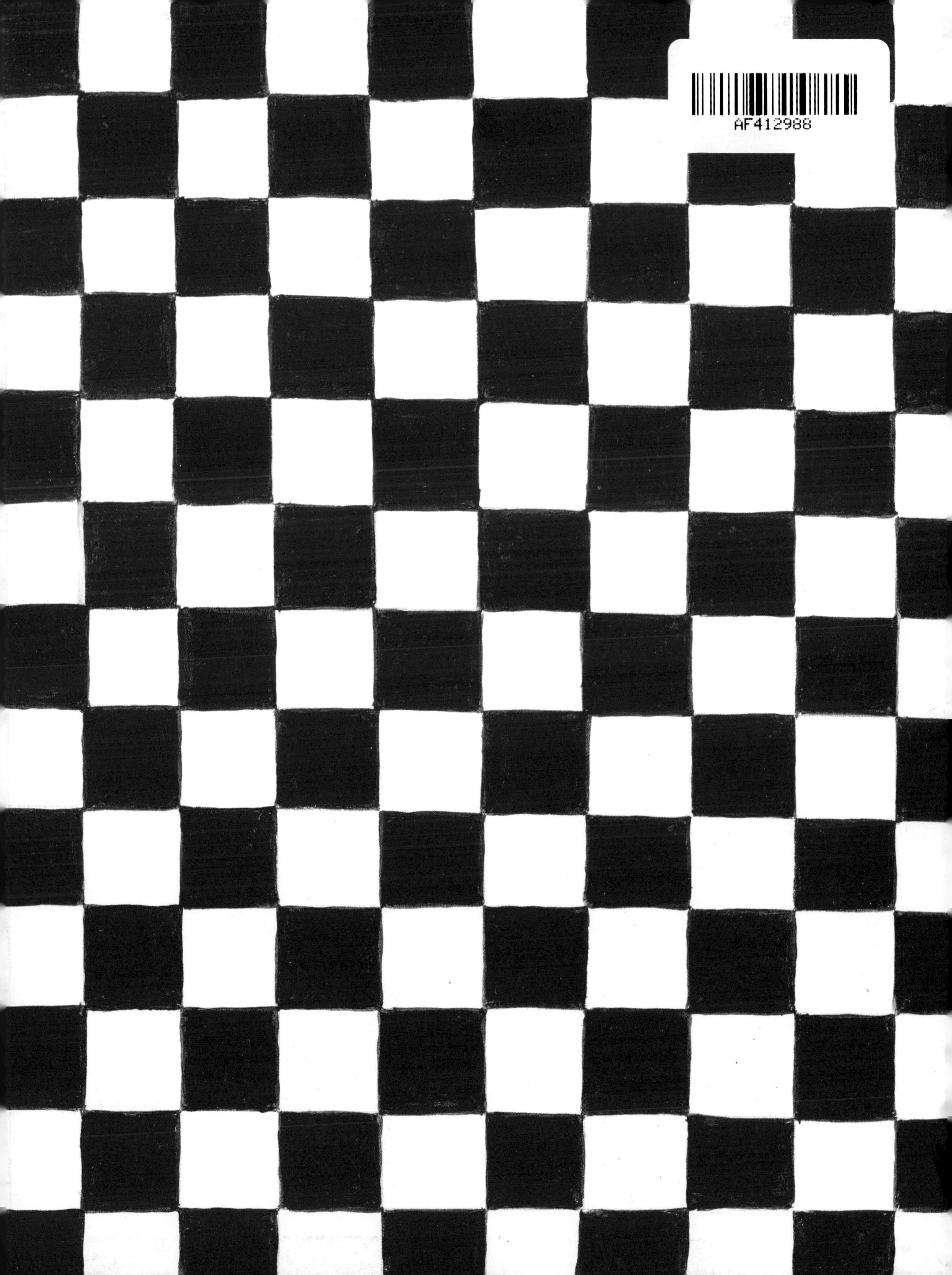

AF412988

Dora Holzhandler

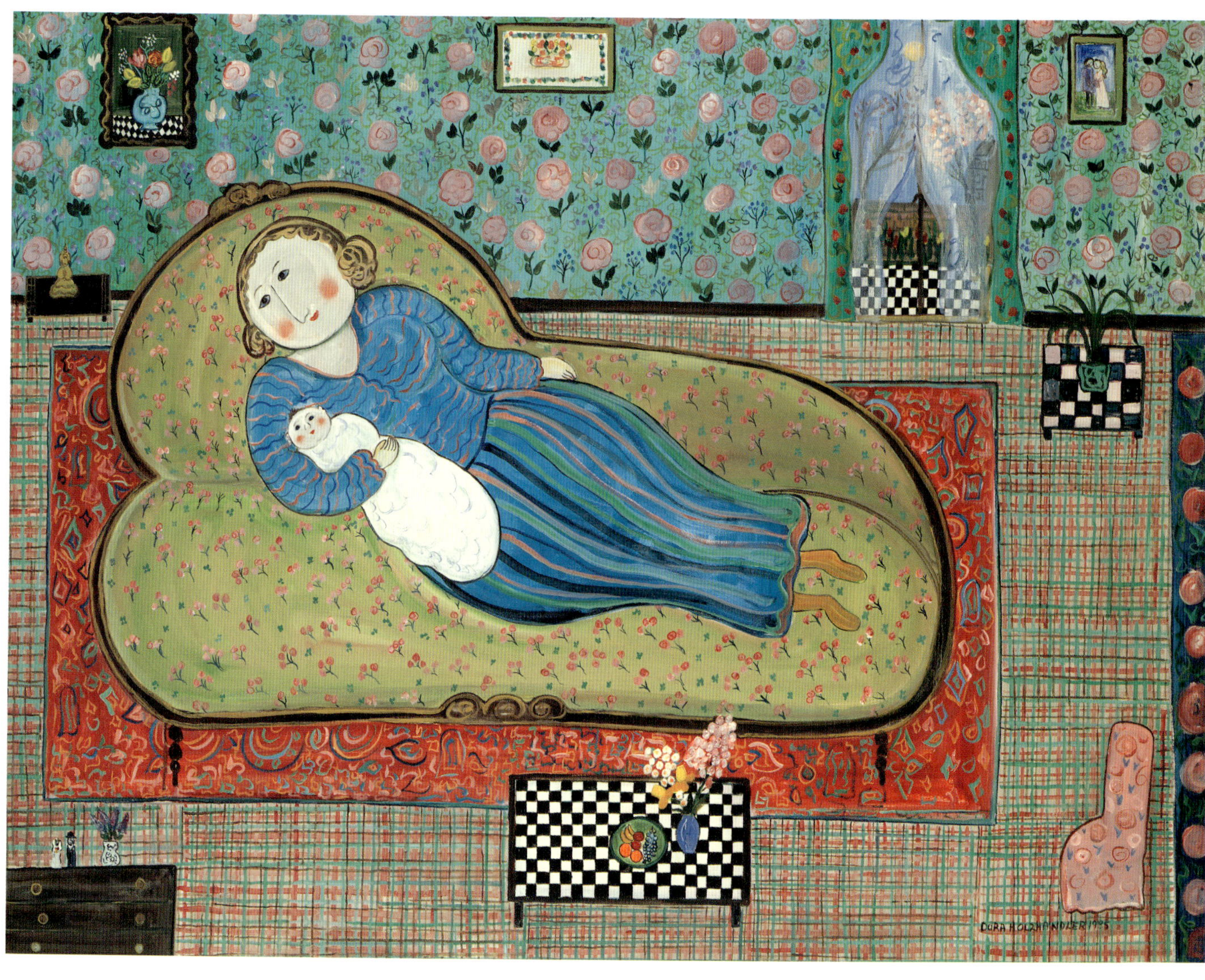

Chapter 2

Plate 1
Hepzibah's New Baby   1985   Oil on canvas   89 x 114.3 cm (35 x 45 in)

You Walk in the Park

Sooner or later let go what you loved, hated or
shrugged off, you walk in the park
You look at the sky, sit on a pillow, count up the stars
in your head, get up and eat.
ALLEN GINSBERG[6]

Parks and gardens are settings for many of Dora's paintings. Traditionally in art and literature, the garden paradise symbolises a pre-lapsarian state of blessedly unconditioned human consciousness. When Dora's three daughters – Amalie (born in 1951), Hepzibah (born in 1956) and Hermione (born in 1966) – were small children, a pattern developed around them. In the afternoons, after listening to children's radio programmes, Dora would let them sleep or rest – this valuable interlude could then be devoted to her painting. Afterwards she would take them to the park; whilst they were playing, she would be able to sit quietly and read from books on Buddhism, especially the Sutras or sacred texts. 'In that way I was truly happy at that time. There was never any conflict in my mind that I should paint more, or indeed that there should be any anxiety about my art.' Motherhood deepened and enriched Dora's vision (though since her children have grown up and left home she has been able to paint a good deal more – her attention undivided). She has described how after Hepzibah's birth she spent the night alone with her new baby, awake in a state of marvellous lucidity, 'very much aware of the truth of the Buddha's teaching'. From heartfelt experiences such as this comes her feeling 'that a mother's love is so near to enlightenment – if this pure love could be spread to the whole world of sentient beings'. The mystery of this pure love passing through the generations is shown in a picture painted almost twenty years later in 1985, *Hepzibah's New Baby* (Plate 1), marking the birth of Dora's grandson William.

In the mid-1950s, the period of early motherhood when she and George discovered Buddhism, 'painting was a background to our life and our life was a background to my painting'. In her many paintings since then of mothers and children in parks and gardens (such as *The Secret of the Golden Flower*, a symbolic picture of a mother holding a sunflower in one hand and her little girl's hand in the other) is found the simultaneous flowering of her own insights as a young mother and as a student of mystical philosophy, especially Buddhism and, as we shall see, Jewish Kabbalah. Though her essential style and subject matter have not altered radically since this time, it has been over the last twenty or so years in particular that she has truly found her own voice – one of an increasingly classical assurance.

In *Children Playing in Sand in Holland Park* (Plate 2), a young mother cradles her baby and watches over children at play. Comparatively tiny in perspective are another mother and baby who are much nearer to us in space. Without a trace of academic realism, every detail (wheel-eyed push-chair, wooden benches rendered in all their municipal graininess, bouncing ball like a suspended globe, paintbrush-swirled-up sand and buckets, russet and flaming trees and irridescent pointillism of leaf-speckled grass) has the unmistakable mark, pitch and instress of reality; it is as though the artist has identified herself utterly with each in turn. What suffuses the whole picture and all its details is the unobstructed loving-kindness of the mother, clothed in Op Art black-and-white checks, in seated contemplation of the world – in this case, children at play within the sandpit's golden orb.

As a visionary who almost never makes preliminary studies for a picture nor draws or paints directly from life or the outdoors, Dora is able to reconstitute in the inscape of her imagination all the poetic constituents of nature and the world around her with a tremendous fidelity and clarity. Each picture remembers the world anew, adhering with non-literal preciseness to the form of forms and also to the atmosphere of atmospheres in terms of climate, weather, season, time of day or night and, above all, light (her treatment of the latter dissolving all barriers between the naturalistic and the numinous). Herein lies the paradoxical mix of creative artifice (arising from a view of the world as a playground or immaculately wrought theatrical setting) and heightened realism that distinguishes her work.

The critic Eric Newton, who reviewed for *The*

The woman is the composition's pivotal figure, one of heightened spiritual and maternal stature. (As such, she has much in common with earth goddesses of ancient religions: the Buddhist Goddess of Compassion Tara; the Queen of Heaven of the Old Testament; the New Testament Madonna; and Kerouac's Lady, as in his lines: 'The universe is a lady / Holding within her the unborn light – Our Lady, Nostre Dame.'⁹) So pre-eminent in scale and focus, such a figure – recurring in different guises throughout Dora's work – surely evokes the artist's own persona. Yet she never looms large at the expense of other characters; indeed, all the men, women and children Dora paints are aspects of innermost self – ageless and beyond sex and duality.

The subject of *Mother and Child in Park* is the interdependence of love and knowledge. The mother's unqualified love for her children is emblematically focussed in the bunch of flowers she holds near her heart; the father's prayerful wisdom is manifested in his sitting in a quiet garden retreat, crowned by a rose arbour. The parents' predominant qualities are not mutually exclusive; rather, they are inseparably wedded. Nor is landscape or nature subsidiary to human values. Each and every particular – blossoming trees, flowers, blossoming motifs on the woman's clothes, repeated checkered patterns on the path, the Jewish eight-branched candelabrum (the *Menorah*) seen through a window, the peacock, even the pram's front wheels (curiously resembling a transfixing pair of eyes) – is a visionary affirmation of the picture's symbolic message.

Dora is aware of the supreme importance in art of what she calls 'symbol consciousness': 'Symbols, like colours, communicate on a cosmic level: a flower, a star, universes and, in the last analysis, the world of microcosms and molecular levels of consciousness. The *Menorah*, for instance, is a Jewish symbol. If you paint a *Menorah*, that's the whole of Judaism. There's also the message of the father and mother and children, the human message. Everything in a picture is very meaningful to me. Subjects are starting points, but what matters is the actual painting itself and the note that it hits.'

Traditional Indian and Persian miniature paintings typically portray lovers, contemplatives, family groups and friends embowered in stately pleasure gardens, enjoying the full fruits and flowers of a felicitous climate. The title of one sixteenth-century Indian miniature,

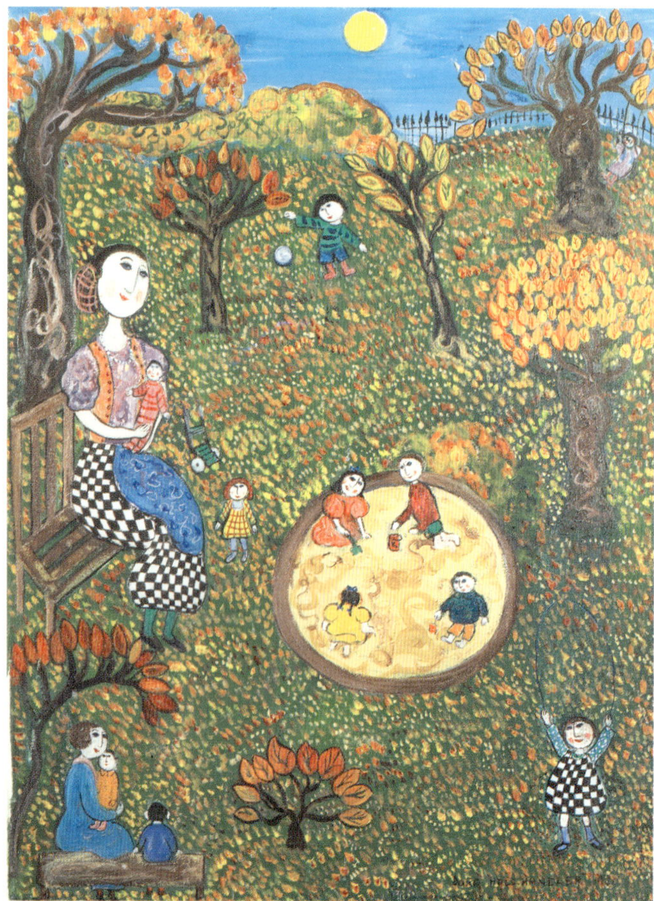

Plate 2
Children Playing in Sand in Holland Park   1982
Oil on canvas   76.2 x 66 cm (30 x 26 in)

Guardian and *The Times* and keenly supported Dora during the 1960s, wrote: '… her method of painting is that of the pattern-maker, oriental in origin, colourful as a Persian illumination, always brilliant but never harsh. These are pictures invented by a mother but painted by a child – a sophisticated but immensely amiable child.'⁷ The novelist Edna O'Brien has written in similar vein: 'Dora is that rare thing – a mother and child in one, as an artist she captures the apparent simplicity of life and infuses it with a depth I find eerie.'⁸ These qualities as pattern-maker and sophisticated-ingenuous spirit are seen to the full in *Mother and Child in Park* (Plate 3). A female figure of giant (but, in the picture's context, entirely natural-seeming) proportions stands on a path of tessellated design, hand-in-hand with her small daughter; a baby son perches next to them in a pram. On a background bench sit a man wearing the Jewish *tallith* (prayer shawl) and carrying a book, and a little boy, also dressed in rabbinical black.

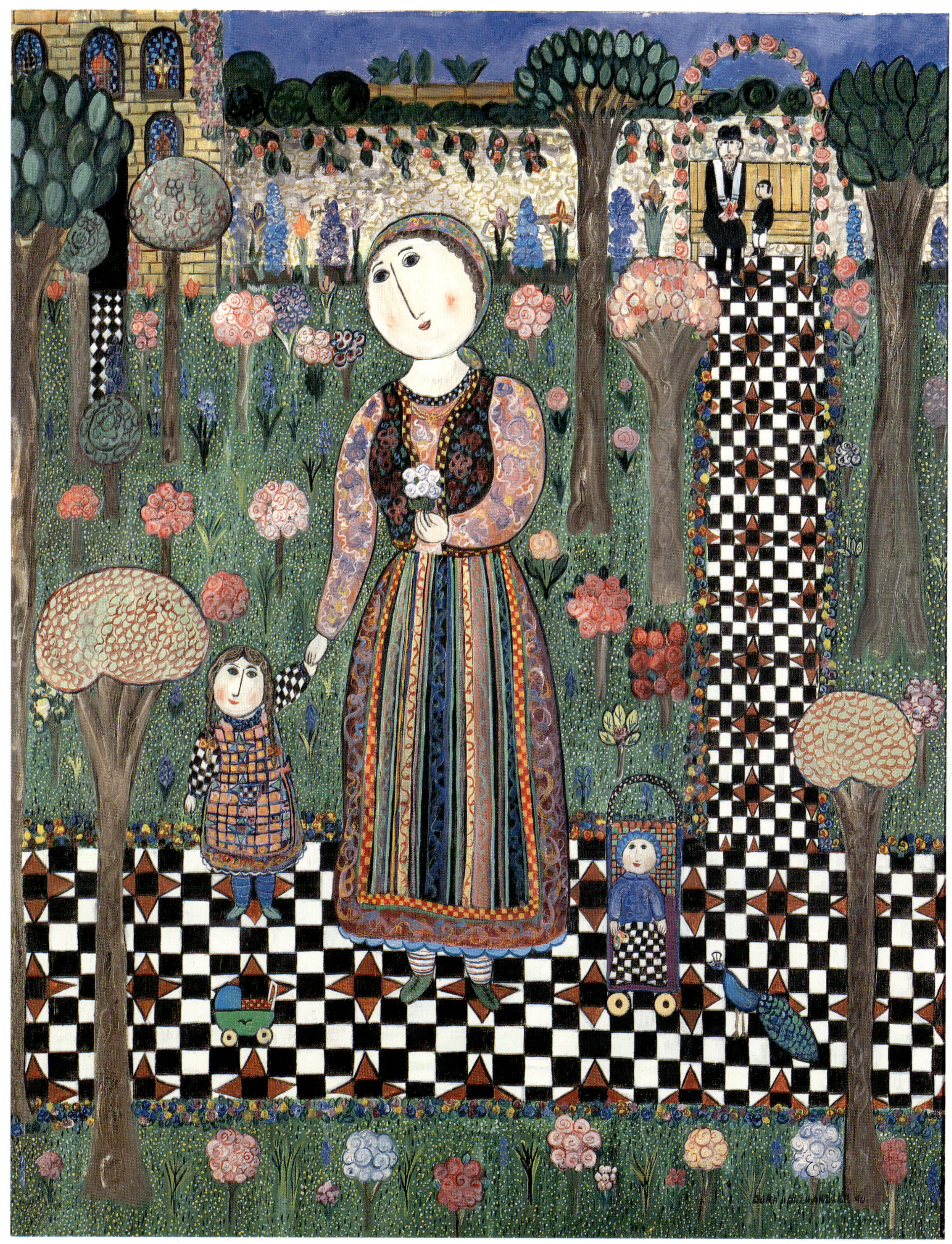

Plate 3
Mother and Child in Park   1990   Oil on canvas   94 x 76.2 cm (37 x 30 in)

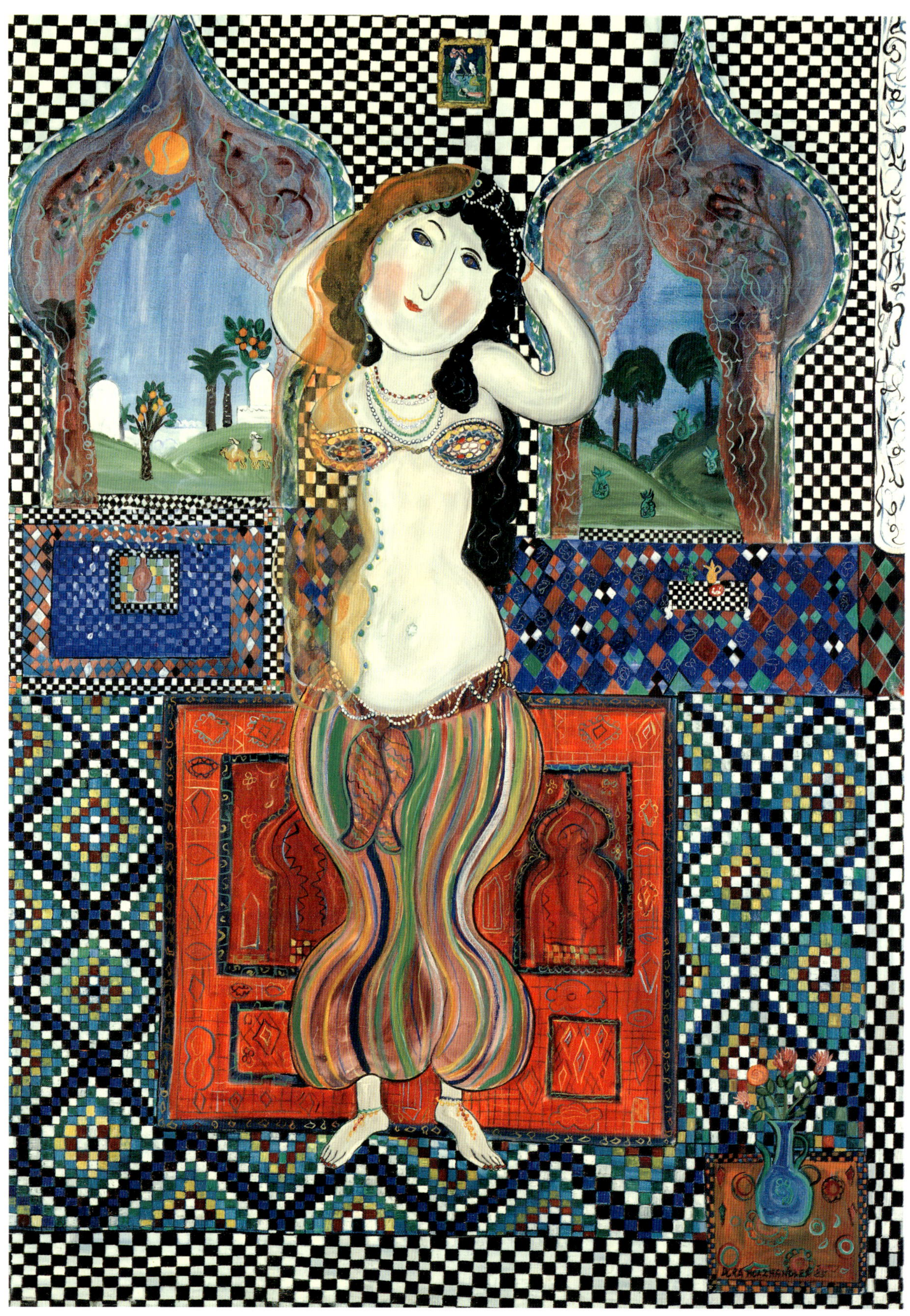

Plate 4
La Danseuse Tunisienne   1985   Oil on canvas
121.9 x 86.4 cm (48 x 34 in)

14 DORA HOLZHANDLER

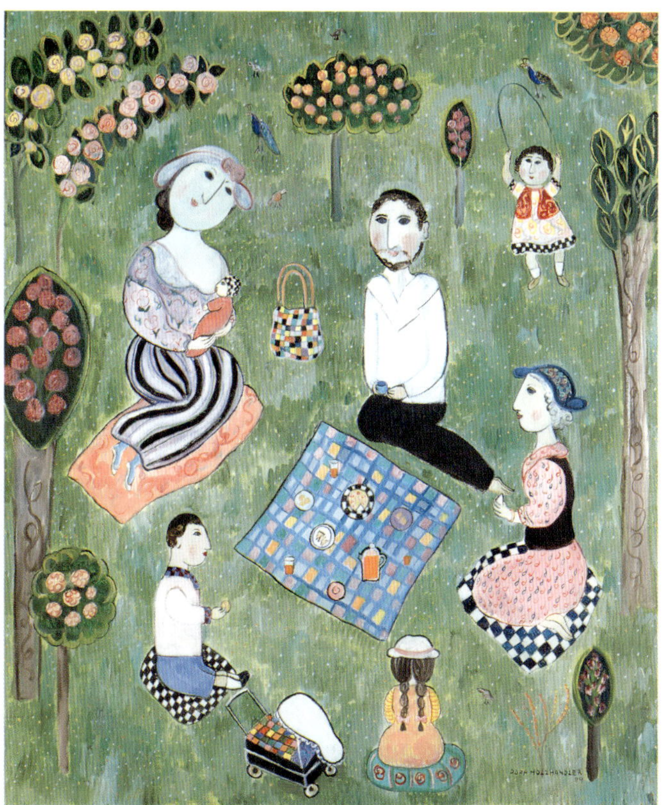

Plate 5
Picnic 1989
Oil on canvas
71 x 61 cm (28 x 24 in)

A Tree Blossoms at the Touch of a Beautiful Woman, sums up the miraculous harmony envisaged in such works. Dora has always enjoyed looking at these pictures, whose origins are both Hindu and Sufi; in the background of her painting *La Danseuse Tunisienne* (Plate 4), made following a North African holiday, is an Eastern miniature picture, demonstrating Dora's innate gifts as an Oriental-like pattern-maker flowing back, as it were, to their source. Her pictures of outdoor meals or '*déjeuners sur l'herbe*' and other *alfresco* tableaux possess a decorative luxuriance and ordered refinement reminiscent both of Near Eastern and French painting (perhaps here is a dual reflection of her roots as a Parisian-born Jew). In her painting *Picnic* (Plate 5), there is, characteristically, no use of recessive perspective: trees, grass, people, picnic-rug, food and drink are all set out with an undifferentiated, shadowless frontality. Aldous Huxley has written: 'In nature, as in a work of art, the isolation of an object tends to invest it with absoluteness, to endow it with that more-than-symbolic meaning which is identical with being.'[10]

Crisply delineated, placed flat and unforeshortened against the variegated grass backdrop, each figure and detail in *Picnic* is seen as firmly rooted in its milieu yet also somehow flowing in serene detachment above. This paradoxical mix of firm-rootedness and fluidity, of concentrated stillness and wave-like motion, gives Dora's work a visionary quality. The world is evoked here in all its 'isness'. The dazzlingly checkered picnic bag, the suckling baby, the man's rosy cheeks, the little girl's extended skipping rope describing an arc of perfect happiness, sandwiches on a plate: all are painted with a detached eye combining elements both of illusionism and discontinuous abstraction (rather as Byzantine painting may be seen to unite Graeco-Roman and Oriental viewpoints). Dora heightens each isolated facet of subject matter almost to the point of abstraction, at the same time accentuating and enhancing, at every level, a sense of shared humanity and universal being.

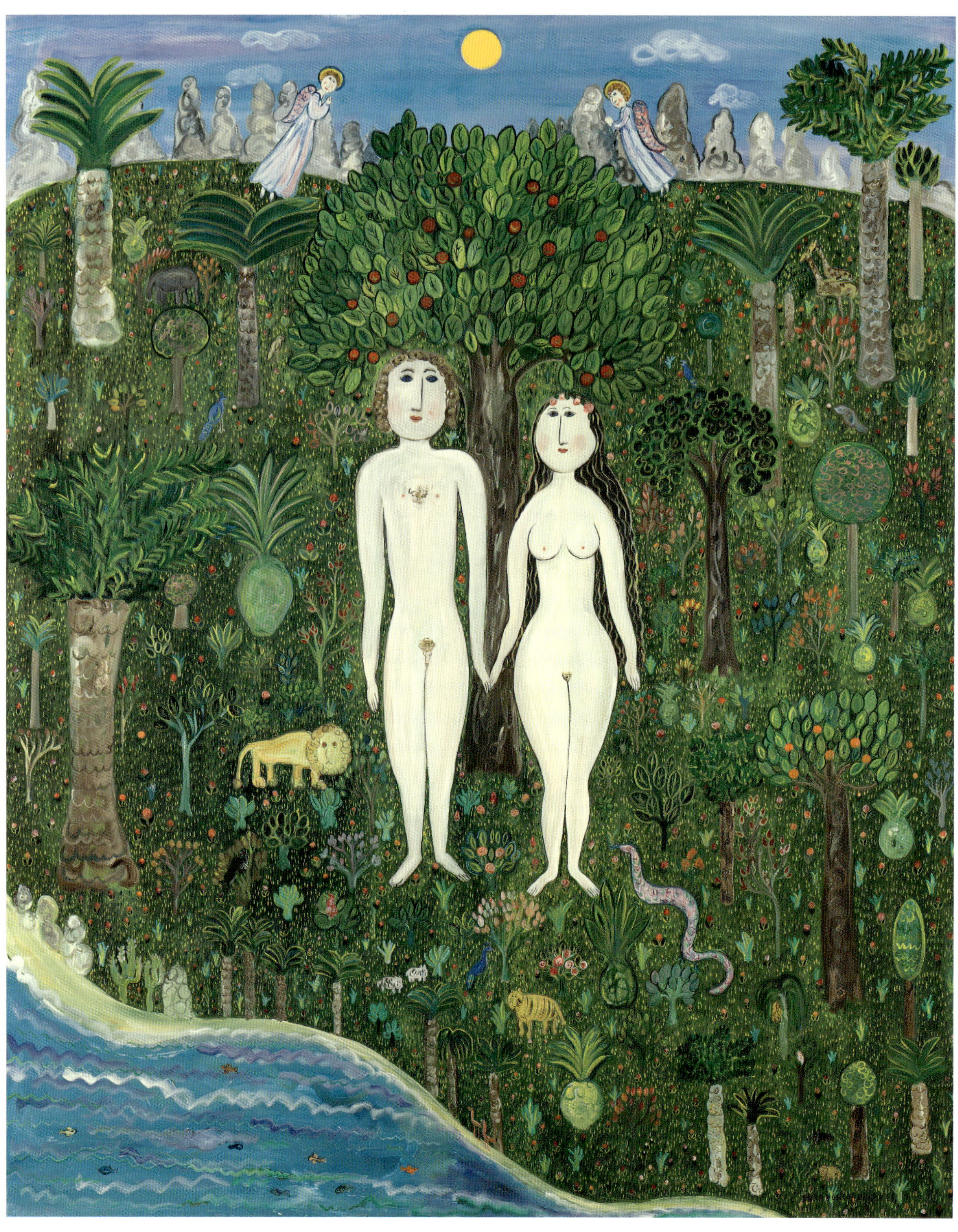

Plate 6
Adam and Eve in the Garden of Eden 1985 Oil on canvas 152.4 x 121.9 cm (60 x 48 in)

The Secret Desire

… the secret desire of our heart is for the lost paradise.
CECIL COLLINS[11]

Dora's subject is original human relationships, whose setting is often the garden. Lovers are central – their unitary state has for her a supreme mystical and human meaning. Several times she has depicted Adam and Eve in the Garden of Eden, standing in naked unself-consciousness before the Trees of Life and of Good and Evil. In the top right hand corner of one such picture is a mini-tableau of The Fall – the grievous going of Adam and Eve from Paradise and 'the cherubim and a sword whirling and flashing to guard the way to the tree of life'.[12]

In the Jewish Talmud, the ancient collection of biblical and legal commentaries, speculative mystics are called 'Those who entered *Pardes* [Paradise or the Garden]'. In the perennial teachings of Jewish mysticism, the Kabbalah (or 'Tradition'), which, in Europe, can be traced back to sources from the ninth century AD (though its origins are in the Old Testament), *Gan Eden* (Garden of Eden) is described as the beginning and end of Creation. According to Kabbalah, it is because of Adam and Eve's striving towards independent ego-existence that a split has happened between the *En Sof* (the Divine Nothingness, or God without End) and the *Shechinah* (the Indwelling Spirit, or God made manifest or immanent in this world). Only when the individual commits him or herself to a whole or holy life can the *En Sof* (known in terms of the male principle) be reunited with His Bride, the *Shechinah* (the female principle), and Creation redeemed in a kind of mystical marriage.

Dora has been much inspired by reading extracts in translation from the Zohar, which is known as 'the text-book of Jewish mystics'. These supreme Kabbalistic writings, which appeared around 1300 (partly in Hebrew, partly in Aramaic), were compiled from a variety of sources by Moses de León of Granada, who died in 1305. The Zohar takes the form of an interpretation of the Torah, or Old Testament Books of the Law. It is a profoundly beautiful and accessible meditation on the mysteries of God and the universe, and the destiny of mankind.

In the biblical Song of Songs, humanity's longing for God is expressed allegorically in terms of the romantic and sexual yearnings of the bride and bridegroom. The latter says of his beloved: 'My sister, my bride, is a garden close-locked, / a garden close-locked, a fountain sealed.'[13] A poem in the Zohar, alluding to the above, describes how the Lord, sitting on the Judgement Throne, 'utters the Name – / The holy, the blessed / Source of mercy for men / And life-giving to all'. A verse follows which speaks of the reconciliation of *En Sof* and *Shechinah*:

> The secret Garden
> In worlds of light hidden
> …
> Where *Shechinah*'s splendour
> From splendour proceeding
> Its splendour sends forth
> To the ends of creation,
> In the fulness of glory
> Is revealed in its beauty
> To the eyes made seeing –
> The Garden of Eden.[14]

The walled garden, the secret garden, is a preferred spot for Dora's pairs of lovers. The radiant splendour of *Lovers in a Rose Garden* (Plate 7) emanates from the multi-coloured roses trailing down the wall, roses 'embroidering' both grass and coverlet, and in resounding patterns of squares on pillows, pyjamas and rug. It is even there in the lovers' rosy cheeks! At the still point of this turning world, so resplendently fertile and gay in design and colour, the lovers are seen to unite in ultimate stillness and flowing peace. (The symbol of the rose is perennial in art and literature: in the rose windows of medieval cathedrals; the 'rosarium', or rose garden, in the *cultus* of Our Lady; roseate bowers of bliss in the Shiraz School of Persian painting; W.B. Yeats's 'Rose of all Roses, Rose of all the World!'[15]; and Gertrude Stein's unarguable affirmation of 'isness': 'Rose is a rose is a rose is a rose'.[16] In Western and Middle Eastern tradition, the rose has a comparable

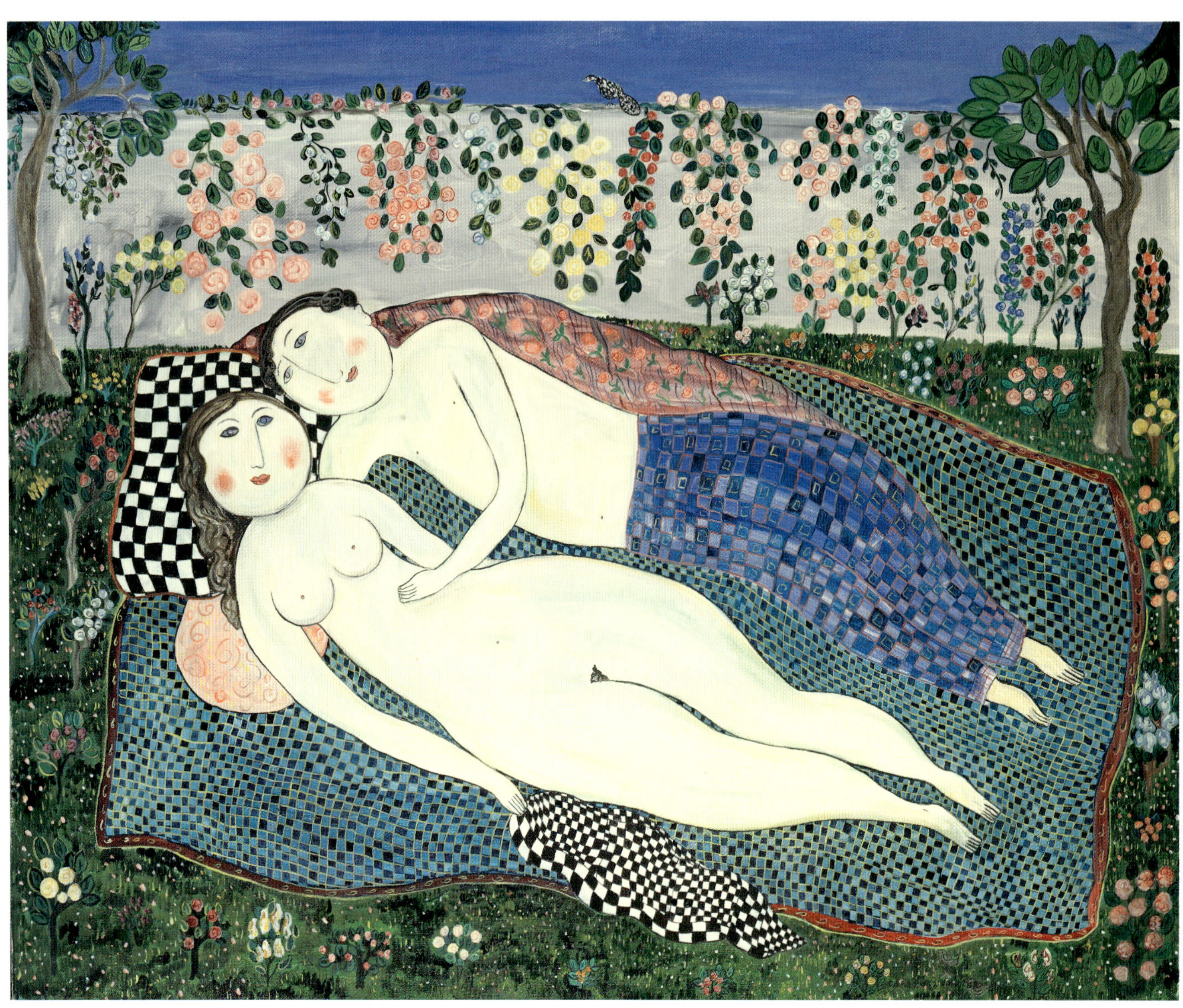

Plate 7
Lovers in a Rose Garden   1985   Oil on canvas   101.6 x 121.9 cm (40 x 48 in)

Plate 8
Succot Meal   1993   Oil on canvas   71 x 55.9 cm (28 x 22 in)

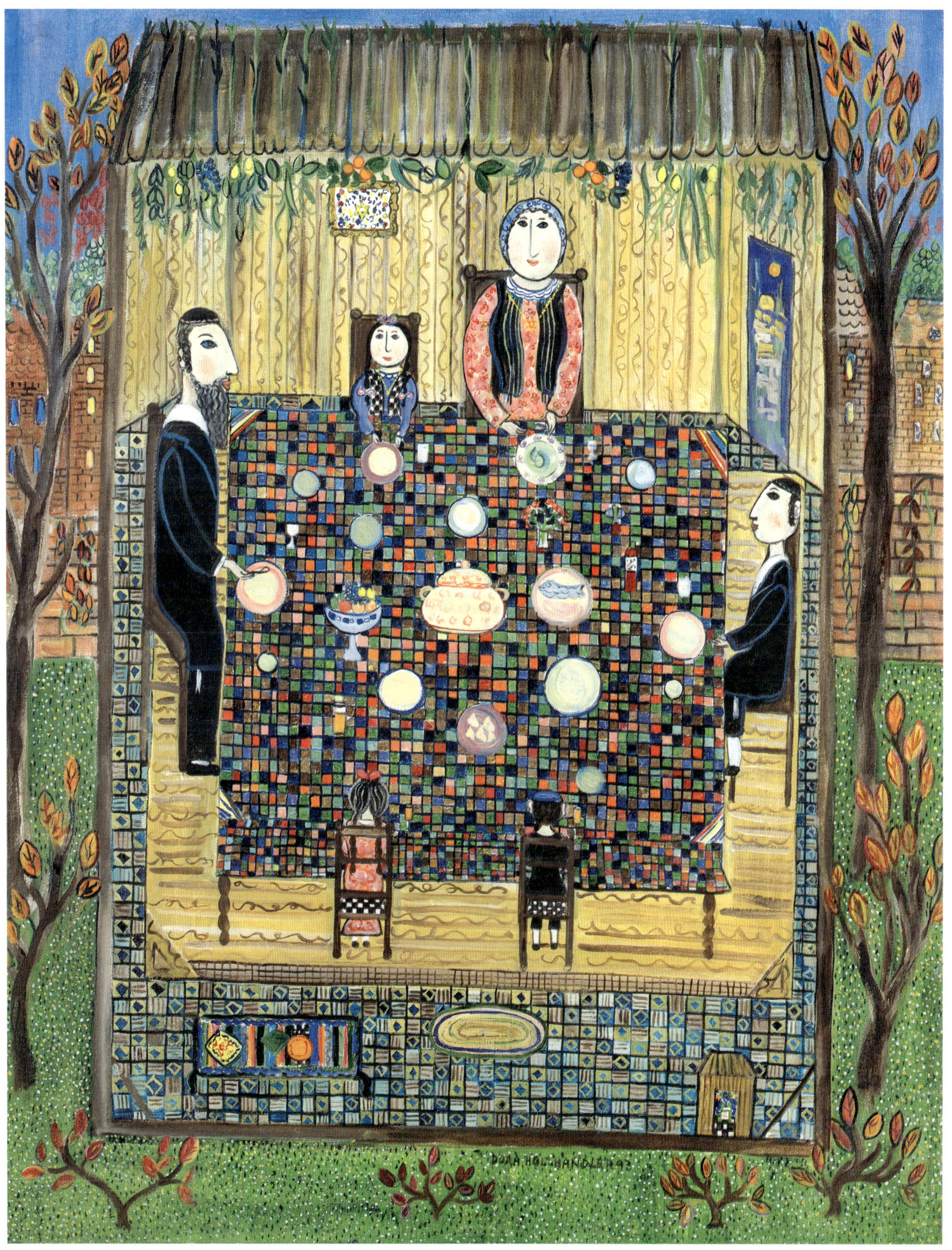

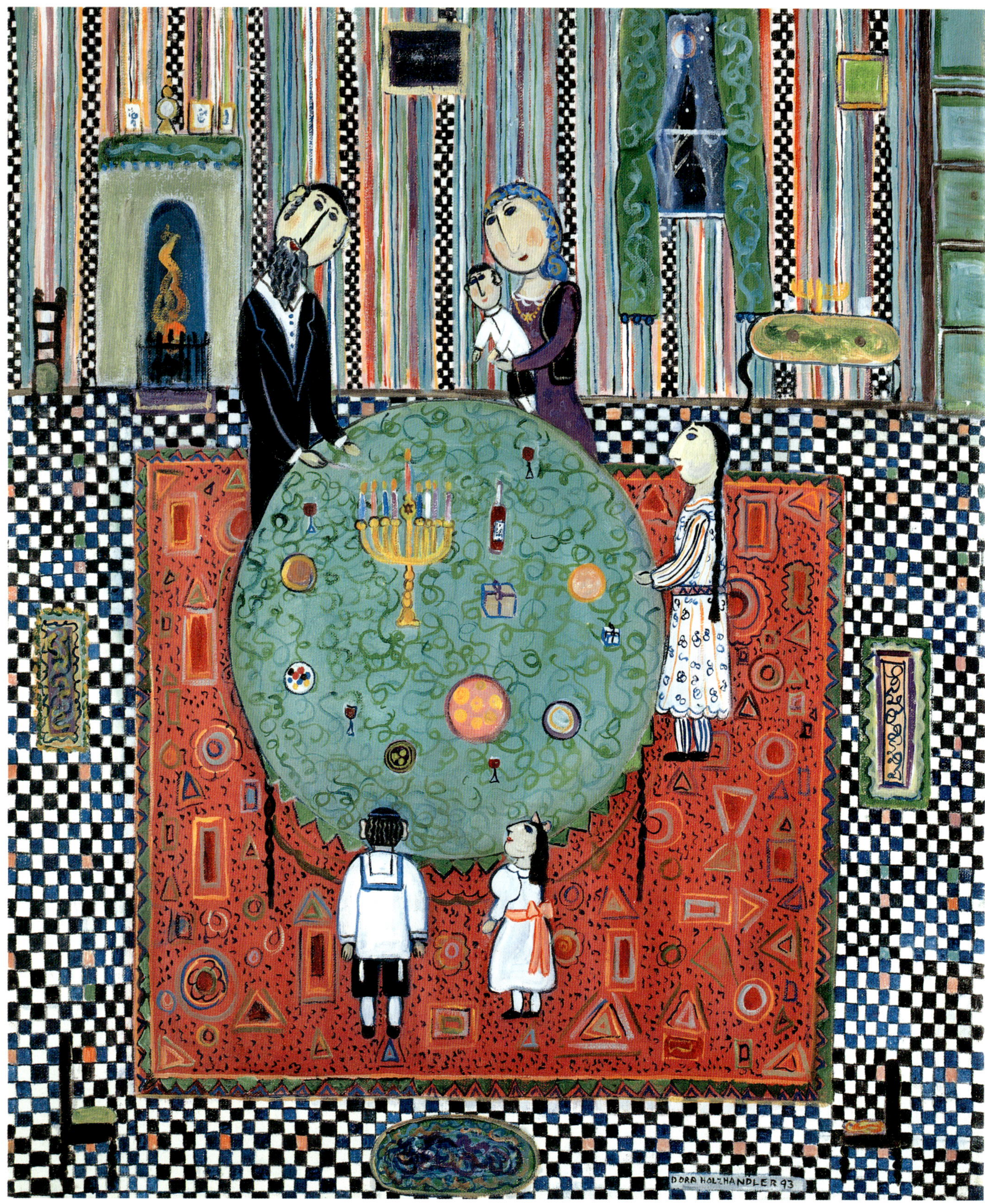

Plate 9
Chanukah   1993   Oil on canvas   61 x 50.8 cm (24 x 20 in)

status to that of the Far Eastern lotus.)

For Dora, *Gan Eden* is not restricted to any particular locality; rather, it is a state of spiritual enlightenment which strips away all distinctions between inner and outer worlds, subject and object, teacher and taught, lover and beloved, in a full realisation of the Void or lucid emptiness of reality. The perfume of Eden permeates not only Dora's garden settings but everything she depicts; its original essence fills her interiors too, not least through the arrangements of flowers and floribundant motifs that proliferate with such decorative exuberance on furnishings and clothing. Indoor scenes often contain a glimpse of paradise beyond – a garden and 'beautifully nuanced skies'[17] often partially revealed through a transparent curtain, the latter's painterly rendering invariably a miracle of pellucidity. A perfect symbol of the paradise that is ultimately neither 'in here' nor 'out there' is the *Succah*, the temporary hut made of twigs and branches, decorated with fruit, flowers and leaves, where the Orthodox Jewish family takes its meals for a week at Succot, the Festival of Tabernacles, commemorating the ancient, desert wanderings of Moses. In her painting of this subject (Plate 8), the circular table platters – appearing like full moons or suns against the night sky's psychedelic grid – are as intrinsic a part of Nature's design as the golden leaves and grass seen beyond the ephemeral room.

In Kabbalah, the Tree of Life (planted in Eden, according to Genesis) is the primordial model whose branches are organised into a sacred pattern, giving expression to the ten divine attributes or emanations known as *Sefirot* – these include *Chesed* (Mercy), *Hokhmah* (Wisdom), *Tiferet* (Beauty), and *Nezah* (Eternity). In any diagram of this Tree, *Tiferet*, also known as the Heart of Hearts, is always shown at the utmost centre. Each of Dora's paintings has its own symbolic heart or core, discernible both in terms of symbolism and composition. In a painting of Chanukah (the Festival commemorating the rekindling of lights in the Temple in Jerusalem in 165 BCE, following its heathen desecration), 'the family,' she says, 'is gathered round the table to light the last candle of the *Menorah*, an eight-branched golden candelabrum. The children delight in the happiness of Chanukah' (Plate 9). It is evening; the moon, illuminating the falling snow, shines through the window. Near the centre of a round green table-cloth stands the *Menorah*, appearing both as a tree in a meadow and (with no qualitative shift) as the golden Tree of Life in a verdant paradise.

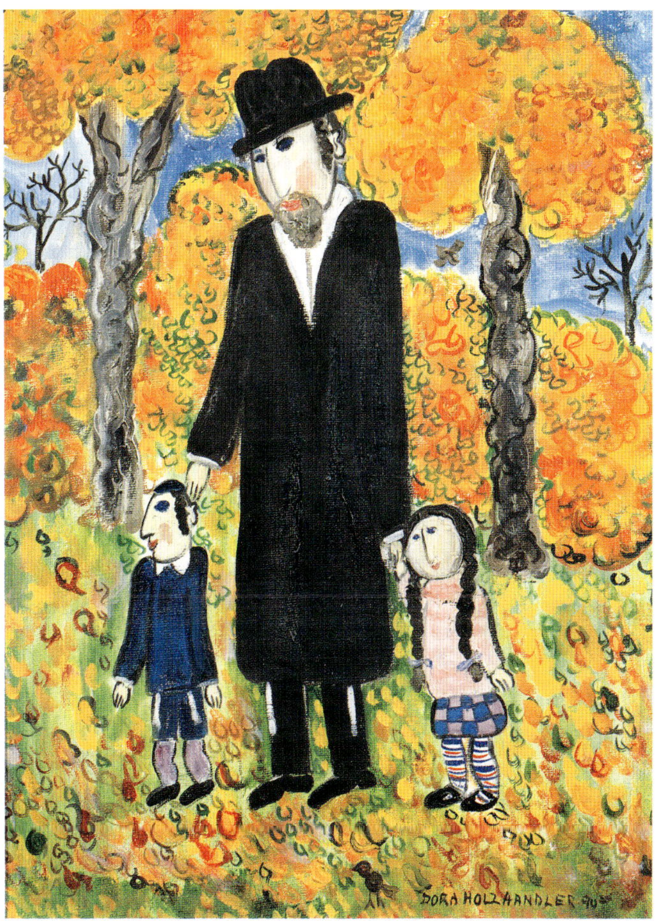

Plate 10
The Park in Autumn   1990   Oil on canvas
40.6 x 30.5 cm (16 x 12 in)

In this instant of blissful illumination, there is a rekindling of innocence and a return to *Gan Eden* within the heart of the home.

Dora's pictures set in gardens and parks take place in all seasons, and portray all the generations. In *The Park in Autumn* (Plate 10), a man is seen out walking with a little boy and a girl. Golden trees and bushes are adorned with little, calligraphic curlicues of orange and green. The grass is strewn with leaves – similar feathery flourishes of varied hues. The scene's burning brilliance is such that it seems almost as if the trees and vegetation are made of gold, some of which has trickled down onto the lawn. Dense, compact, consummately realised right down to the gnarled nub and the sere leaf, Dora's autumnal trees are also irradiated by the lustre of another dimension. Such flaming foliage has much in common with Golden Age descriptions made by mystics in many traditions. The gentle fatherly figure

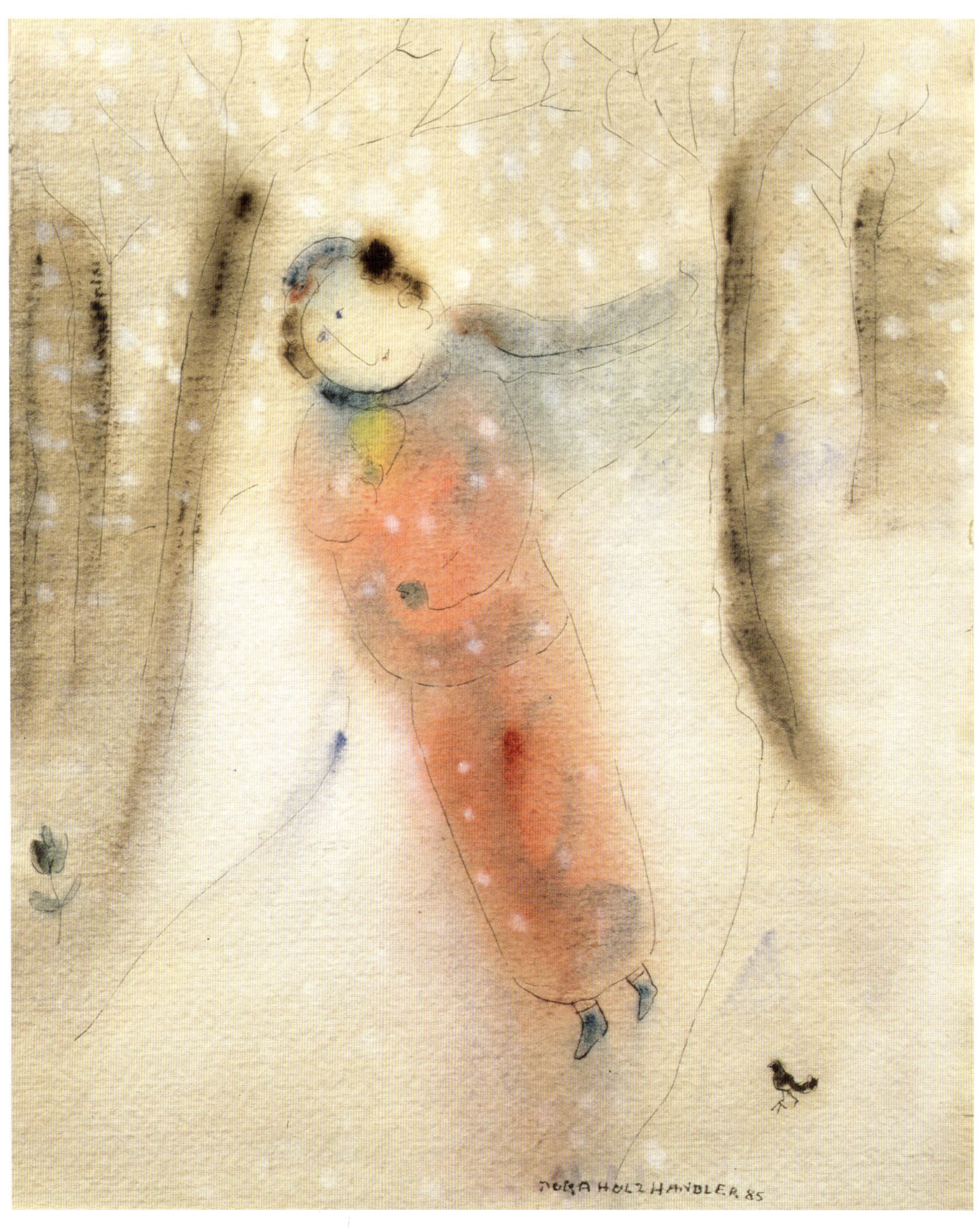

Plate 11
Lady with Mimosa in Snow   1985   Watercolour   35.6 x 30.5 cm (14 x 12 in)

22 DORA HOLZHANDLER

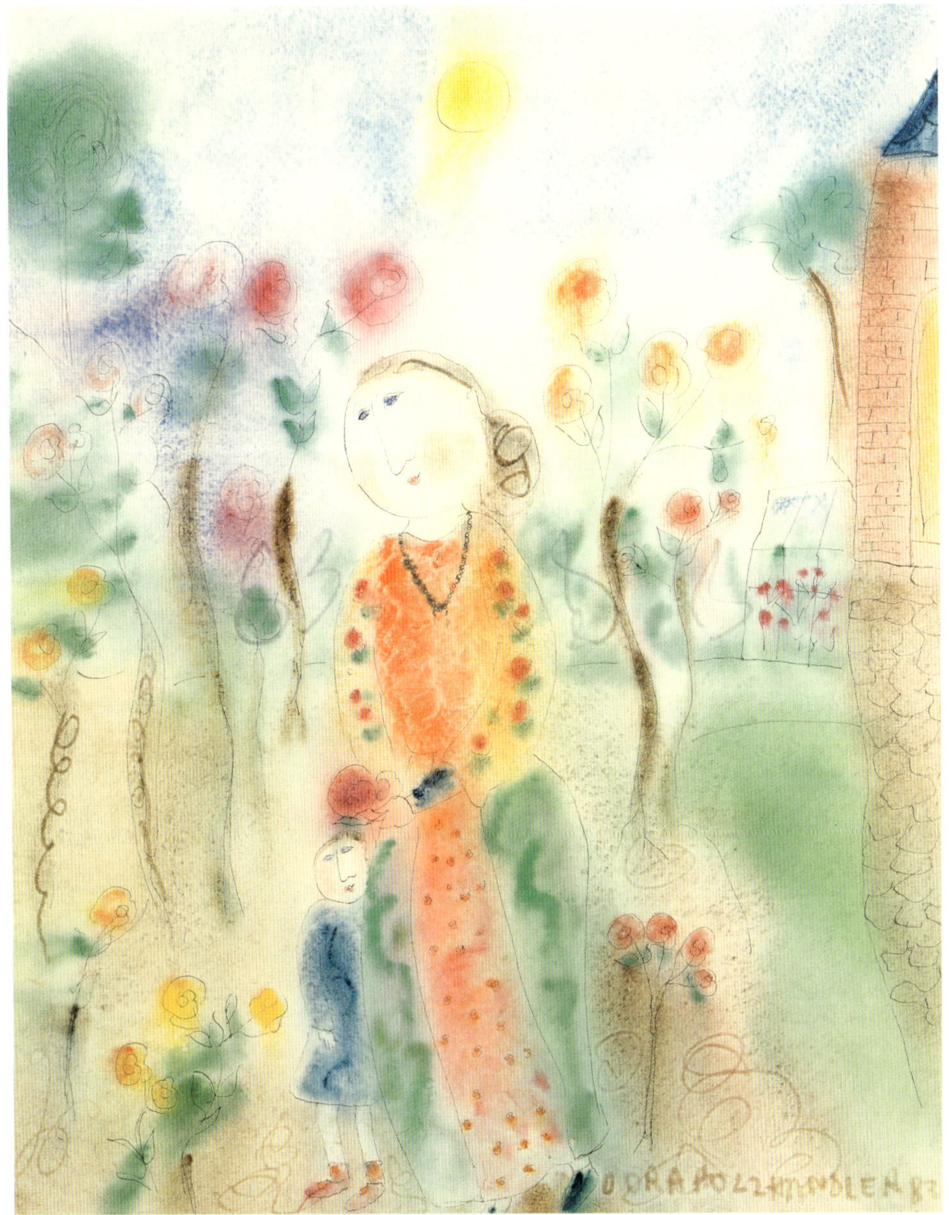

Plate 12
Walk under a Pale Sun
1983   Watercolour on paper
30.5 x 20.3 cm (12 x 8 in)

here, in black and white Chassidic garb, forms a severely monumental presence against the scintillating backdrop.

In bleak midwinter, the trees are bare and the garden covered in snow. Dora is always happy when the first snows fall in Holland Park, and she eagerly rushes to paint a world made anew in 'Arctic Confidence'.[18] Watercolour seems particularly suitable for evoking the drifting, coalescing, transient world of ice and snow. In *Lady with Mimosa in Snow* (Plate 11), the subject, wrapped warmly in red with a blue scarf, is delineated by a fine ink binding line against the cold, stark, monochromatic background. The snowflakes melt on her –

white coalescing with red, yellow and blue. Her head is inclined, partly against the buffeting cold but essentially in a meditative tilt. The yellow mimosa aglow between her heart and throat is a vivifying symbol of the beauty (*Tiferet*) at the picture's core. A solitary female figure, meditating in a garden, is one of Dora's recurrent subjects. The nearest parallel perhaps is the example of Chinese and Japanese women artists and poets who, over many centuries, have made deeply personal and symbolic self-portraits, which show them – in lone delight with the Alone – contemplating their own true nature within Nature.

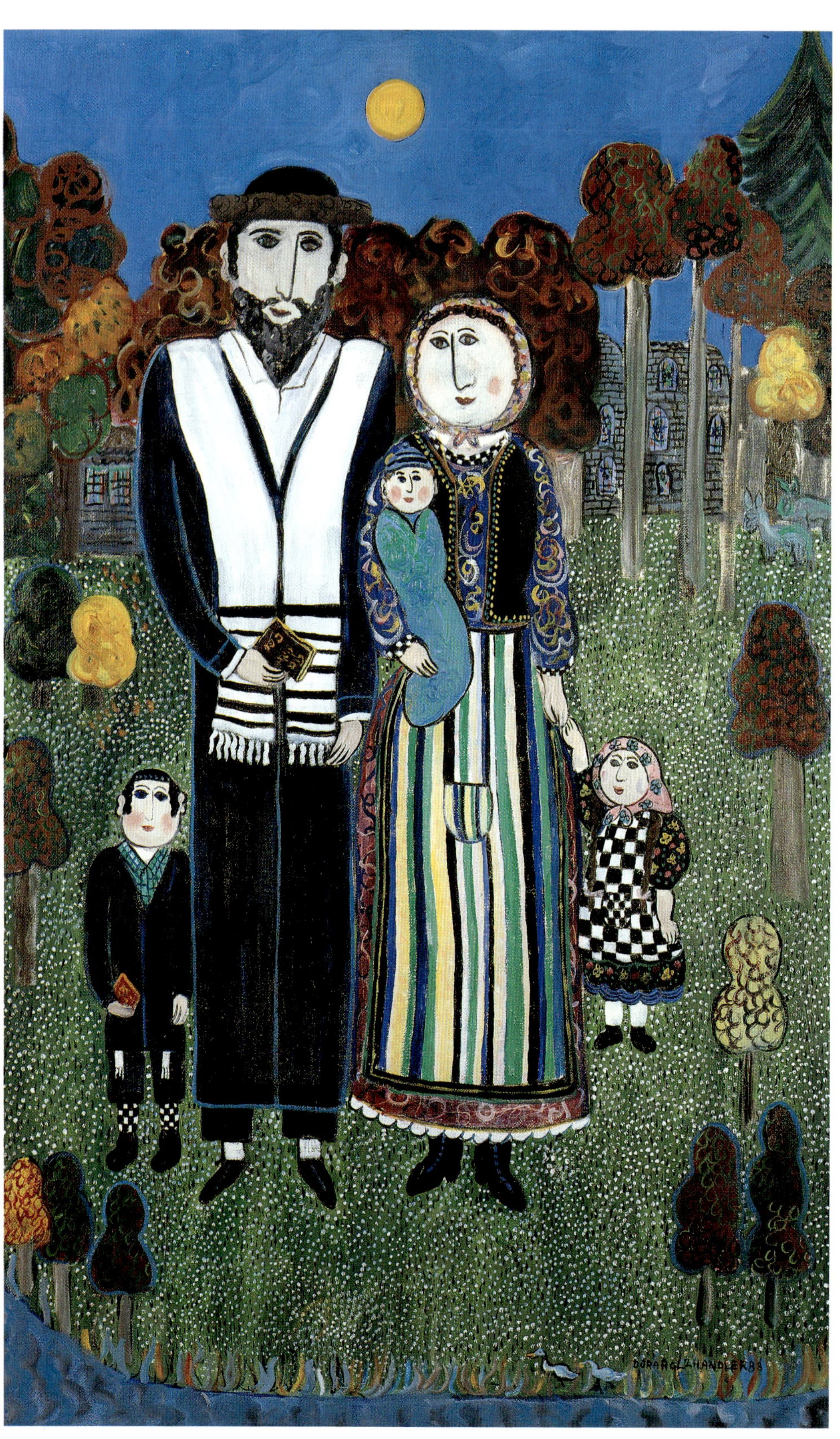

Chapter 4

Plate 13
My Grandparents in Poland
1988
Oil on canvas
88.9 x 55.9 cm (35 x 22 in)

The Old Place

Little wanderer, hie thee home.
WILLIAM BLAKE[19]

Dora's father, Sehia Holzhandler, who came from Warsaw, and her mother, Ruchla Rochman, from Otwock, a small town near Warsaw, met as refugees in London in 1927 and were married the same year in a synagogue there. Sehia had been married before and had six children by his first marriage. He had acquired British nationality and fought in the British army in the First World War – he was proud of his war service. Dora's maternal grandparents had lived in Hanbury Street near Brick Lane in London's East End, and attended a synagogue there; Dora was named after her mother's late mother, Devorah Miriam, who died not long before Sehia and Ruchla were married. A few months after their wedding, Sehia, a handbag-maker by trade, and Ruchla, a seamstress, moved to Paris, where Ruchla's brother already lived, and were joined there by Ruchla's father. They settled in the Belleville *quartier*, near the Place de la République, home to a large immigrant Jewish population.

By 1897, more than five million Polish and Russian Jews had been confined under Tsarist rule in the ruthlessly circumscribed swathe of territory, the Pale of Settlement, which lasted until 1917. Anti-Semitic pogroms, sanctioned by the authorities in Moscow, were common throughout the period; hundreds were killed. As a result, between 1880 and 1914, more than 2,000,000 Jews from Russian-ruled lands emigrated to the United States, about 200,000 to Britain, and 60,000 to Palestine. A minority of the Russian and Polish Jews were prosperous, middle class and reasonably assimilated into gentile, urban society. The vast majority were poor, still devout, and Yiddish-speaking, dwelling in urban ghettoes, shtetls and small farming communities; their principal contact with their non-Jewish peasant neighbours was through trade. These factors did not, however, tend to reflect political leanings: some Jews of all classes had strong Zionist aspirations, while others held radical, left-wing views.

Aspects of this now-vanished world exist today only through works of art: in Marc Chagall's magical paintings of childhood in the provincial Russian town of Vitebsk; in tragi-comic contemporary stories from Poland by Isaac Leib Peretz (1851-1915) and Shalom Aleichem (1859-1916); in the novels and short stories of Isaac Bashevis Singer (1904-91), which embrace not only the shtetl but the whole cosmos; and in Roman Vishniac's haunting photographs of timeless Central and Eastern European Jewish communities taken just before the Second World War.[20]

Born in Paris, brought up there and in Normandy and London, Dora has never visited the Jewish Poland of her forebears except in the light of her imagination. However, as emigrants, her parents and grandparents carried with them the flavour, the perfume, the music of their heritage. Much of her childhood was permeated by this atmosphere. On returning to London from her first visit to Israel in 1987, Dora commented that 'all around it was my paintings come to life! The Jewishness of life is exactly the same in Israel as in London or Poland or New York.' Her brilliantly subdued painting *My Grandparents in Poland* (Plate 13) is an archetypal remembering of what made her family what it was. The background holds a synagogue with its stained-glass windows, set with Star of David designs. In the foreground are two fantastically diminutive geese (goose being, along with carp, a main staple of Polish-Jewish Sabbath and festive cuisine). The father and boy's Orthodox garb and prayerbooks, and the mother and daughter's floral and geometric patterned clothes, represent twin, wedded strands of Polish Jewish identity: Chassidic and Polish folkloric. The picture's sturdy verticals – both in the attenuated human figures and the tall, slender tree trunks – suggest the upright dignity of a way of life rooted and emerging in blessedness.

Folk-art in the Russian-held parts of Poland had blossomed following the abolition of the feudal system there in 1864. (A similar process had happened earlier in areas governed by Prussia and Austria.) Religious icons, painted and carved furniture, rustic pottery, primitive toys, paper cut-outs and embroidered costumes filled the wooden homes of the newly emancipated Catholic peasantry. Even the most mundane

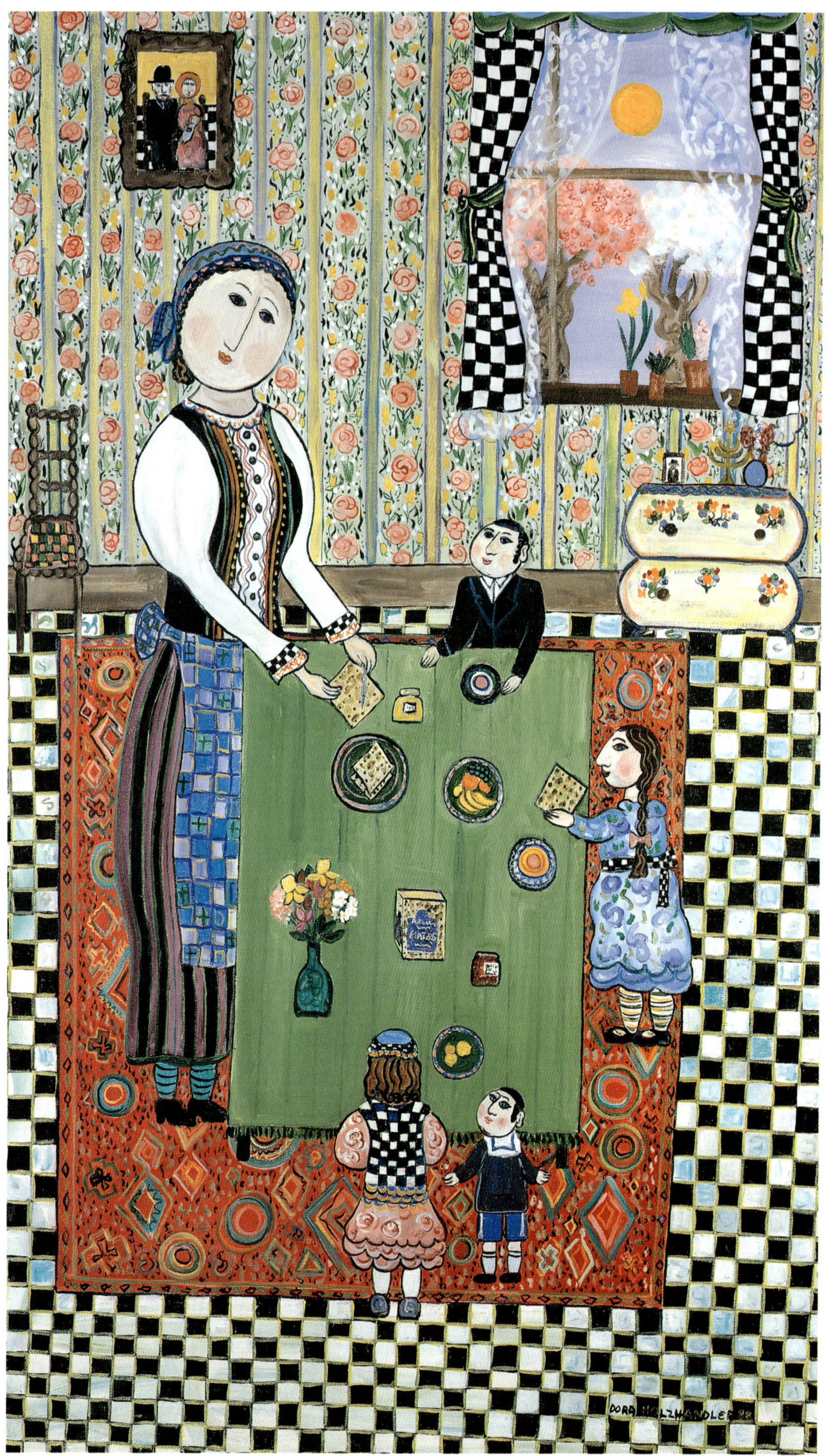

Plate 14
**Mother and Children
at Passover** 1988
Oil on canvas
106.7 x 66 cm (42 x 26 in)

artefacts were carved and incised with dazzling arrays of star, sun, snowflake, lozenge, herring-bone, arrow and other patterns, and zoomorphic, vegetal and floral motifs. Anonymous peasant artists gave expression to an often archaic, even pagan attachment to nature, and an awesome sense of death and regeneration. In fact, a good deal of the country's folk-art (Catholic imagery excepted) was made to order in villages and small towns by Jewish artisans, tailors and carpenters especially, whose skills were highly prized. The naive, intricately ornamental art of the paper cut-out (which has long-standing Jewish Ashkenazi and Sephardic roots) was widely practised among Poles of all backgrounds in the mid- to late nineteenth century.

Photographs of Dora's mother, Ruchla, as a young woman, show her holding a bunch of roses or garlanded with flowers and costumed in different styles of Polish folk-dress, long ribbons cascading down from her neck. Dora has inherited a Central European folk-art instinct, with its fertile employment of floral, geometric, vegetal and micro- and macrocosmic motifs. Peasant icons, naive in perspective, rich in religious devotion, unselfconsciously interfusing figuration and decoration, are close to her own way of seeing (no matter that their outlook is Catholic). When Dora's paintings were shown in the exhibition *New Frontiers of Naive Art in Europe*[21] in London in 1984, it was illuminating to see them hanging near the pictures of Poland's greatest *naif*, Nikifor (1895-1968), and the simple, angelic icons of a peasant woman, Katarzyne Gawel (1895-1982), who lived near Cracow. The degree of artistic neighbourliness is uncanny.

In Dora's picture *Mother and Children at Passover* (Plate 14), every detail speaks of the generations – and of the regeneration of hope. A recurring feature in her work is that of small pictures within the greater picture, each a further imaginative uncovering of the subject's background. Here, a portrait on the walls shows the grandparents of the children who are about to eat *matzoh* (unleavened bread which is eaten at Passover, recalling the unleavened loaves taken by the ancient Jews fleeing Egypt). Flowers are ubiquitous, and abstract patterns are endlessly reiterated. The mother's costume and a painted chest of drawers appear Central European; the carpet Middle Eastern. The picture's overall effect is of a Polish-Jewish folk aesthetic set within the borders of a Persian miniature. But note that the *matzoh* box – painted with magical immaculateness – is recognisably that of Rakusen's, a modern English

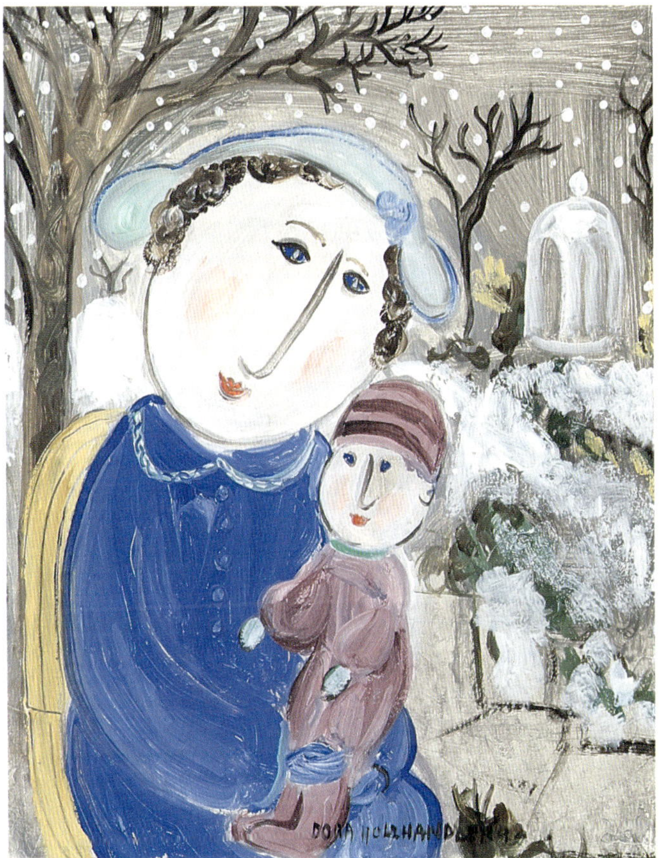

Plate 15
Mother and Child in Winter in the Park of Buttes Chaumont, Paris   1992   Oil on board   22.9 x 17.8 cm (9 x 7 in)

Kosher food manufacturer; as we have seen, Dora's sense of Jewishness is not confined by time or place.

Dora's earliest childhood is evoked in *Mother and Child in Winter in the Park of Buttes Chaumont, Paris* (the hilly park situated near her childhood home), one of many pictures depicting this most primal relationship (Plate 15). The polarity between the mother's soulfully inclined countenance, lit by a 'love … so near to enlightenment', and the child's fresh, pert, innocent features, is moving beyond words. The falling, dissolving snowflakes form a soft, gentle pattern, equivalent to the impalpable melody playing between mother and child. (In another picture of the same subject, an exquisite coalescence of falling snow and pink, cascading blossoms happens.) The snow-covered cupola in the background is a small temple or pavilion overlooking the park and, indeed, much of Paris. Dora recalls that later on, when suffering from a childhood illness, she was (on some neighbour's advice) 'wrapped up and taken to Buttes Chaumont in the snow; how beautiful it was. What that outing did for my illness I do not know, but my little heart was filled with joy.'

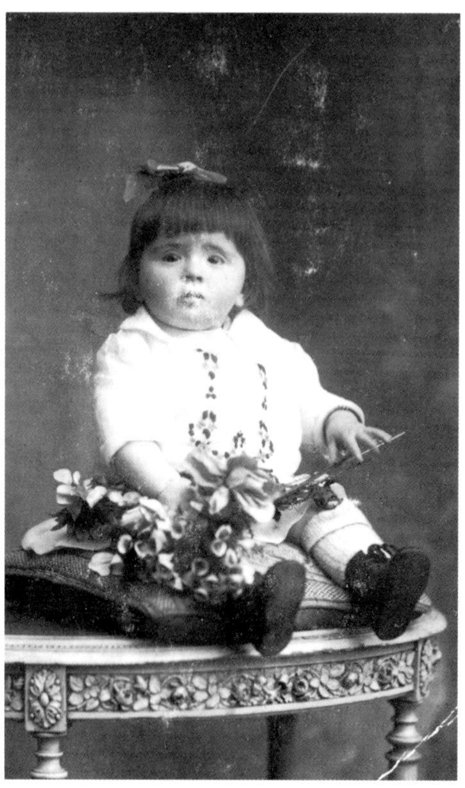

'22-3-29 De Petite Dora Holzhandler'

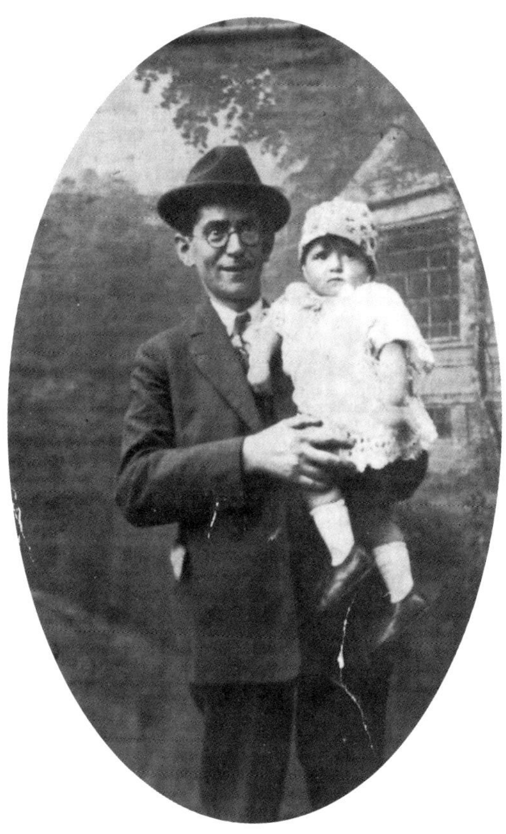

Dora with her father Sehia 1929

Sadly, Sehia Holzhandler's trade suffered during the Great Depression, and so, in straitened family circumstances, Dora was sent as a baby to live with Catholic foster-parents on a Normandy farm. She cannot now visualise their faces, though she stayed there for nearly five years, but recalls from that time 'a feeling of lightness and happiness. I was not spoilt but I was loved. I can remember learning to walk, I can still remember falling a lot and the bandages on my little fat knees. I can remember the hot summer sunshine, the flowers, the smell of them, and the sound of bees and other insects.' Her real mother, whom she called 'Maman Paris', visited her periodically, and Dora was about five when a terrible trauma occurred – she was taken back by 'Maman Paris' to live in Belleville.

To a degree, this was her own Fall from Eden – a literal and psychic happening that has recurred at intervals during her life. Her paintings of mankind living in easy harmony with birds and beasts of the field, evoke 'the feeling of lightness and happiness' she describes experiencing as a young child, and can also be seen as part of an ancient tradition. Adam Naming the Animals and Eve Naming the Birds, and a Peaceable Kingdom of creaturely reconciliation, were favourite subjects among Dutch, Flemish and Italian Masters. Edward Hicks (1780-1849), the American primitive painter, painted perhaps one hundred versions of 'The Peaceable Kingdom', recalling Isaiah's biblical prophecy that, one day, led by the messianic child, 'the wolf shall lie down with the sheep, and the leopard lie down with the kid; the calf and the young lion shall grow up together, and a little child shall lead them; the cow and the bear shall be friends … the infant shall play over the hole of the cobra, and the young child dance over the viper's nest … so shall the land be filled with the knowledge of the Lord.'[22]

Dora's own version of *The Peaceable Kingdom* (Plate 16) is, in a way, reminiscent of the visionary, naive art of Hicks and his contemporaries, such as the English artist John Miles of Northleach, yet it possesses a uniquely commanding lightness of touch. All the trust and grace of unspoilt childhood is here in this non-maudlin representation of infants in etherial white gowns – one leading a lion, another riding a turquoise-eyed leopard, and yet another toying with a serpent. The innocence expressed, however, belongs to more than just the early stages of life; it shows the integration of all aspects of the human psyche (including our animal propensities – leonine, tigerish, wolvish,

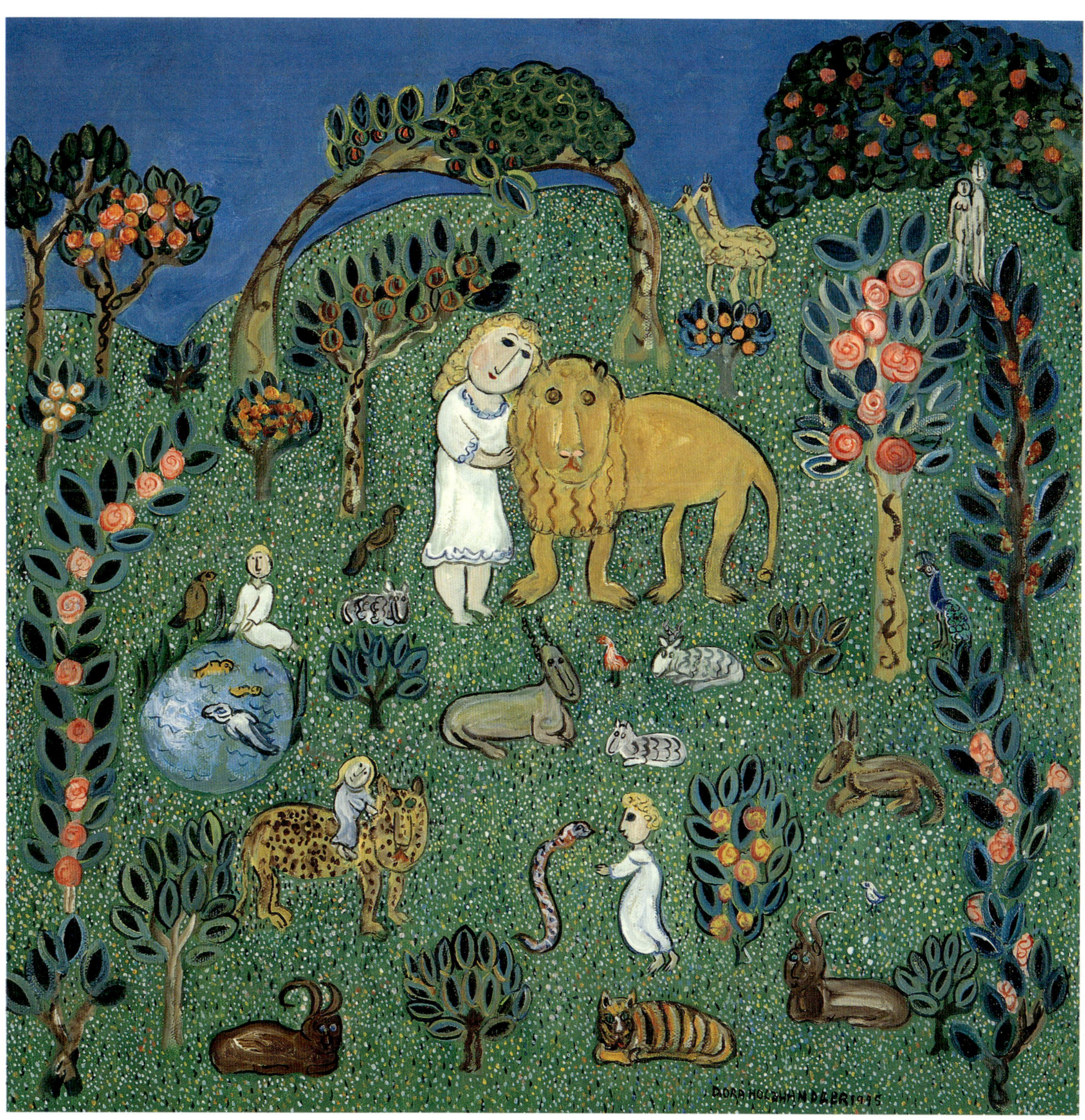

Plate 16
The Peaceable Kingdom   1995   Oil on canvas   45.7 x 45.7 cm (18 x 18 in)

asinine, lamblike and the rest) in an ultimate understanding. As such, it reflects 'the peace that passes understanding' that, one day, according to prophecy, all may have knowledge of.

The lion's ferociously wise stare, the woolly harmlessness of the little lambs, two trees on the horizon intertwining as if in an embrace, toysomely mature stances of the pretty infants: such details make the viewer want to laugh with a kind of transcendent amusement. In this way, her pictures are extremely releasing and liberating to behold. They are full of a radically all-embracing humour (the antithesis of frivolity or flippancy) based in wordless perception. In the top right of *The Peaceable Kingdom* are Adam (in Hebrew, *Ha-adam*, meaning 'material' or 'the earth') and Eve (in Hebrew *Chava*, derived from the word for life), transfixing us with looks of unutterable openness. Their vulnerable nakedness awakens our compassionate concern – especially in light of our knowledge that they will have to leave Eden for an existence bound by the exigencies of time and space. For her, Dora says, 'the Peaceable Kingdom is the Garden of Eden regained. We've left Eden. Only having suffered and meditated can we return to the new Eden.'

Viewing the painting *Adam and Eve in the Garden of Eden* (see Plate 6), we can play the joyous game of exploring Eden ourselves from the artist's weightlessly fluctuating viewpoint, searching out, amid prodigiously embroidered lushness, the sentient toys of paradise: a turquoise peacock here, a pair of miniscule giraffes there, a wild cat climbing into a tree curiously no bigger than itself, two pelicans infinitesimal in scale on the banks of a near river in whose ruffled waters (freely evoked through a calligraphy of long, wavy, multi-coloured lines) sport tiny but proportionally enhanced fish. Unidentifiable perhaps according to a naturalist's criteria, Dora's sometimes imaginatively hybridized flora and fauna still strike us as straightforwardly, unfantastically real, seen simply as if for the very first time as we awaken in paradise. The generous stature and pivotal stillness of Adam and Eve's moonbright forms make the point that it is human consciousness which is at the heart of an Edenesque vision of the world, shown here manifesting itself endlessly in waves of purposeless gaiety.

Synonymous with Eden are her visions of the godly groves of ancient Greece and Rome. Her *Judgement of Paris* (Plate 19) (in which the mortal herdsman Paris, faced with the three goddesses Hera, Aphrodite and

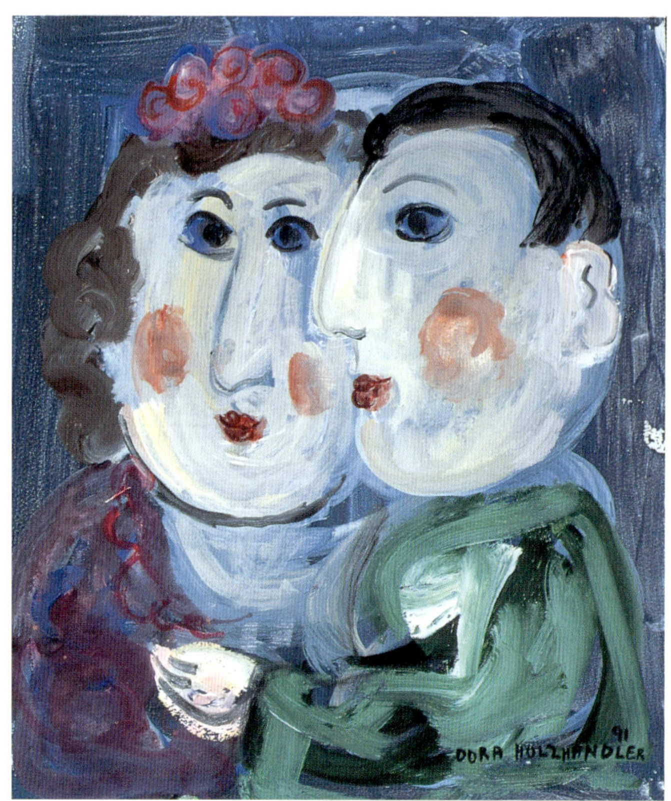

Plate 17
Lovers   1991   Gouache on paper
25.4 x 15.2 cm (10 x 6 in)

Athene, offers an apple to 'the fairest', Aphrodite, thus setting in motion the turbulent emotions among the gods that led to the Trojan Wars), is set in a rolling paradise, topped by a little white temple like that in her own Parisian childhood park.

The vinous intoxication enjoyed by naked, garlanded nymphs and Dionysian males in Dora's Bacchanalia, as they move to the Arcadian rhythms of goatish Pan's pipes, is equivalent to the holy folly and abandon of her (albeit heavily clothed) dancing rabbis. The sweet and wildly merry countenances of the revellers in *Bacchanale* (Plate 20) (accompanied and impersonated by tiny winged infants – the cherubs of European Christian art) are uproariously freeing to the viewer. With concise wit, Dora has penned little bunches of grapes, some stained a light purple, as dainty, bobbly, bloomy accessories for those on a self-liberating spree. The nearest modern relations to Dora's dancers are the frolicsome Fools of Cecil Collins, the English visionary painter whom Dora has always admired and respected.

In classical and biblical antiquity (from the Platonic 'music of the spheres' to the Aeolian harp, from

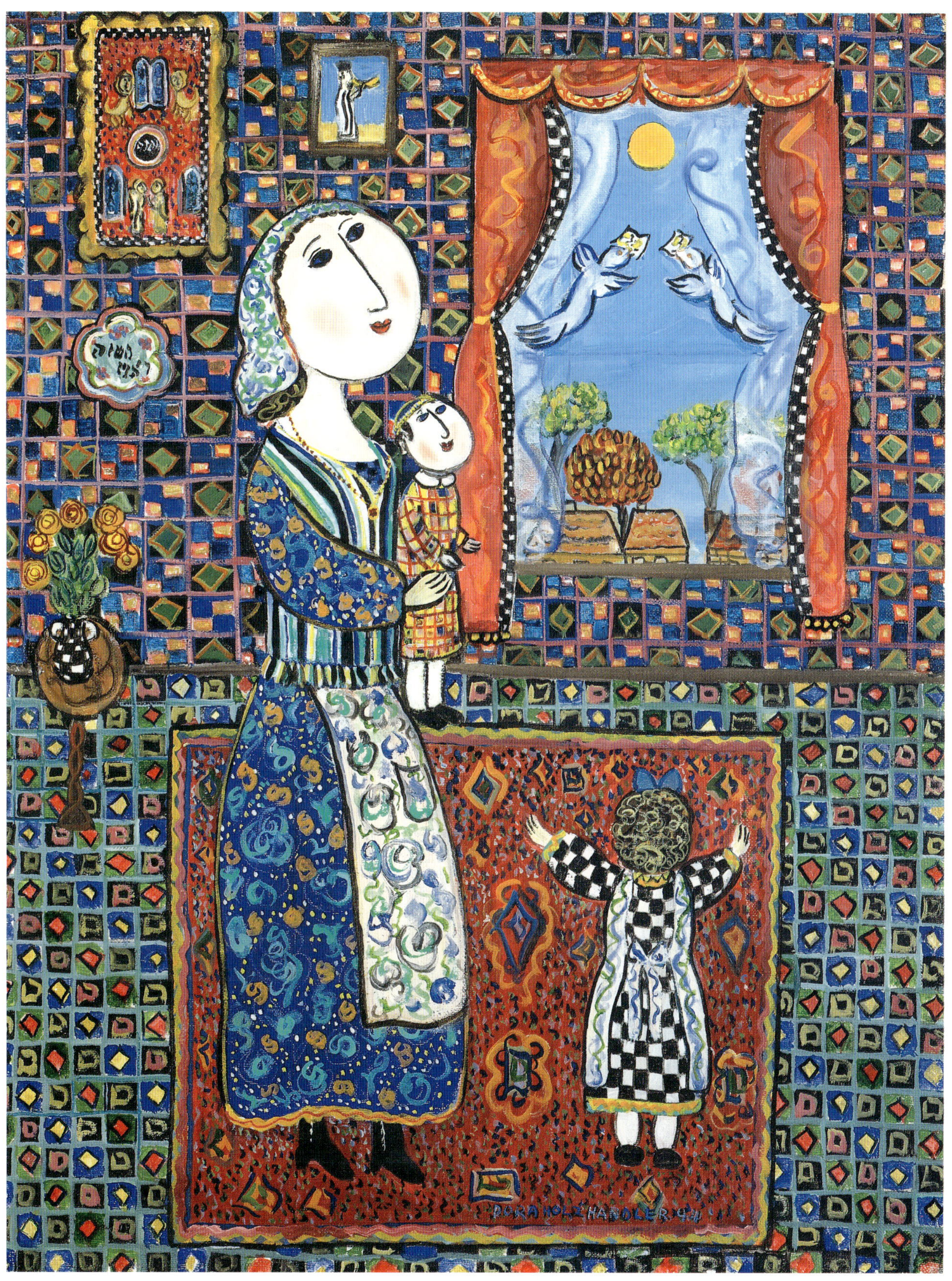

Plate 18
Rosh Hashanah   1994   Oil on canvas
38.1 x 25.4 cm (15 x 10 in)

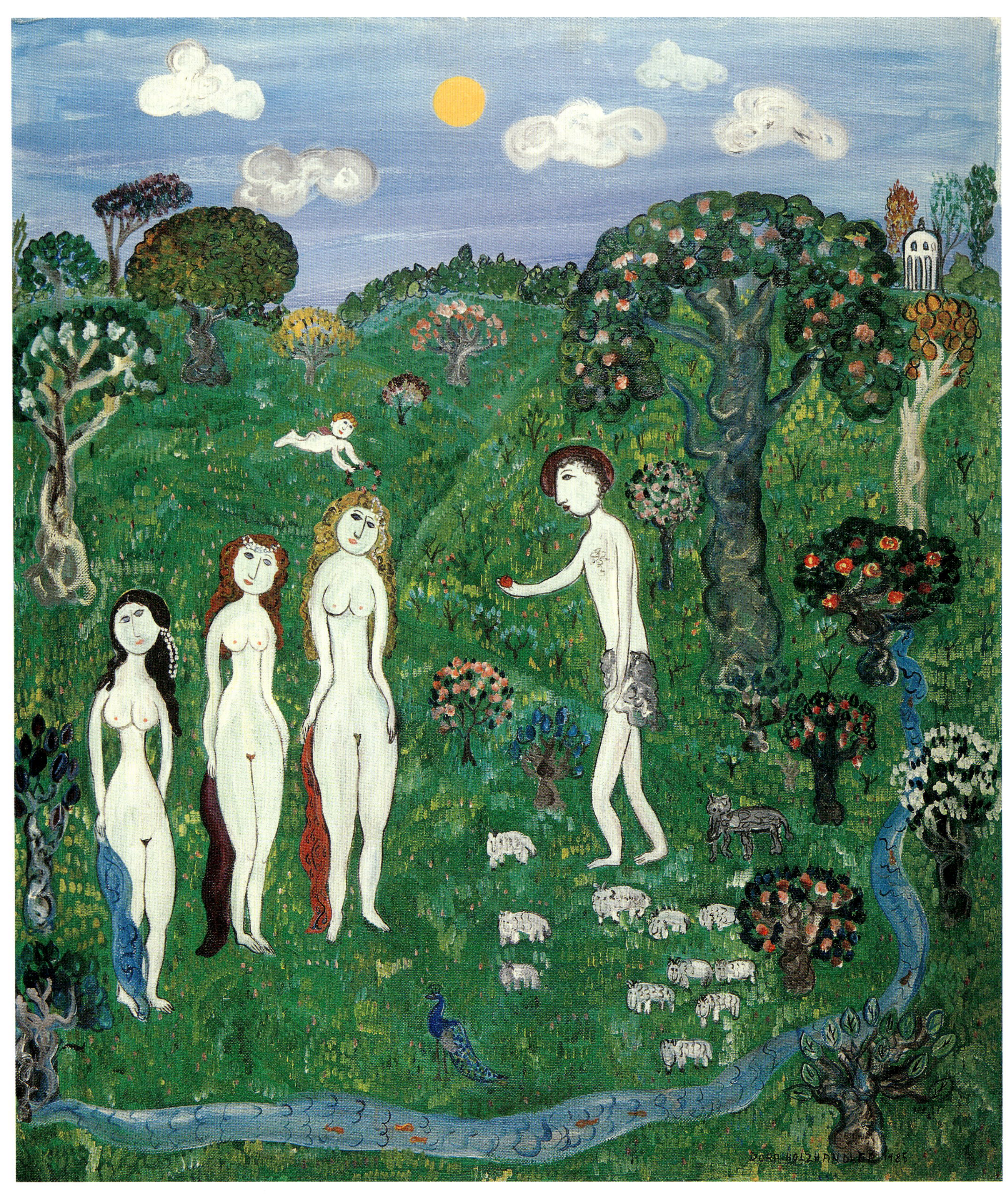

Plate 19
The Judgement of Paris   1985   Oil on canvas   81.3 x 66 cm (32 x 26 in)

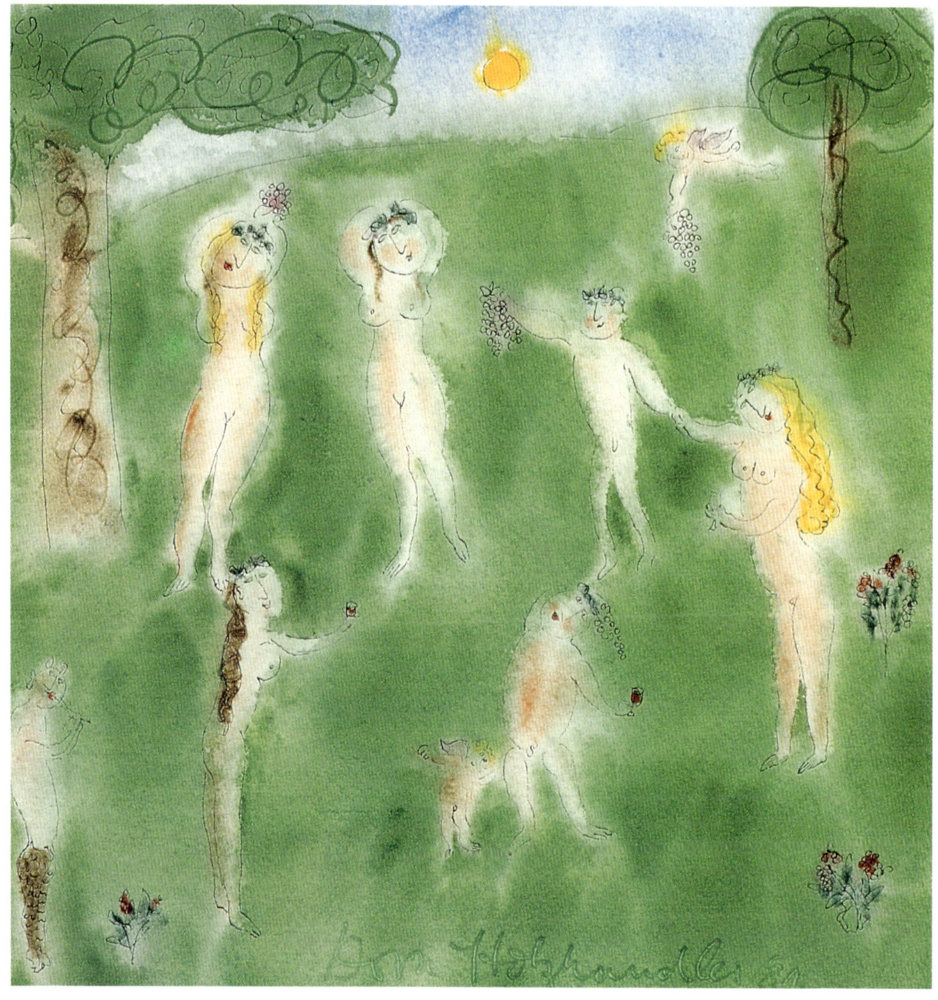

Plate 20
Bacchanale 1984
Watercolour on paper
27.9 x 30.5 cm (11 x 12 in)

Orpheus to David the psalmist, it was an accepted truth that the created universe dances perpetually to a cosmic tune. Indian and Persian miniaturists, Botticelli and Fra Angelico, Chagall and Matisse all excelled in picturing rhythms of the communal dance, instinct with celebration. In Dora's pictures of Bacchic revellers, Cornish floral dancers, wedding guests literally elevated to the sounds of a *klezmer* violin, and rabbis exultantly light on their feet at Simchat Torah (Festival of the Law), the figures are embodied by a soaring stillness, a quiet inwardness that is dynamically moving. Even the trees in such paintings seem to surge and vibrate to the festive strains. But Dora is not a pantheist who believes that nature – animals, trees, birds, flowers etc – is all one; for her, 'it is the human being that's all-important, without it coming from the ego. It's that point of intellect where it's not the merging of all nature, but it's as if all there is is one's empty mind.'

Flora, the Roman goddess of fertility, flowers and vegetation in general, is the subject of some of Dora's most fecund paintings. From 'one's empty mind' comes tremendous vegetal and floral profusion in an oil portrait of the barefoot goddess being showered by flowers from above by a tiny cherub (Plate 22). An orange-tree forms a brilliant solar constellation, each fruit a phosphorescent reflection of the vast globe above. The picture's hallucinatory depth of colour (its dark lights, its radiating sombreness) has a transporting power like that seen in medieval stained glass.

Another oil, *Flora Reclining*, is aflame with splendour upon splendour: in the yellow sun above; Flora's golden, flowing hair; trees like burning bushes; leaves like tongues of flame; the fiercely protective foreground lion. Counterpointed against these are the sky's cool blue, the pale, creamy pink of Flora's lovely form, and the fleecy grey of grazing sheep. Dora's gods and goddesses are both archetypes and real, non-idealised, fully recognisable individuals. The bliss of yearning inherent in this graceful portrait cannot be accounted for simply in terms of notions of sexual and romantic desire (though they play their part); its origins lie surely in an even more secret communion.

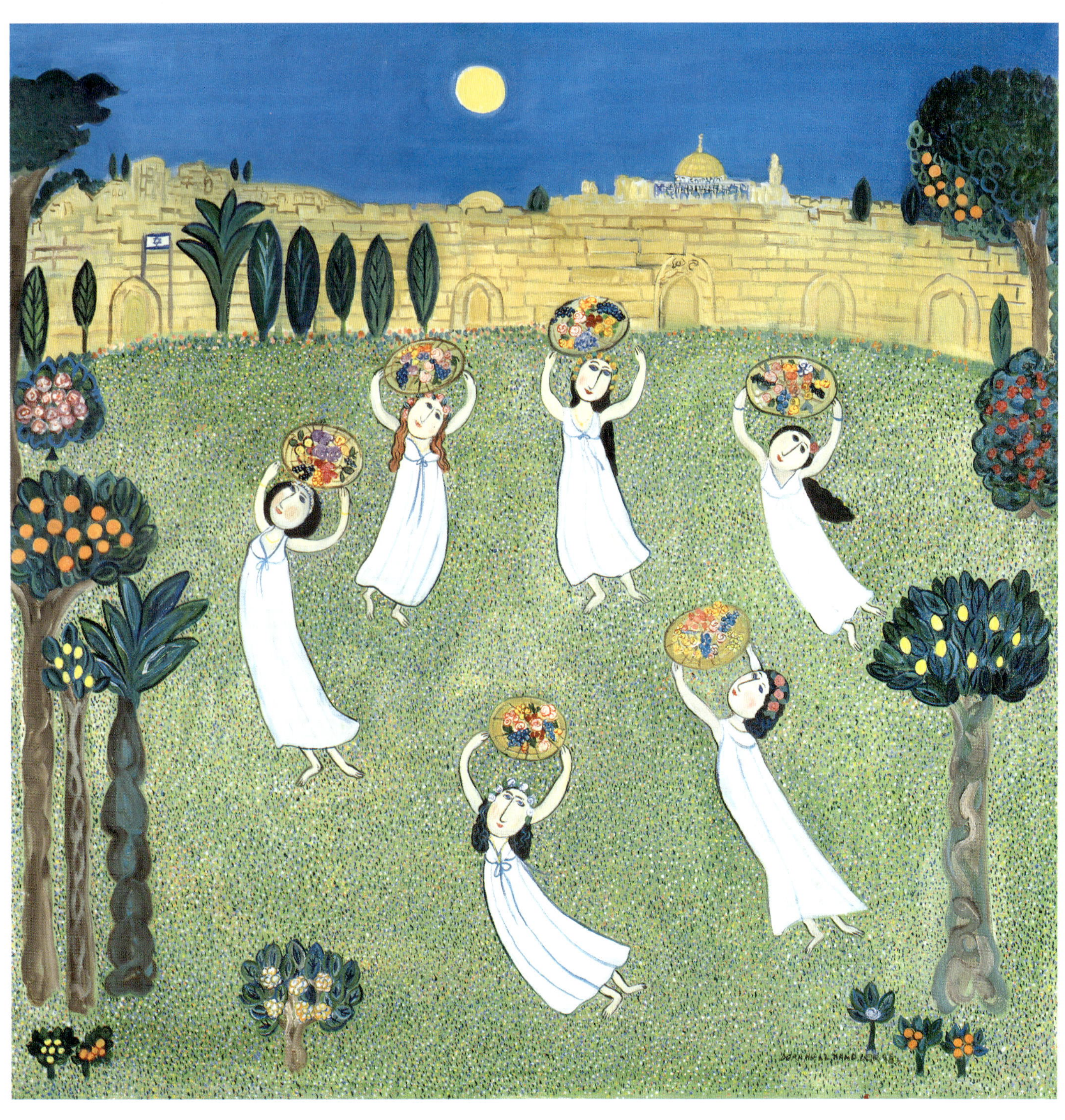

Plate 21
Young Girls Dancing at Shavuot   1993   Oil on canvas   71 x 71 cm (28 x 28 in)

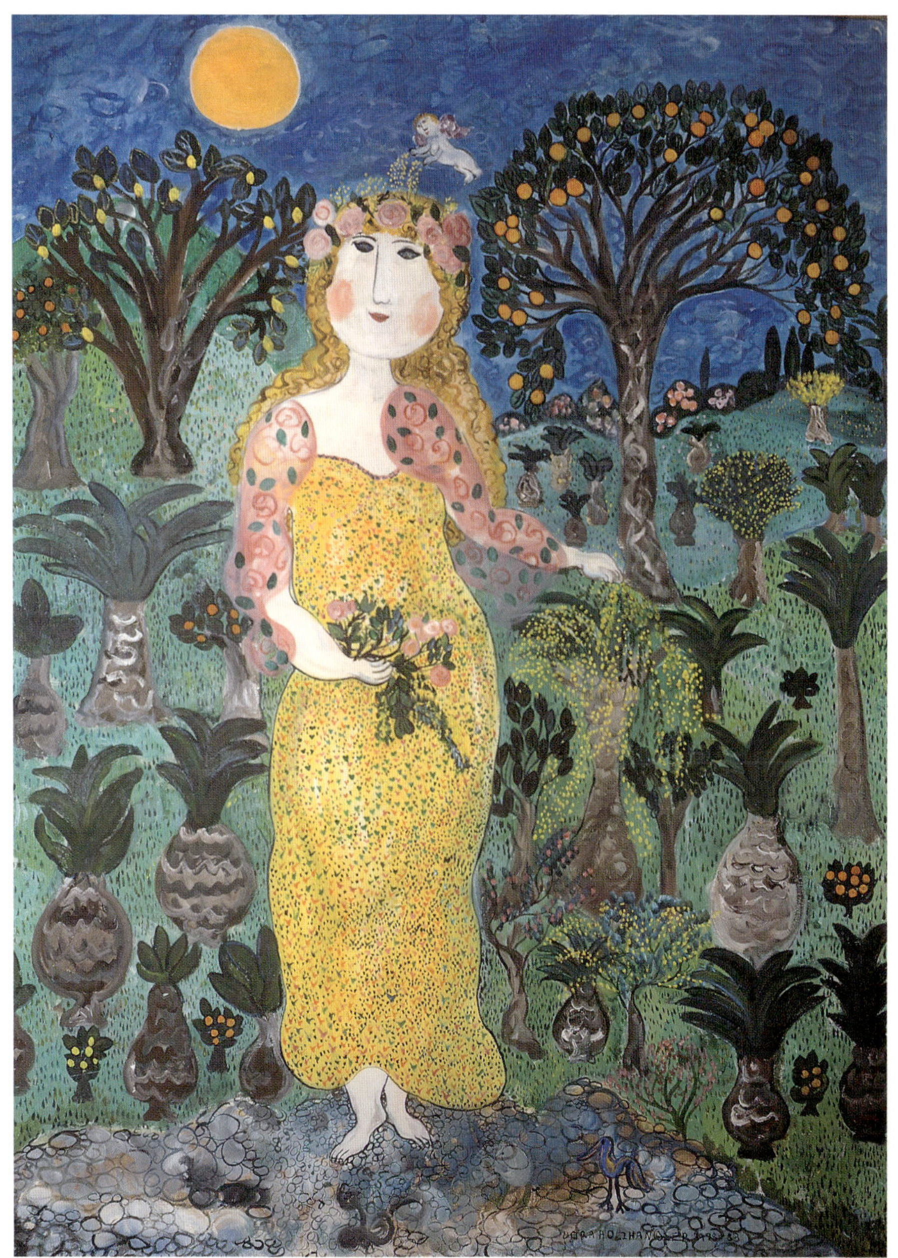

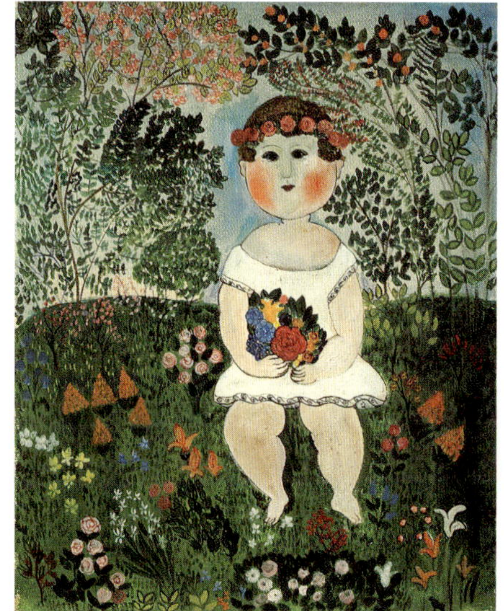

Plate 22
Flora   1978-83   Oil on canvas
88.9 x 71 cm (35 x 28 in)

Plate 23
Baby Flora   c.1976   Oil on canvas
35.6 x 30.5 cm (14 x 12 in)

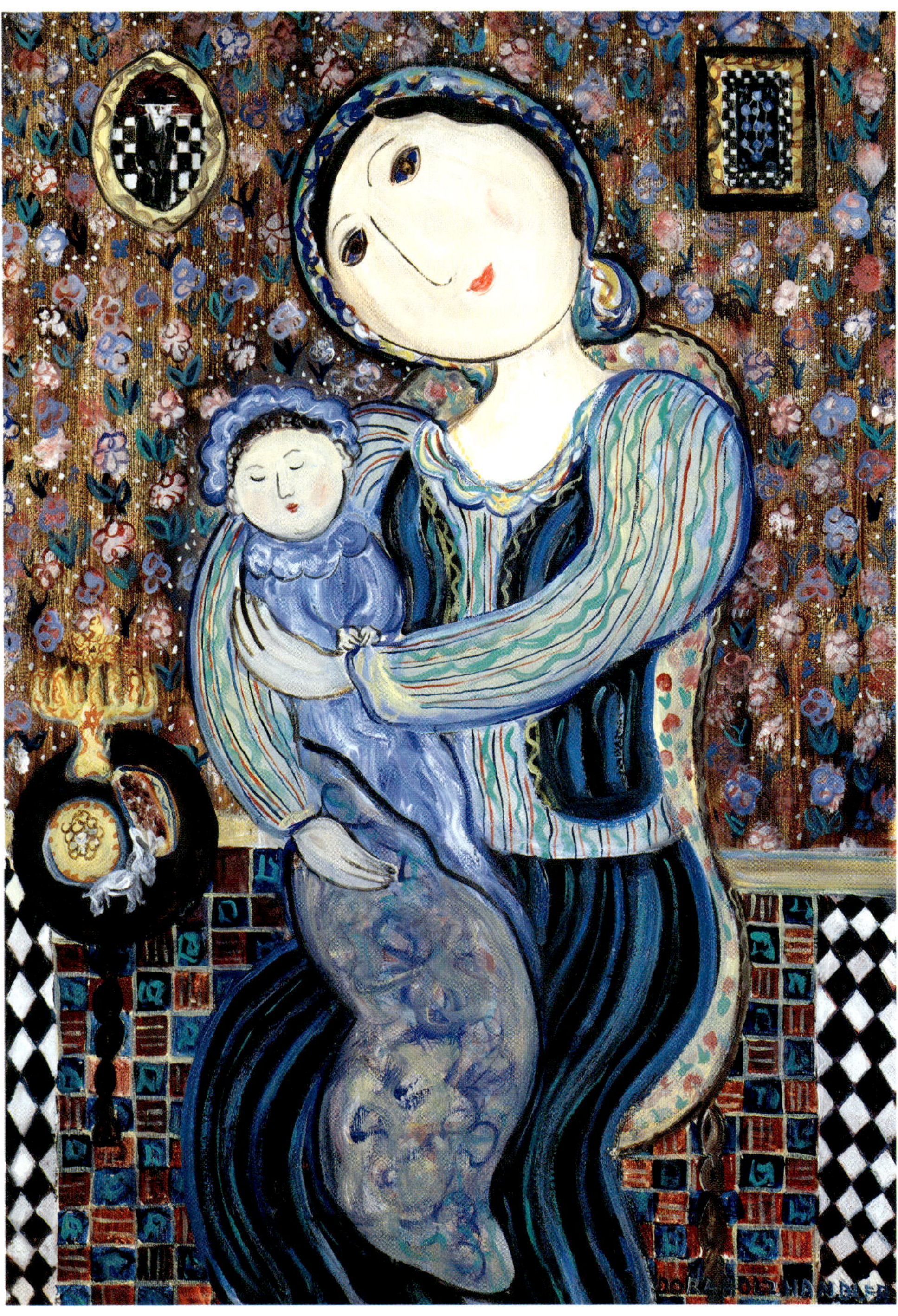

Chapter 5

Plate 24
Rozhinkes mit Mandlen (Raisins and Almonds)   1994   Oil on canvas   48.3 x 33 cm (19 x 13 in)

Toy Boxes in Paris and London

Not for a moment was that Table to remain empty, since blessing does not rest upon an empty place.
THE ZOHAR[23]

Some time around her fifth birthday, Dora was removed from what she calls 'my idyllic existence in the Normandy countryside, and suddenly plunged into the strangeness of life in Paris, in Belleville, in a poor Jewish family. I found grown-up brothers and sisters [six siblings from her father's first marriage], there were also aunts, uncles and cousins … it was rather terrifying.' Her foster mother did come and visit her in Paris a few times; 'once she brought me a toy dresser with little cups on it'. The family suffered from economic hardship. 'I suppose,' she says, 'I would now be considered a very underprivileged child.' Soon afterwards, Dora's father fell ill, and left for England (taking with him his other children) to have medical treatment there. Dora stayed in Paris with her mother, who supported them with her work as a seamstress. Dora was often ill with tonsillitis and during the day was left alone at home, 'but I was not too unhappy with this situation; lying in my little bed, I watched the sunlight coming through the windows and felt quite content. I loved to draw and had crayons and paper, and I remember once my mother bought me a little modelling set that consisted of tiny sticks with which one could build houses.'

One day her cousin Blanche gave the five-year-old 'a shoe-box containing a little plastic doll with a wardrobe of clothes'. Dora's response to this gift gives us a clue to the transfiguring essence of her work. She loved dressing the doll in its different clothes, 'and I still keep from this time a sort of bliss that sometimes comes over me when all the world seems simply one great toy box and everything is tiny and delightful – people are simply lovely dolls with real clothes, real hair (golden, black or white), real shoes of leather – the sky is real, the clouds and the flowers. But it is still a lovely toy; of course I am one of the dolls.'

Uprooted as an impressionable young child, Dora was simultaneously introduced to new realities – Parisian and Jewish. Being 'plunged' suddenly into 'the strangeness of life in Paris … in a poor Jewish family', has helped her, she believes, look objectively at what it is to be Jewish. While, on the one hand, she considers Jewishness her inheritance, in another respect she views it with detachment: 'it's still a sort of theatre for me. That's one reason I paint these pictures, I suppose, to explain it to myself.'

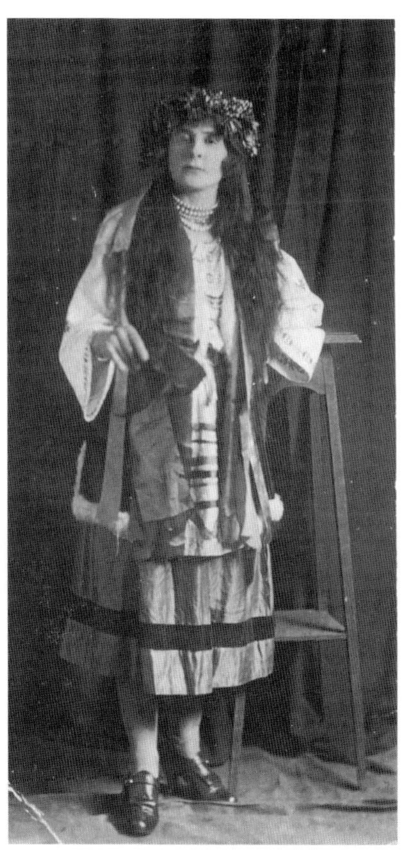

Dora's mother Ruchla

Her mother she describes as 'a really old type of Jewish lady from the Polish shtetl. She was full of beautifully embroidered Yiddish curses' and curious superstitions and magical beliefs that would not be out of place in an Isaac Bashevis Singer story. She had unfulfilled ambitions to be an actress and singer, and sang Yiddish songs to her little girl. 'When I hear that music now,' says Dora, 'I go right back – absolutely.' Two paintings have been inspired by the Yiddish lullaby, '*Rozhinkes mit Mandlen*' ('Raisins and Almonds') (Plate 24). A partial translation reads: 'In a corner of the Temple, the widowed daughter of Zion sits, rocking her only son Yidele to sleep. She sings a tender lullaby: "Under Yidele's cradle stands a snow-white kid. The kid has been to market. That will be Yidele's calling too – trading in raisins and almonds. Even when you are rich, Yidele, remember your mother's lullaby." '[24] In a gouache version, the mother, clothed in ultramarine, rocks and lullabies her baby to sleep against a Prussian-blue sky a-sparkle with crescent moon and stars or snowflakes. Above the small dish of hope (containing symbolic raisins and almonds) hovers a miniscule, snow-white kid with wide, red eyes of sweet astonishment.

The second version is set indoors, and glistens throughout with the *Menorah*'s refulgence; in the candlelight, bare, white canvas shimmers through the wallpaper's soily brown. On a small, round side-table are candelabrum, dishes of raisins and almonds and, tremulously perched on domestic mahogany, the pocket-sized kid, its tender limbs, trunk, face and ears each a whorl of white. The picture's lyrical message is not simply about remembering 'your mother's lullaby' (though that is central) but also one of being mindful of Zion (or one's spiritual heritage) and the mystical origin of all things. (An extended metaphor in the Zohar springs to mind here: the spiritually awakened human soul is described as a newborn baby recognising its mother for the first time.) Each part of the painting contributes to that one end (or beginning): on the wall, a portrait of an aged rabbi and a Kabbalistic diagram; abstract, calligraphic designs on the floor (resembling reiterated *alephs*, the first letter of the Hebrew alphabet); and, above all, the primordial illumination (like the background glow irradiating the universe, which scientists talk about) transfiguring every detail.

Buttes Chaumont was her Parisian playground. 'I loved playing in the sand and my greatest love was Guignol, the French Punch and Judy show. When I was well, I went there every day. As a child, I used to think India was at the other side of the park!' From that year she lived in Paris, 'most of all,' she says, 'I remember my grandfather, Zaida, my mother's father. I loved him.' (Zaida is the Yiddish word for grandfather.) Zaida was a devout man (descended from a long line of Polish rabbis), who attended synagogue frequently. Often he would take Dora to Buttes Chaumont, telling her stories in Yiddish like those by Shalom Aleichem. One of her earliest memories is of her and her mother meeting Zaida in the street; he was carrying a bunch of roses. This memory inspired a gouache, painted in 1991. White-bearded, black-garbed, Chassidic in essence, Zaida offers the flowers to his daughter and granddaughter. The roses' bloody hue stands out starkly against the chalky complexioned buildings, road and sky. It is as though he is offering them his loving heart.

Dora only knew Zaida from the time she came to Paris from Normandy until she departed about a year later for London with her mother. But he moved and impressed her deeply. The figure of the white- or grey-bearded rabbi recurs in many paintings (especially post-1986) set in different locales, for example Holland Park, by Jerusalem's Wailing Wall, Buttes Chaumont. *Rabbi with Roses* (Plate 25) is an oil painting with all the flourishing richness of her gouaches. The tenebrous colours – browns, greens and blacks swirling around like wisps of smoke – seem curiously apt for depicting a rabbi's mystical study. With one hand touching the roses (their container meaningfully placed adjacent to two holy books), it seems as if the rabbi is offering the viewer a gift of the wisdom that flowers in his secret heart of hearts.

Over the years, Dora has returned often to Paris. The humming rue des Rosiers in Le Marais (see Plate 26), with its Jewish bookshops, kosher restaurants and delicatessens, and, above all, its Orthodox inhabitants, attracts her, recalling her Belleville childhood. The statuesque woman in her painting *Lilies of the Valley, Paris* (Plate 27) is, in many ways, a symbolic representation of Maman Paris wrought large. The blue of her skirt reflects Dora's pleasure in a 'blue that is very French, a colour I love', an ultramarine or lapis lazuli seen, for example, in Limoges enamelware. Sacré Cœur is seen on the horizon; to the right, with its miniature white temple echoing the church's form, is Buttes Chaumont in all its declivitous entirety. The magic of the picture is such that the viewer can imagine, as did Dora as a child, that India is beyond the horizon, 'at the other side of the park'.

Whereas she thinks affectionately of England as being like 'an overgrown garden', she says she likes 'the French way for things to be neat, orderly, everything in its place. The philosophy is neat. I try to do that in the paintings.' She likes the way that trees in

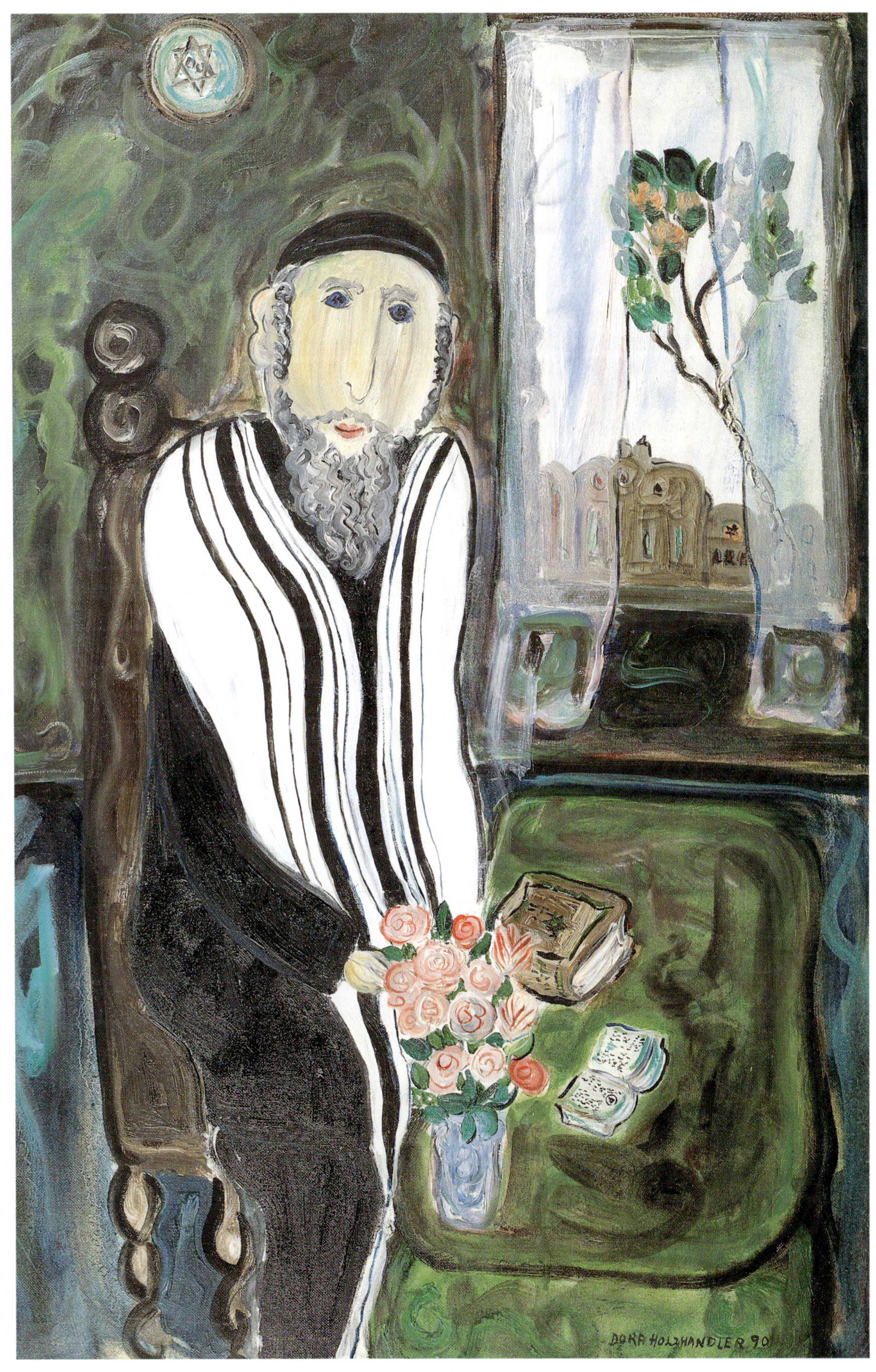

Plate 25
Rabbi with Roses   1990   Oil on canvas   76.2 x 50.8 cm (30 x 20 in)

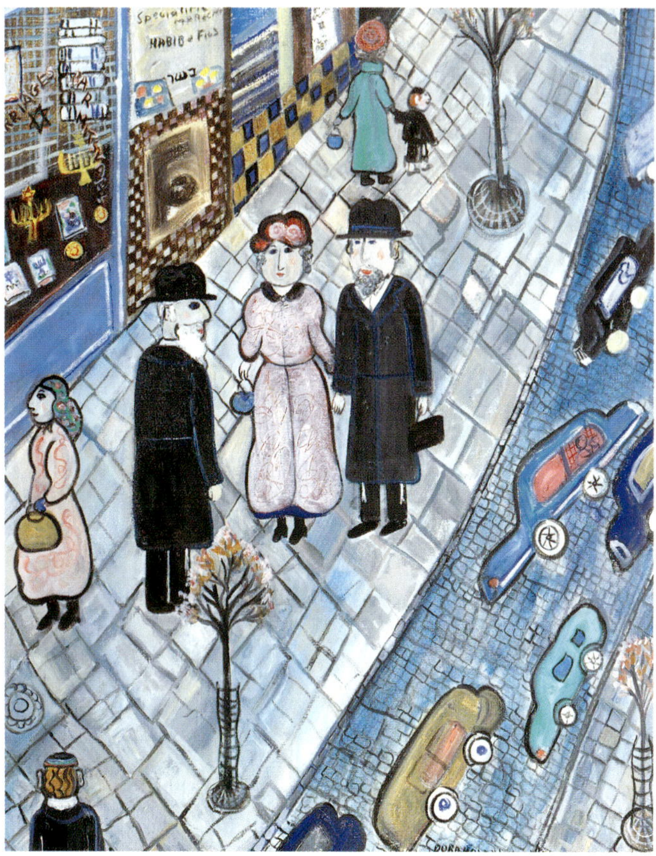

Plate 26
Rue des Rosiers   1992   Oil on canvas
53.3 x 43.2 cm (21 x 17 in)

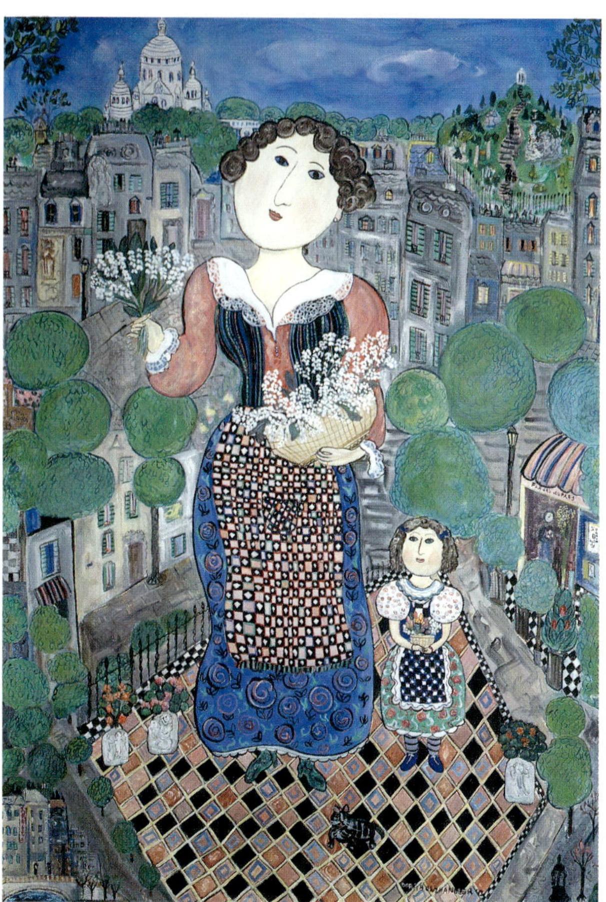

Plate 27
Lilies of the Valley, Paris   1992   Oil on canvas
101.6 x 86.4 cm (40 x 34 in)

a formal French garden are planted with a precise, medieval geometry, and a simple meal there – an omelette, wine, a peach – can be presented with as much care as an elaborate flower arrangement. She loves the 'much more luminous Paris light' dissolving barriers between subject and object, and identifies 'a Parisian quality of things: toy-like, charming, the little bunches of flowers – it's very special, sweets and little patisseries like little jewels, little toys'. What she denotes as Parisian 'lightness and humour' have been starting points for many watercolours and gouaches, including, notably, pictures of an impeccably proper *'Jeune Femme'* promenading in the Jardins de Luxembourg with a clipped poodle of outrageous chic, a waiter observed balancing trays of drinks – against all conceivable odds – between café tables, with uncanny balletic finesse, and extravagantly voluptuous nightlife spectaculars – resembling, at least in outline, Hindu temple carvings of dancers – inspired by photographs

of 1930s Josephine Baker musicals.

Soon after Dora's sixth birthday in March 1934, she and her mother left Paris to join her father and Dora's half-brothers and sisters in London. At first she was homesick for Paris; London, by comparison, seemed a much murkier, sootier place. They lived in Highbury in north London, and later moved to a flat, near a street market and opposite a synagogue in Dalston in the East End. Dora had to learn English, which proved difficult as her parents spoke Yiddish at home. 'I remember the first day at school, children were chanting what I thought to be a religious chant but what turned out to be the arithmetic tables.' Her father, who was now in reasonable health, had a job, and the family enjoyed a quite settled existence until the outbreak of War. London's East End was, in the early 1930s, still home to about 80,000 Jews (about a third of London's Jewish population), and was full of synagogues, tailoring workshops, street markets and Turkish baths; the Yiddish

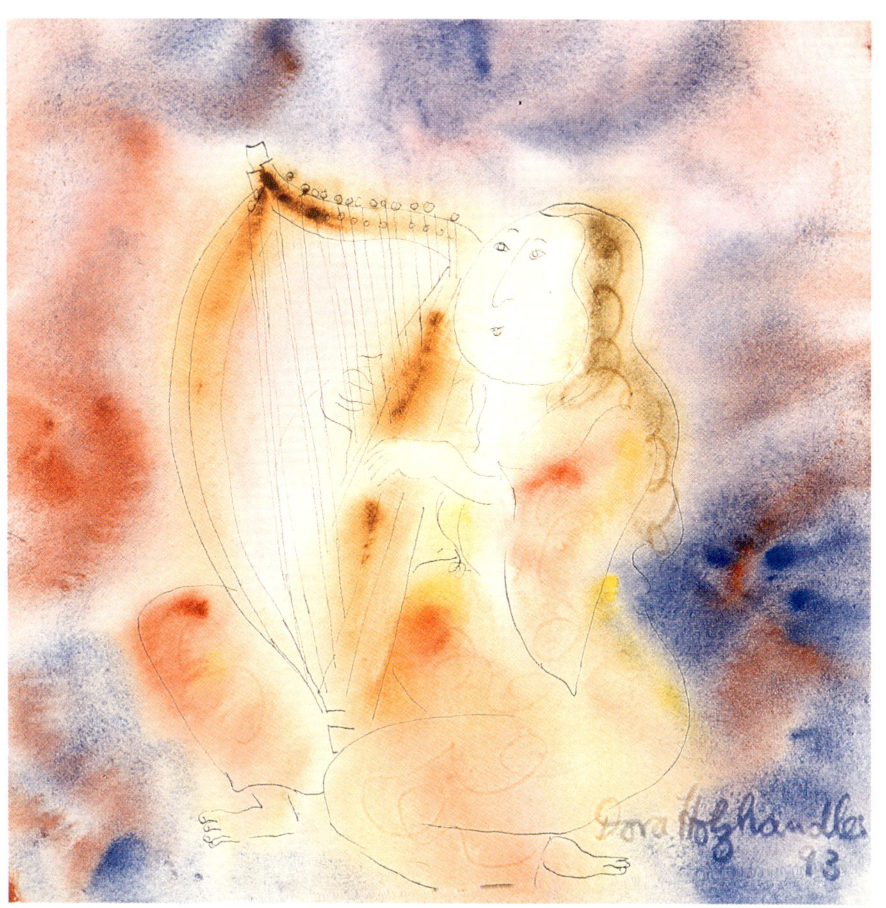

Plate 28
The Harpist 1993
Watercolour on paper
27.9 x 27.9 cm (11 x 11 in)

theatre, with many famous guest stars from Eastern Europe and the United States, and Yiddish newspapers thrived there too. As the inhabitants prospered, they moved in greater numbers to the North London suburbs; after the War, the exodus into Anglicised middle-classdom became unstoppable.

After the peaceful rural idyll of her earliest years, followed by the year in Paris, when she was often ill and left alone in 'a kind of meditative state', 'Jewish life in the East End was very vividly imprinted on me. Instead of being a baby born into it, I was a six-year-old looking at it, noticing it very much.' In her many paintings of Jewish life, Dora is both 'a six-year-old looking at it', and her mature self contemplating her origins with a renewed and refreshed understanding.

According to Genesis, after the Creation of heaven and earth, 'God blessed the seventh day and made it holy, because on that day he ceased from all the work he had set himself to do'.[25] The Jewish Sabbath has immemorially been a day of rest, peace and simple joy for the whole community – irrespective of social status. Even for the poorer Jews of Eastern Europe, Shabbat was a day of music, prayer, wine to drink and good things to eat – the latter scrimped and saved for, purchased and prepared during the hard, unstinting labours of a sometimes hungry week.

In the Zohar, it is written: '… the Holy People must direct its mind towards the supernal world, and prepare for the Lord of the House a bed, a table, a stool, and a candlestick, in order that perfection and harmony may reign undisturbed every day, both above and below.'[26] As we shall see, each of these essential domestic items figures centrally (though certainly not according to any preconceived plan or method) in Dora's pictures of the Jewish Sabbath and other Holy Days or Festivals, and indeed throughout her representations of the miraculous nature of everyday reality.

First we buy the meat
and then we buy
the pot
Haiku BY JACK KEROUAC[27]

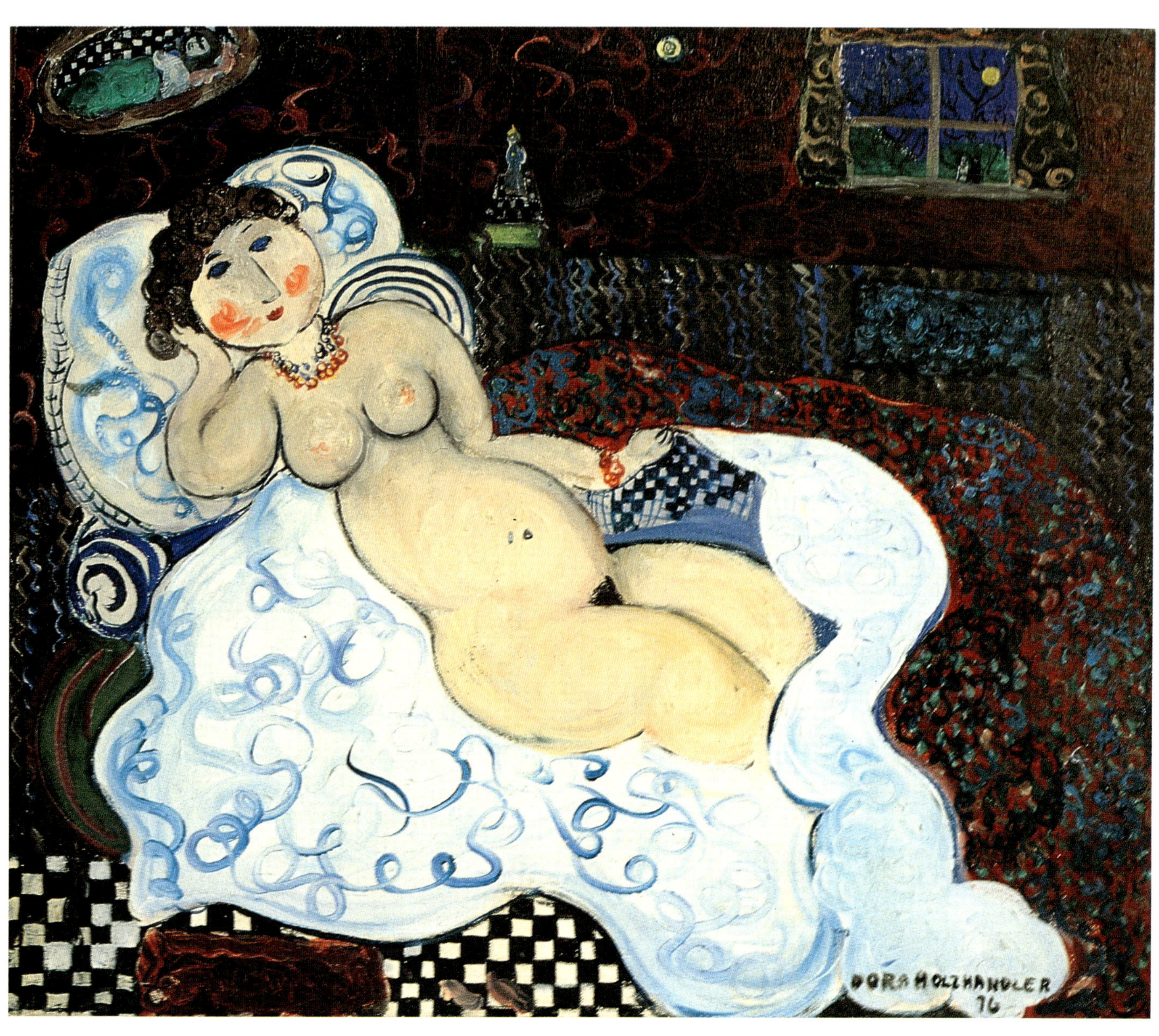

Plate 29
Nude Lady   1976   Oil on canvas   50.8 x 61 cm (20 x 24 in)

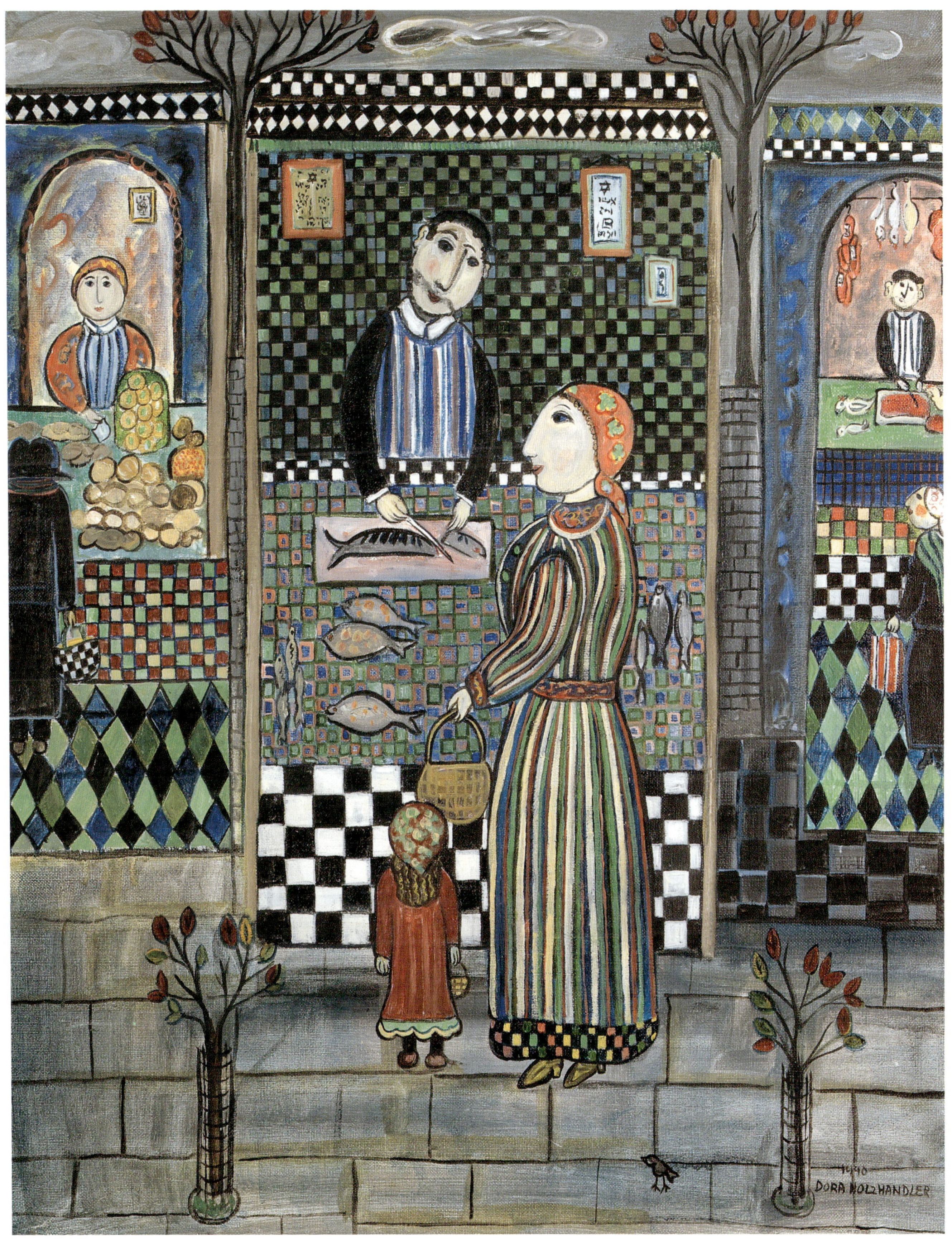

Plate 30
Shopping for Sabbath   1990   Oil on canvas   66 x 53.3 cm (26 x 21 in)

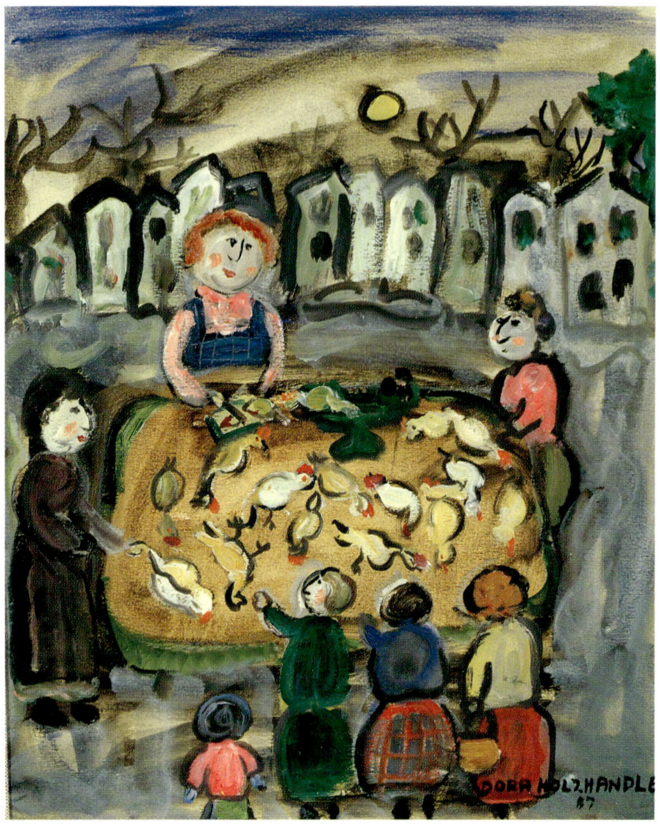

Plate 31
Chicken Market   1987   Oil on paper   33 x 27.9 cm (13 x 11 in)

In *Shopping for Sabbath* (Plate 30), mother and daughter are at the fishmonger's, a kind of booth or stall, on either side of which are a baker's and butcher's. Dora enjoys the neat and toy-like appearance of shop merchandise displays. Once, walking past cuts of meat and carcasses in a butcher's window, she remarked to me how uncannily they resemble tiny, expertly carved and painted wooden models from a typical Victorian model butcher's shop. In this painting, fish, loaves and meat have this triple quality: they are miniature models, wooden toys, to be appreciated for their concentrated painterly and sculptural qualities; they glow like polished stones (dabs of colour on red-spotted fish and on green-iced buns piled up under a glass dome resemble gems glimmering in neutral settings); they are real, bulky foods of raw, pungent immediacy. At the heart of the formally triangular relationship here between fishmonger, mother and child, a bloody knife severs the fish's head. From the focal point of the dead fish's eye arises the mystery of seeing which fills the painting: this has its origins in the mother's limitless love for her offspring, inseparable from a radically incisive awareness of creaturely vulnerability and

'death's tremendous nearness'.[28] The butcher's stall has taken on something of the recessive box-like form and spiritual centrality of the synagogue Holy Ark.

Each Thursday, Dora would go with her mother to buy a chicken for Shabbat. She recalls 'the grey cold of winter as a background to a crowd of Jewish ladies picking and haggling over a pile of chickens'. This scene is represented in an oil on paper, *Chicken Market* (Plate 31), depicted with a brooding spontaneity more typical of her works in gouache. *Fish for the Sabbath* (Plate 32), a gouache, shows a woman in blue (with rivetingly blue eyes), indicating which fish she wants to buy. The bare, black trees, the bleak, gusty atmosphere of cold greys suffused with dusky pinks, the piles of dead chickens and fish, combine to give such pictures a moody, peasant vigour, a highly numinous, unceremonious earthiness – one unconfined to the East End, or to Belleville or to Jewish Warsaw but rather emanating from a timeless shtetl in the mind's eye.

Each Friday at midday, Ruchla would prepare the chicken and fish for the Sabbath meal. 'She'd tear out the chicken liver and throw it straight on the gas flame, then give it to me to eat. Other bits the cat used to get.' This is in fact the scene portrayed in *Preparing for the Sabbath* (Plate 35). On the wooden kitchen table-top, shown in flattened perspective, are raw ingredients: carrots, chicken and fish (a Yiddish newspaper with its Hebrew script, in which the purchases were wrapped, is there too). Plates, pans, chopping board and food on the plain boards form a sparsely abstracted and meticulous still-life, set against background fields of dense irridescence. Loving-kindness illumines every part of the marvellously matter-of-fact domestic scene – the mother's apron, the 1930s light fitting, the family portraits and the inexpensive looking rugs etc – reaching an almost intolerable brightness in the hearth flames, red roses on a side-table and the golden *Menorah* on the kitchen dresser. Here truly '… the fire and the rose are one'[29] – along with the red, enamelled pans, raw carrots and red-necked chicken.

Dora recalls that 'in London, my life became that of a little Jewish girl … on Friday afternoons, the Jewish children were allowed to leave school early to be home before nightfall for the Sabbath … On Friday night my mother lit the candles to commemorate the Sabbath evening. There was a white table-cloth and we ate chicken soup and *gefilte* fish.' In many a Jewish childhood, the family meal on the Sabbath and at Festivals, notably the *Seder* at Passover, is perhaps the supreme

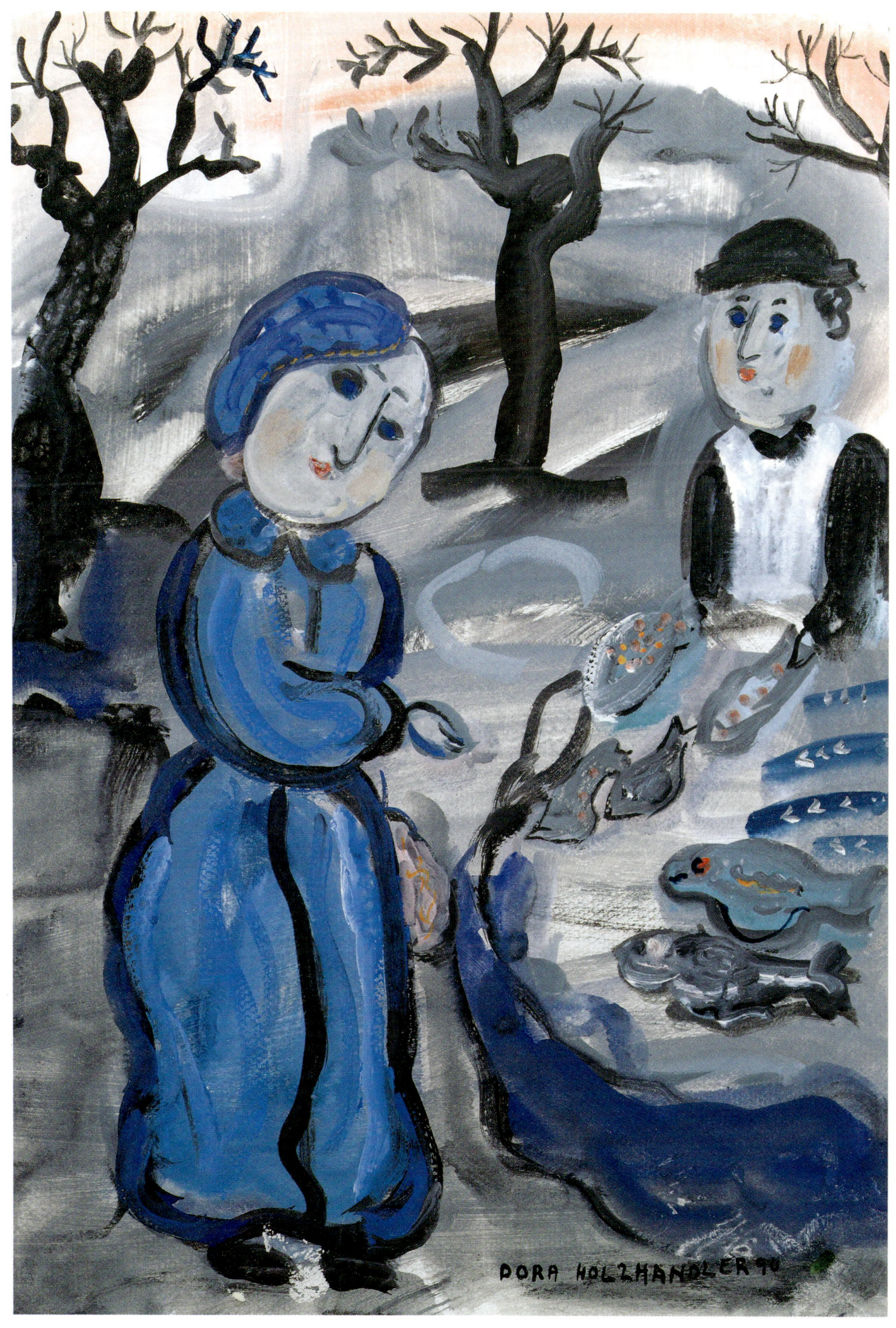

Plate 32
Fish for the Sabbath   1990   Gouache on paper   44.4 x 31.7 cm (17$\frac{1}{2}$ x 12$\frac{1}{2}$ in)

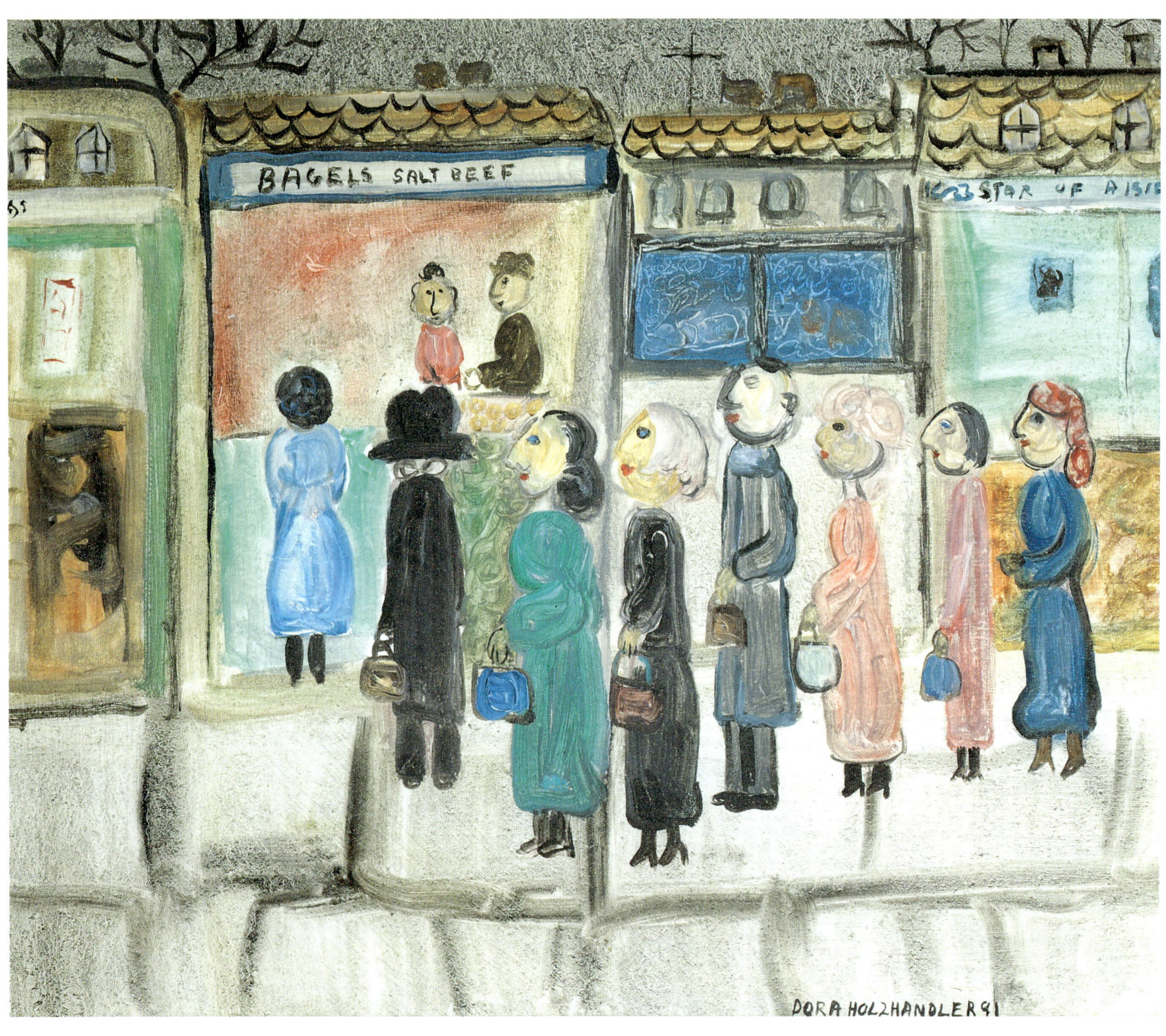

Plate 33
Queuing for Bagels   1991   Oil sketch on board   25.4 x 40.6 cm (10 x 16 in)

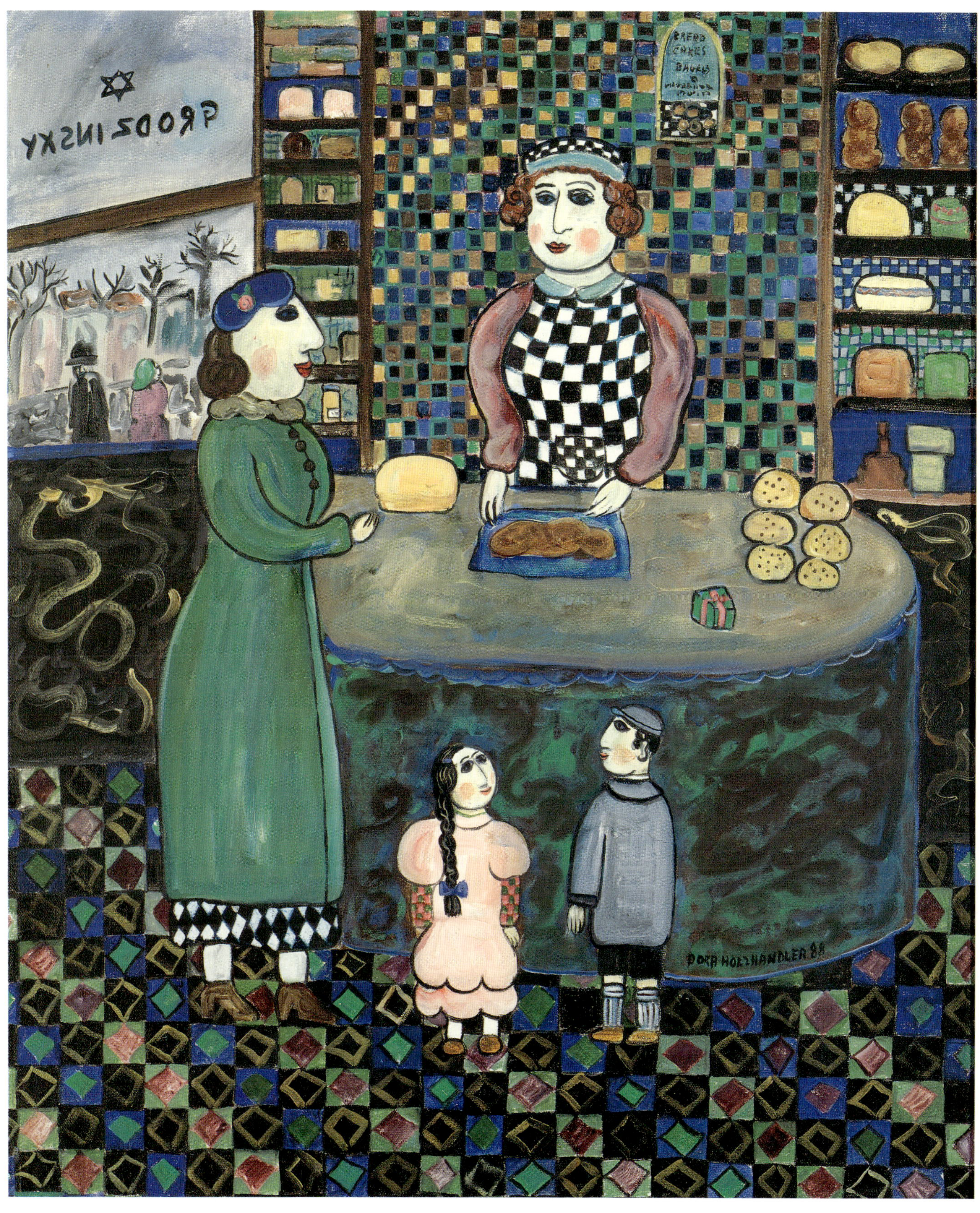

Plate 34
The Grodzinski Bakery   1988   Oil on canvas   61 x 50.8 cm (24 x 20 in)

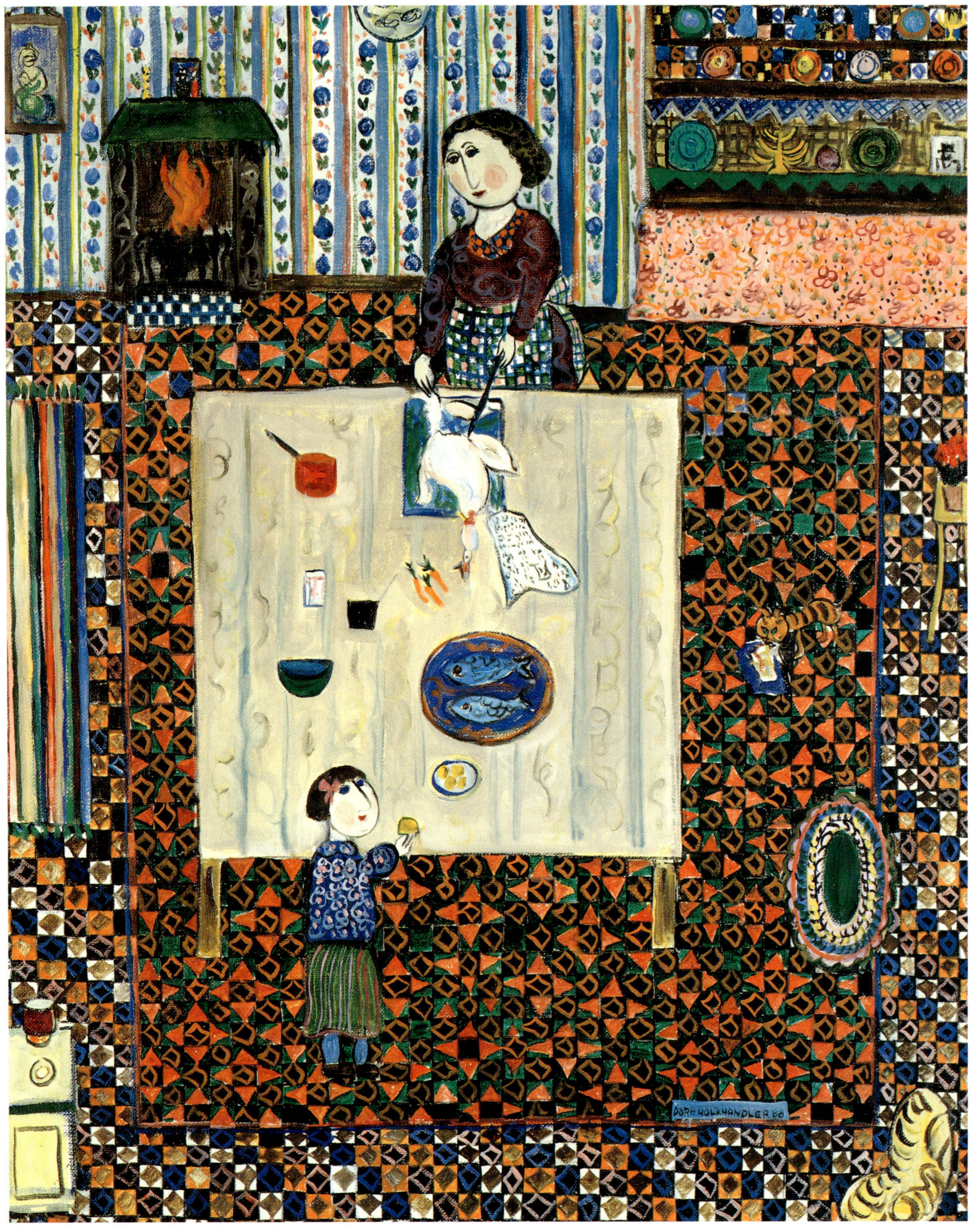

Plate 35
Preparing for the Sabbath   1988   Oil on canvas   63.5 x 53.3 cm (25 x 21 in)

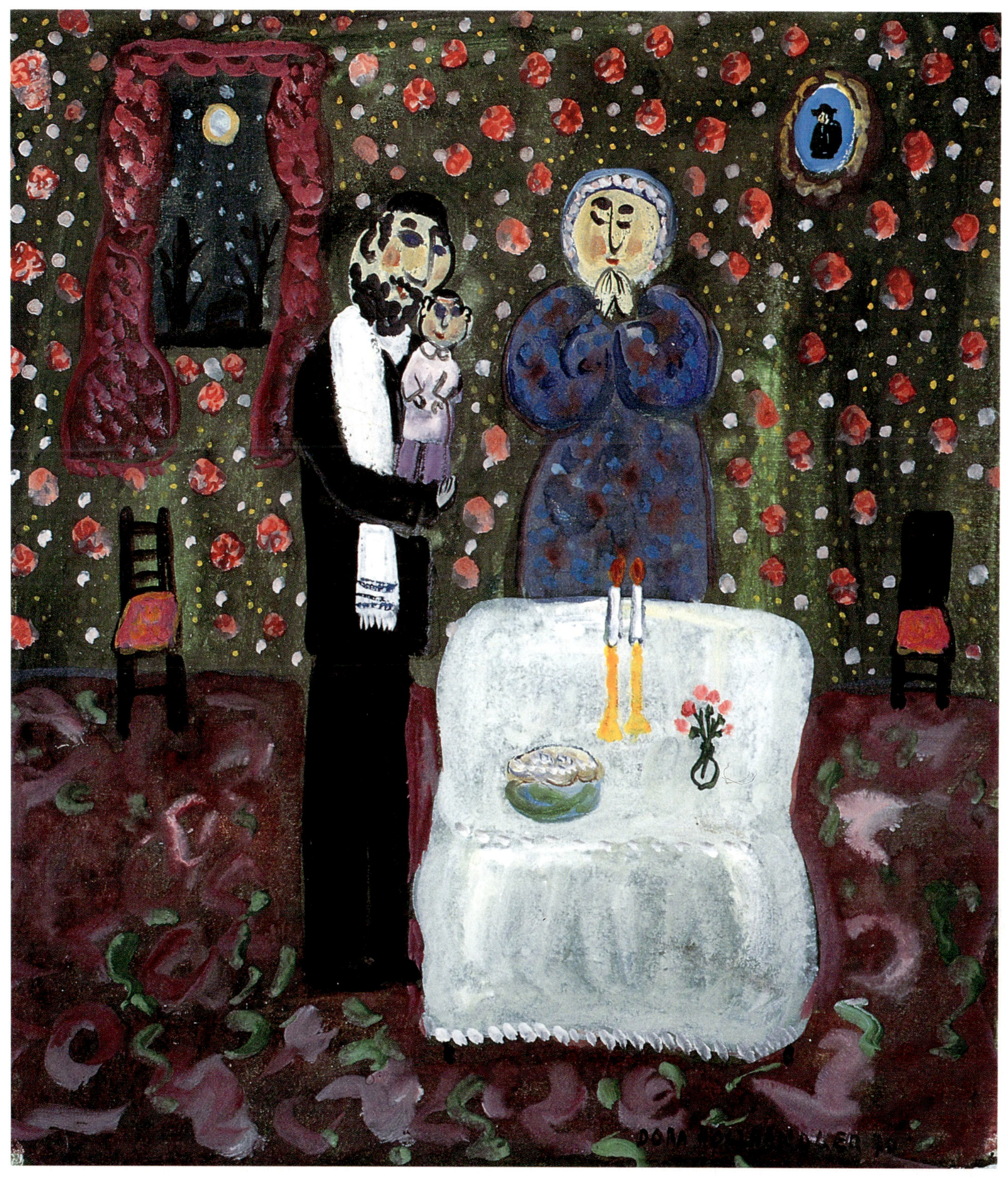

Plate 36
Sabbath Candles   1990   Gouache on paper   30.5 x 20.3 cm (12 x 8 in)

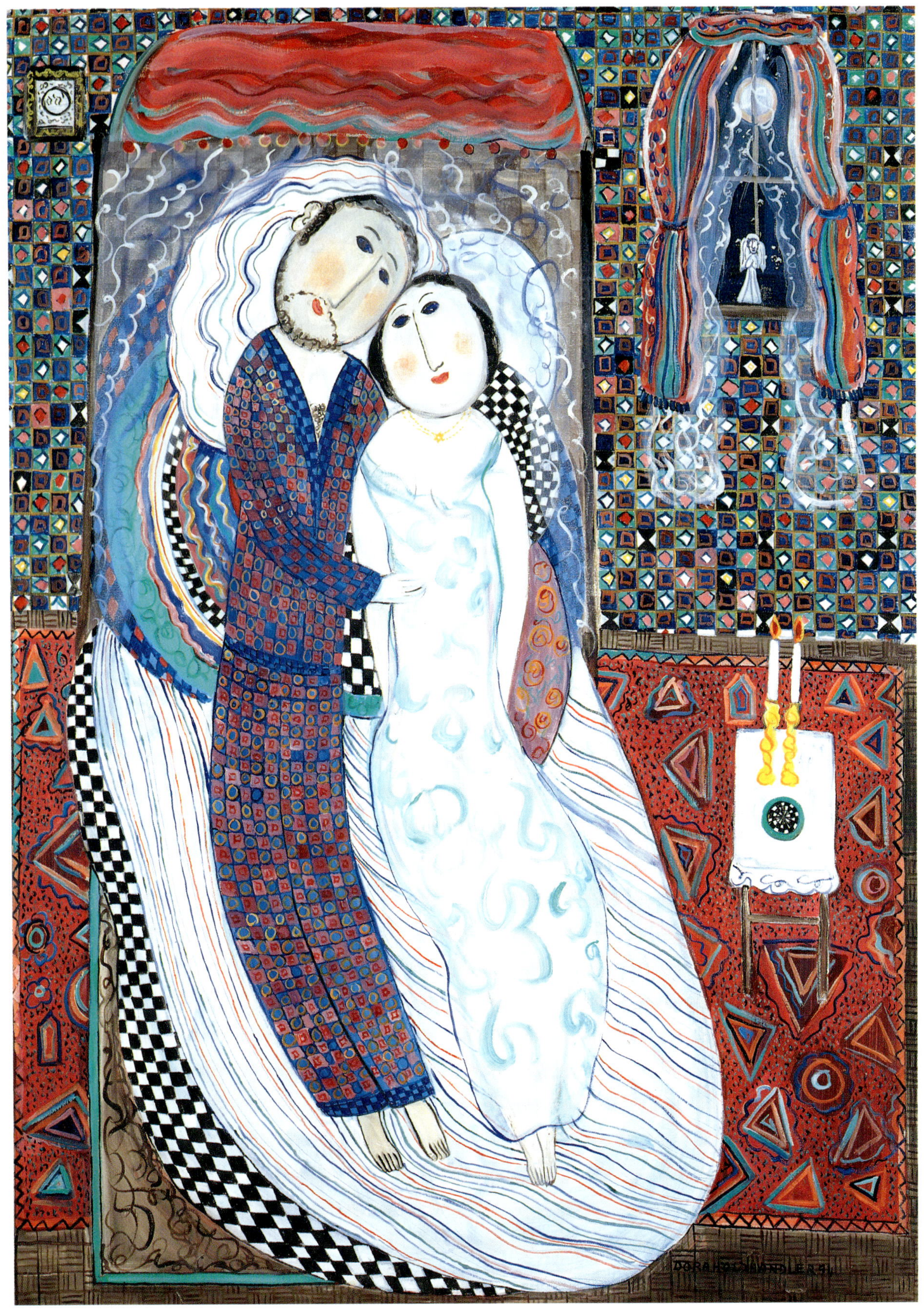

Plate 37
Friday Night Lovers　1994　Oil on canvas　91.4 x 66 cm (36 x 26 in)

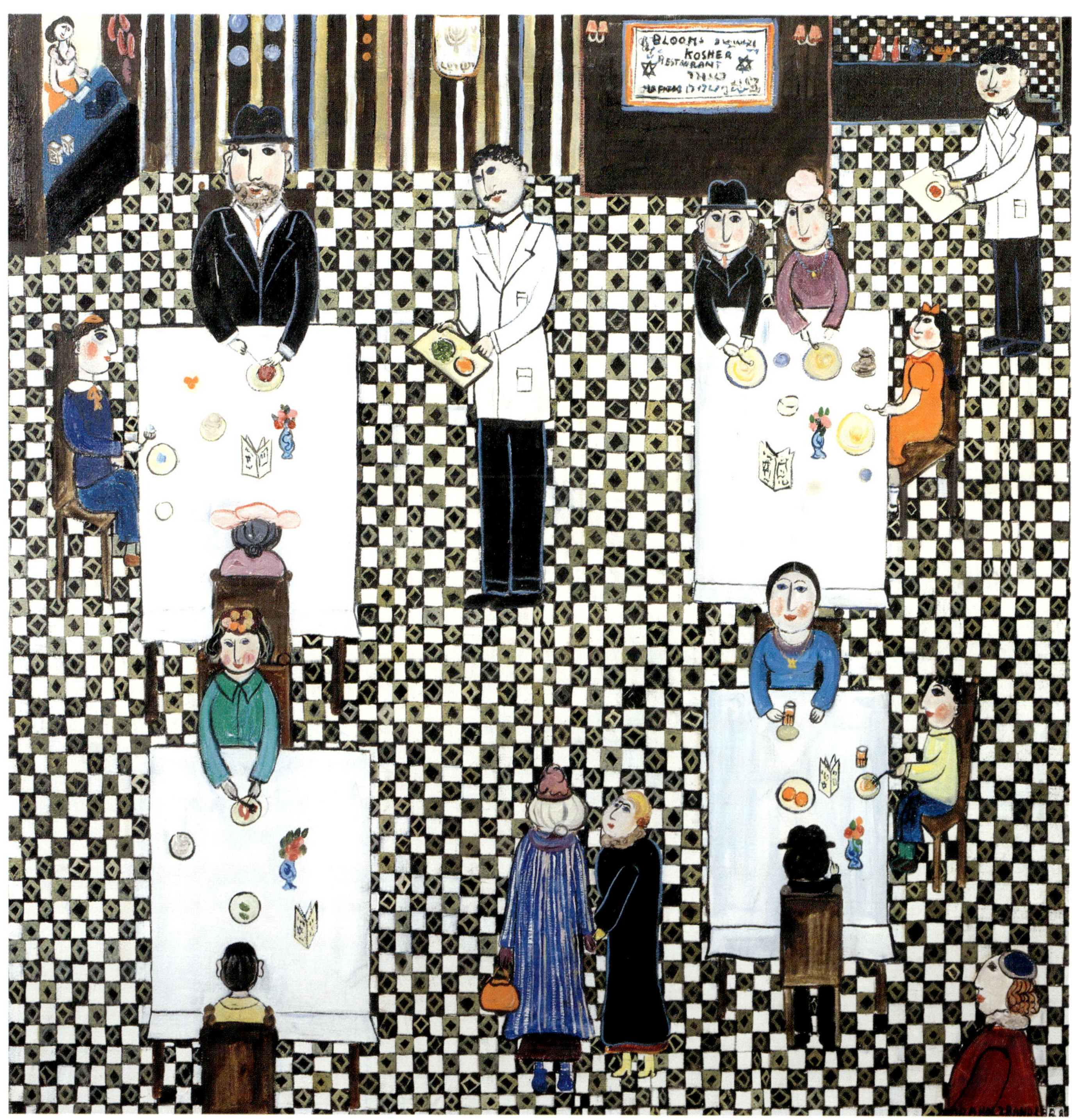

Plate 38
Bloom's Restaurant 1987 Oil on canvas 61 x 61 cm (24 x 24 in)

memory of memories. In the Zohar, such occasions have a mystical symbolism: 'A man's table, used rightly, secures for him participation in the bliss of the world to come, a sufficiency of nourishment in this world, and also additional power and excellency in the right place, and withal, it causes him to be remembered favourably before the Ancient of Days.'[30]

The mother saying a prayer over the newly lit pair of Sabbath Eve candles: this is the subject of numerous portrayals of great inward power and concentration by Dora (Plate 36). A Kabbalist hymn is often sung on this occasion, inviting the *Shechinah* to come to the table as a bride, 'adorned in ornaments, jewels and robes … with the beautiful candelabrum shining on our heads'. Hence Dora's picture of *Friday Night Lovers* (Plate 37), in whose candlelit embrace (in a room enrobed, ornamented and bejewelled with heavenly complexities of colour and patterning), a stillness beyond the powers of human conception is known.

The Hebrew word *Seder*, meaning 'order', is used for the Passover meal as it denotes a prescribed ritual order. Dora's pictures of Sabbath and festive meals are primordially ordered, in terms of composition, structure and meaning. Their form is mandala-like, with, at centre (usually), a large white square or rectangle (the pristine table-top) in a field of patterned reds and other colours (a sacred space, like a Persian carpet, demarcating the grounds of Paradise), itself set within black-and-white checkerboard perimeters. (In her picture of the interior of Bloom's Kosher Restaurant (Plate 38) – now sadly closed – in London's Whitechapel district, the mandala form has shifted somewhat so that there are four small tables set against a background of black and white squares; the mandala is serviced, so to speak, by two sadly debonair waiters poignantly stranded on the psychedelic floor, each holding forth Kosher offerings on a tray.)

In Dora's table pictures, big expanses of festive, white table linen (close examination reveals also a subtle admixture of sky blue) are set with candles, bread, fowl, fish, and ritual accoutrements. Everything is in its proper place; indeed all the family members – grandparents, aunts, uncles, parents, children – are also in their set position according to hierarchy, mother and father usually presiding, with the tiniest offspring often seated with their backs to us, their feet dangling adorably above the ground (as such, it appears that they are both fixed and airborne). In one *Sabbath Meal* (Plate 41), pride of place is taken by a baby – impressively quiffed – seated in a high-chair. Each participant is a known person – a purely imaginative creation who is also a wholly knowable and individuated human being, rooted in childhood familiarity. In these pictures, the sense of order is cosmic, natural and flowing; the 'philosophical neatness' predominating is measurable both in abstract terms and according to the geometry of inseparable human relations.

A glorious precedent to Dora's family meals can be seen in examples from the *Haggadah* (literally 'narration'), an illustrated manuscript telling the story of the Passover deliverance. Remarkable *Seder* portrayals occur in the many beautiful versions of the *Haggadah* from medieval Spain and Germany. Jewish Sephardic manuscript illumination, which came principally from the Islamic-influenced cultures of Spain and Portugal, is notable for its complexities of geometric language – fine filigree and lattice work, and flourishing arabesques. A decorative, Sephardic component, merging with Ashkenazi folkloric qualities, as manifested, for example, in traditional Central European Jewish devotional artefacts, is at the heart of Dora's style. This is not something she has arrived at consciously; her design sense emanates from a deep, pattern-making level of the mind.

Dora has always paid homage to the square as a form of paradisical enclosure (as in a walled garden, a courtyard or a dining room) and as a focal point of human relations (as in the Sabbath table or a canopied bed). Often the four-square is seen to contain the circular – a dish, say, on a rectangular table, the sun or moon viewed through a window, a spherical flower-bed or sandpit in a square garden layout, the curved faces of lovers lying on a bed. Similarly, the circular – a dish, a round table or cushion, a circular rug resembling an enormous rose – is often set within checkered confines. In one picture, a mother, child on her knee, is seen blowing soap bubbles into the air; she is the procreator of worlds, a whole planetary system of orbs of glittering illusion swimming through the air against a fixed universal grid. For a drawing of a wool shop, Dora composed ('knitted' or 'embroidered' are perhaps more apt words) hundreds of multi-coloured balls of wool, each one demarcated within its own square aperture. She says she has early childhood memories of seeing a floor composed of black and white squares, and of Art Deco-ornamented household jars and containers (so popular then in French kitchens); such patterns now carry for her a mystical meaning.

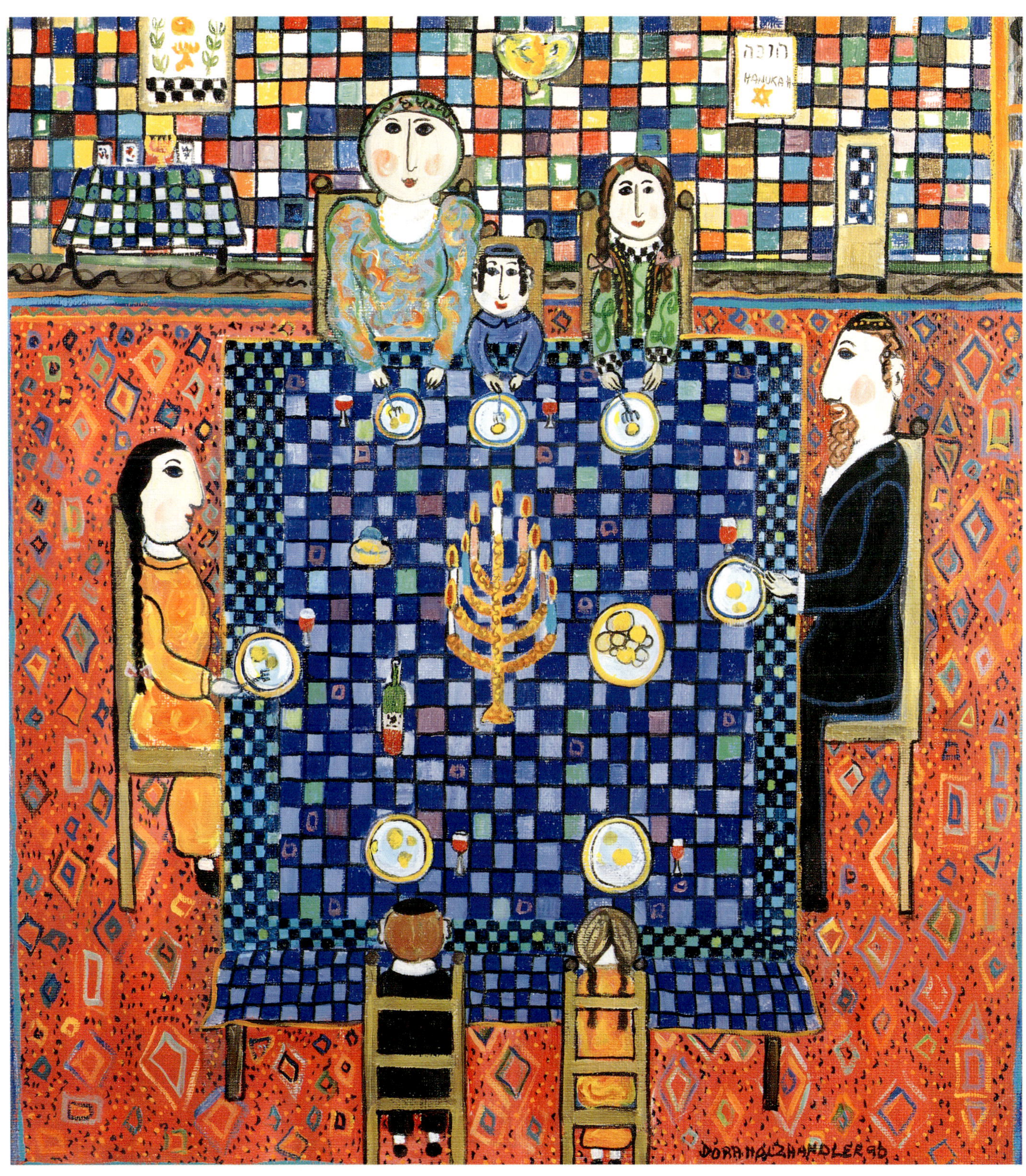

Plate 39
Chanukah   1990   Oil on canvas   40.6 x 38.1 cm (16 x 15 in)

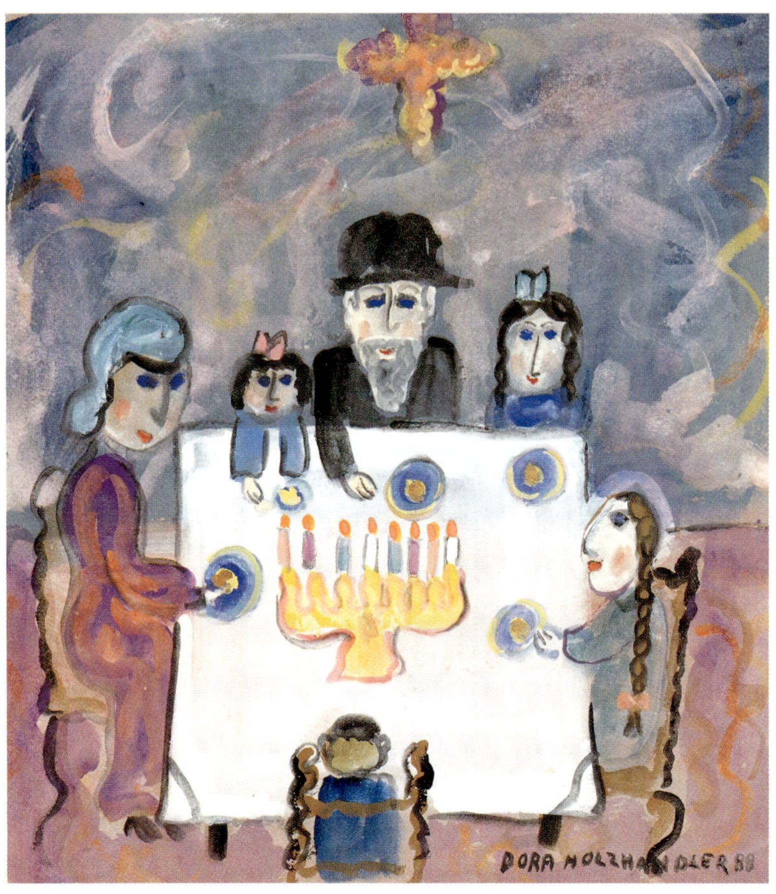

Plate 40
Chanukah   1988   Gouache on paper
29.2 x 26.7 cm (11½ x 10½ in)

In *Sabbath Candles* (Plate 42), the moon glimpsed through diaphanous curtains, round dishes on the giant lozenge-shaped table, the family members' moon-like countenances set within the greater picture's rectangular sub-divisions: each is an example of a mythical geometric operation in action – in this case, a circle is being squared, so to speak. A converse operation is apparent too in the semi-circling of the square seen here within the checkered, domed border of what is either a picture or a wall mirror. Elsewhere, in other works, reiterated, checkered designs are manipulated into star, cross and diamond formations. Dora has an intuitive sense of what is known as quadrature (a technique traditionally used by designers of mosaic pavements), the geometric manipulation of patterns of squares through a basic four-fold or more complex six-fold symmetry, a Byzantine-like operation centred on the hexagon. These transformations – symbolising the ultimate union of polar opposites, light and dark, earthly and heavenly realities – incalculably move the unconscious mind.

To mark the close of Shabbat, the family partakes in the ceremony of *Havdalah* (Hebrew for 'distinction') (Plate 43). Toasts from wine glasses filled to overflow-ing (a measure of blessings to come) are drunk by the adults; a traditional silver spice tower, arrayed with jingling bells and a flag on top, gives off a perfume intended as an aromatic intimation of paradise. On the wall is a picture of two lions holding the tablets of the Ten Commandments, resembling in its insistent and spirited gaucheness the customary design on a *Parokhet* (a curtain hung before the Holy Ark in the synagogue) or on a Torah scroll mantle, with a difference in that Dora has also portrayed two angels (whose representation would be taboo in a synagogue setting). Dora enjoys looking at antique artefacts by craftsmen – silversmiths, embroiderers, wood carvers etc – whose work has traditionally adorned Jewish homes and synagogues.

In *Havdalah*, much of the composition is filled with black-and-white checkered grids, each tiny square fringed with a slender line of twilit, pinkish brown, reflecting the last rays of the sun seen (through the window) as it descends behind the honeyed walls of Jerusalem. Thus the Sabbath's stirring final glow is seen to permeate the design of the whole picture, a synaesthetic evocation of the bedazzling, perfumed music that fills the celebrants' hearts and minds.

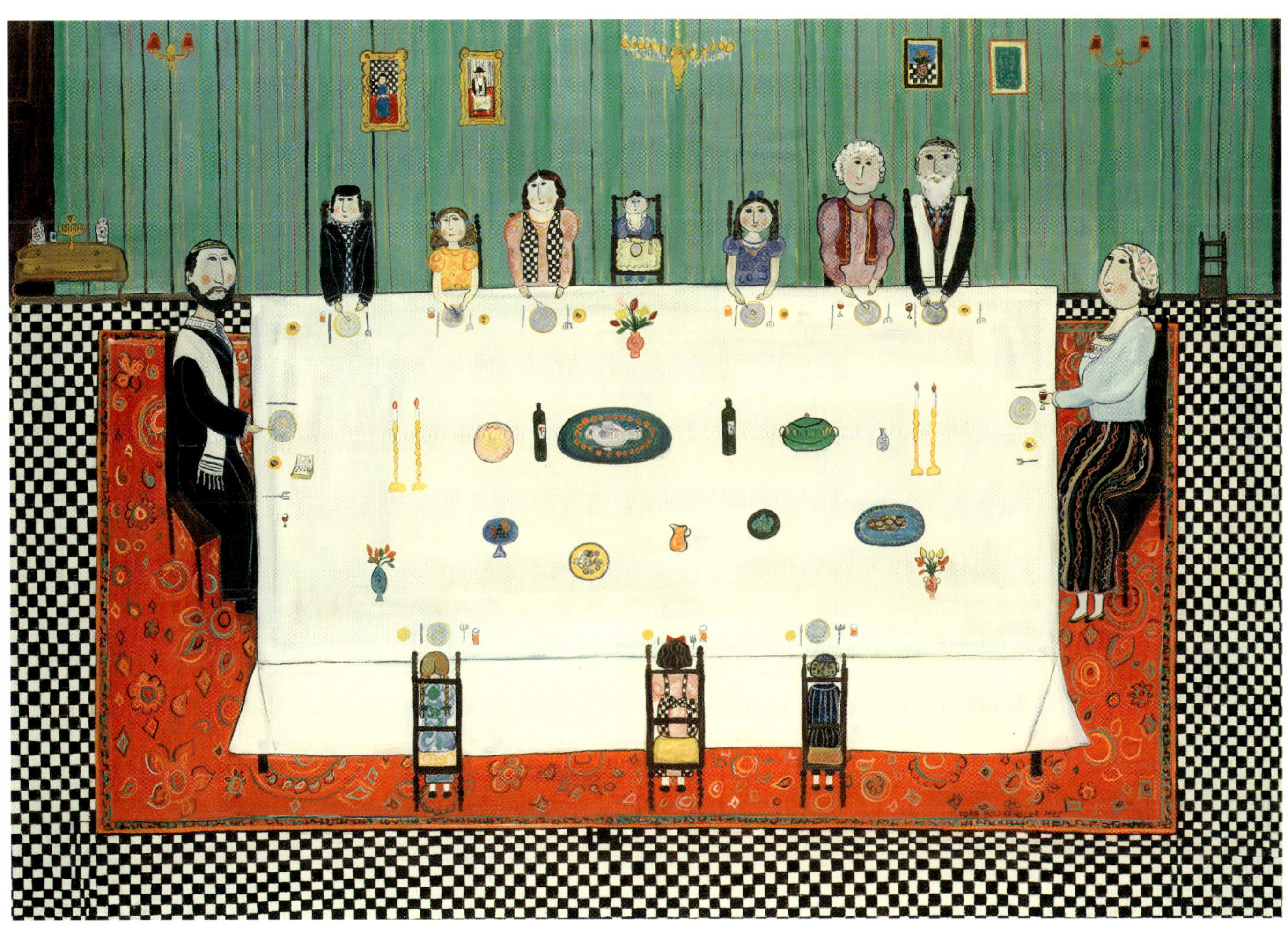

Plate 41
Sabbath Meal 1985   Oil on canvas   91.4 x 132 cm (36 x 52 in)

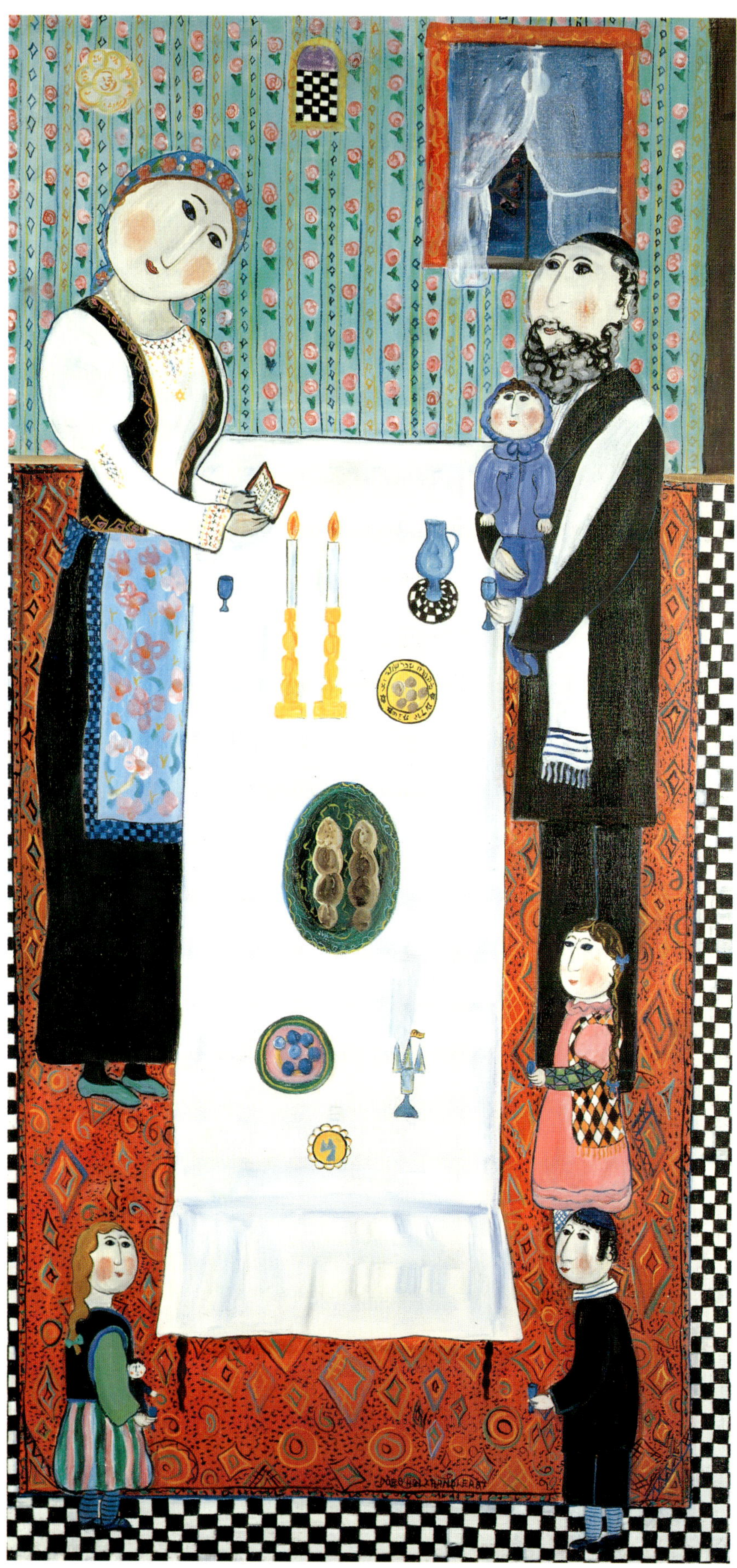

Plate 42
Sabbath Candles   1987
Oil on canvas
139.7 x 63.5 cm (55 x 25 in)

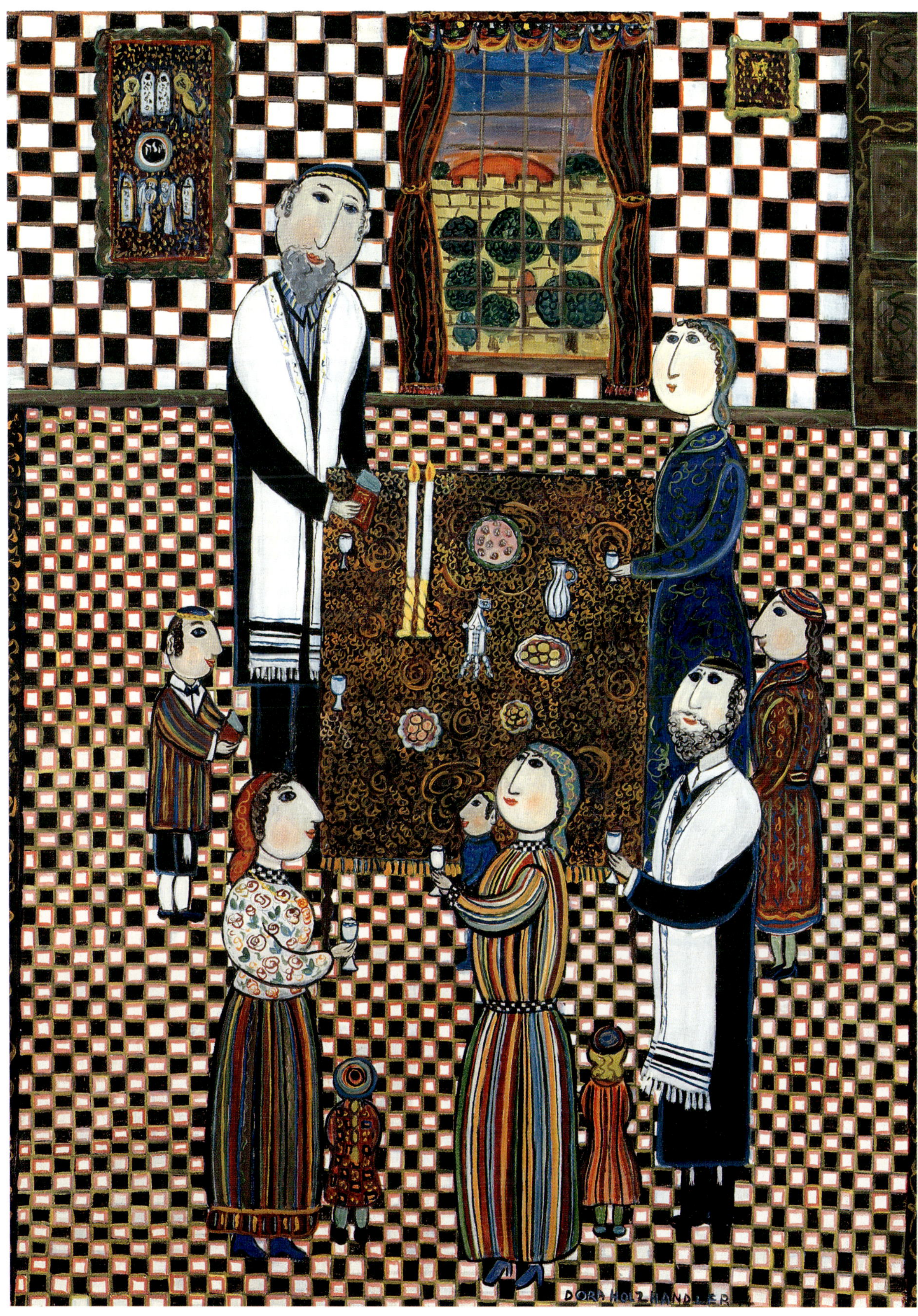

Plate 43
Havdalah   1994   Oil on canvas   76.2 x 61 cm (30 x 24 in)

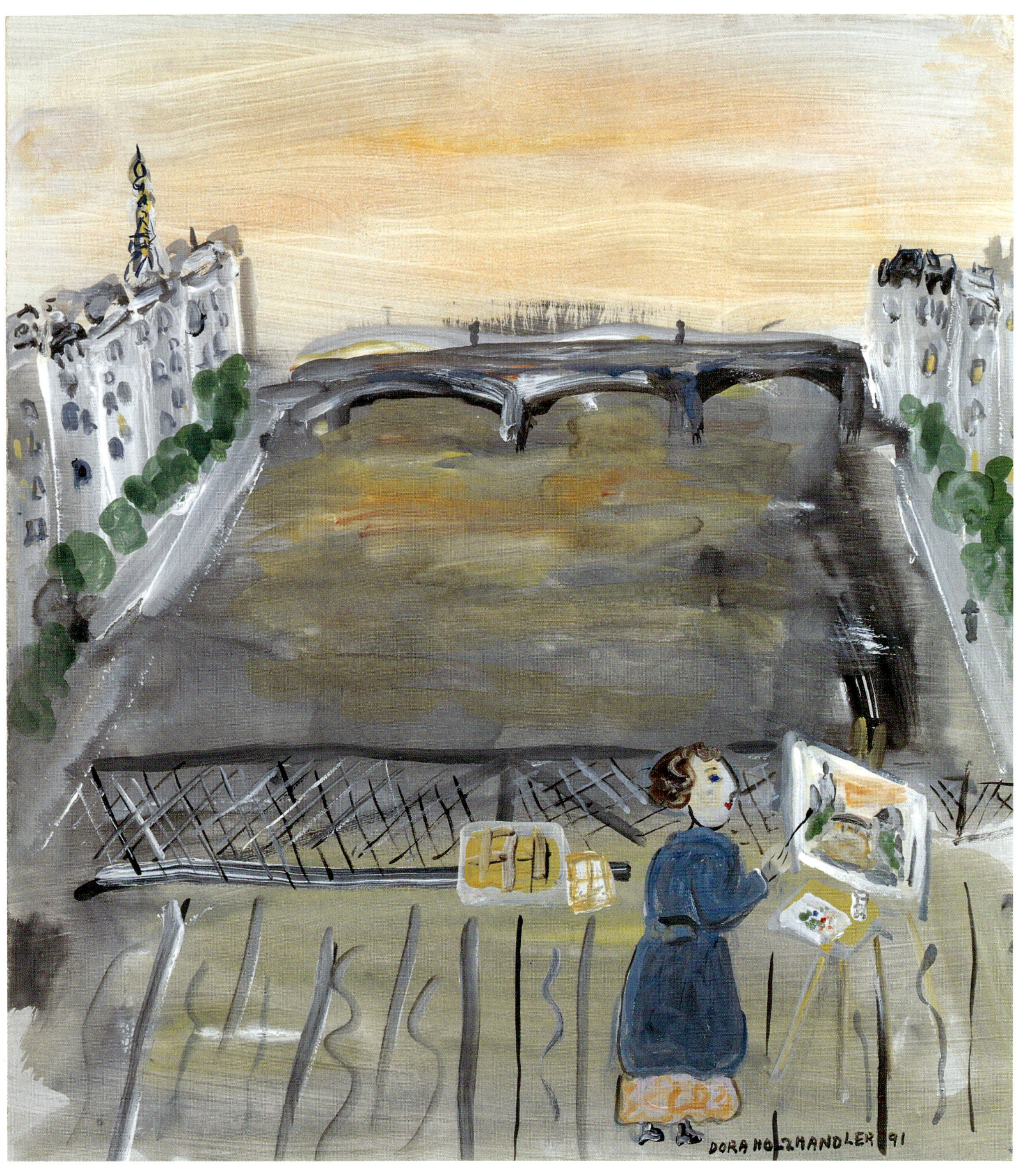

Chapter 6

Plate 44
The Artist in Paris   1991   Gouache on paper   41.9 x 36.8 cm (16$\frac{1}{2}$ x 14$\frac{1}{2}$ in)

The Lion for Real

The Lion for Real
ALLEN GINSBERG[31]

In early September 1939, in common with thousands of other London children, Dora – now eleven years old – was put on a train, wearing an identity label round her neck, and evacuated to the country. 'In a few hours we arrived in Norfolk, in Walpole St Andrews. Mrs Green who took me and two other little girls was a nice lady, a farmer's wife. So the original pattern of my life seemed to begin again, I was once more with foster parents separated from my parents.'

Dora recalls hearing Chamberlain's broadcast announcing that Britain was at war with Germany. She felt 'as if a great black cloud invaded my mind … I wept bitterly, thinking of my grandfather, aunts, uncles and cousins in Paris.' Her teacher in Norfolk, 'a sweet, dark-haired lady full of concern for her evacuee charges' tried to comfort her, telling her 'that although the Germans might invade and occupy France, they would never reach England'. At this, 'of course I wept even more'. Her premonition about her relations in Paris proved justified: her beloved grandfather, Zaida, and her eldest half-sister Marcelle and uncles, aunts and many cousins all perished in Auschwitz.

The Greens were a kind couple, and the three little Jewish girls who came to stay with them were well treated. Dora recalls weekends spent on a farm near Wisbech where 'we three little girls full of delicious country food, and rosy and happy from skipping and running through the fields, were given a pair of flower clippers and told to help by picking dahlias to take home. This was indeed paradise.' It was in the Greens' house that Dora enjoyed her first English Christmas – 'a real country house Christmas, lots of children, games, a log fire and all good things'. On Sundays, the Greens took Dora and her fellow evacuees to a Methodist Chapel. 'I was rather concerned about this reversal of my religious background … I felt a bit "dissociated" – Jesus did not seem to be including me in all this benevolence.'

Echoing her earlier incarnation as 'Maman Paris', Ruchla soon brought Dora back from the countryside

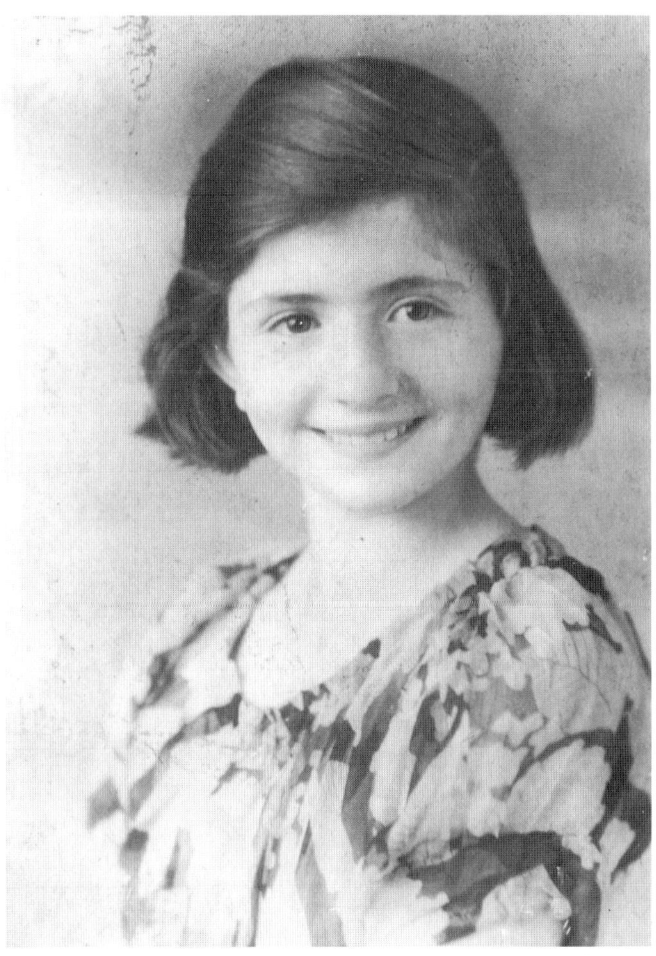

Dora on her thirteenth birthday

– in this case to a London about to undergo the Blitz. After many nights spent in air-raid shelters, Dora and her mother were sent to live in Bury St Edmunds in Suffolk. When Ruchla returned to her husband in London, Dora stayed on, boarding with a family, becoming especially friendly with the daughter, Audrey. 'There are photographs of me at thirteen looking pretty and composed, with permed hair and a sweet smile with little china doll teeth. Religion occupied my mind quite a lot. Audrey said she would become a nun, and to me Jews and Christians seemed to be in a universe apart.'

As a small child in Normandy, Dora had no toys to play with nor can she recall ever drawing or painting then. Instead, 'I spent my time contemplating the sky and the flowers and the animals and insects and birds'. When she came to Paris aged five, she began to draw: 'I remember that having crayons and paper meant happiness, but I also remember that this world of mine was something that I wanted to keep secret.' During her wartime years in Norfolk and Suffolk, she drew little. In fact, her only experience then of art was a depressing one. At her secondary school in Bury St Edmunds, she was made to draw a still-life of an iron bucket and floor cloth. The dreary monotony and over-literalness of the exercise, the 'killjoy' teacher lecturing on the modelling of these dirty greynesses and their shadows, made her heart sink.

Back in London at the end of the War, Dora started reading books on art and visiting the National Gallery: 'I sat up late at nights drawing self portraits with a mirror!' Her bedroom walls were covered in reproductions of works by Van Gogh, Gauguin and Renoir. She had rediscovered what she calls 'my luminous world of art … the glorious paradise of it', and decided she wanted to become an artist. Then 'a great happening' occurred; her cousin Momo, who (possessing a British passport) had been interned along with other British nationals at a camp at Vittel, came to stay with her aunt and uncle in London. Momo had made many friends among artists and musicians at Vittel, and some of them were now living in Kensington and Chelsea. Momo introduced Dora to notable figures like the sculptor Morley Troman and a Russian princess who was now Lady Sofka Skipwith, and to a new world of 'houses and rooms painted white and ablaze with flowers and paintings and *objets d'art*' – a far remove indeed from the darkly introverted, modest interiors at home.

Now seventeen years old, with long, golden brown hair and an attractive figure, Dora was considered by her new friends a perfect artists' model, told she was '*une vraie Renoir*'. Momo soon found her own room in Chelsea, 'to which cultured paradise,' Dora says, 'the 22 bus from Dalston Junction took me daily'.

To her mother's disapproval, Dora obtained a French visa, and in the summer of 1946 she and Momo went to stay with Momo's family who, after the Liberation, had settled in a pretty villa outside Paris. Dora became particularly close to her Aunt Cécile (who was Russian-born and highly cultured) and her cousin Lionel (who later went on to become a renowned Yiddish folk singer in France). Cécile had had the foresight to leave for the unoccupied South of France with her children (except for Momo, who was interned) just before the Nazis invaded Paris; her husband, Dora's Uncle Henri, had stayed on in the capital, and was one of 80,000 French Jews who – in many cases through Nazi collaboration by the French police – died in the Holocaust.

After some coaching, Dora learnt to speak French again, and enrolled on a literature course for foreign students at the Sorbonne; she also studied drawing at an Académie Libre called La Grande Chaumière. The beauty of Paris and its resurgent post-war air enthralled her. She spent time visiting the studio of two of Momo's friends, epitomes of the modern 'artist', and posed for them; their rather self-conscious style and authoritative talk of '*tons recherchés*' rather mystified her, but all the time in Paris her secret understanding of art grew. One day, however, while doing botanical drawings in the Jardin des Plantes, she unthinkingly licked her paint brush which had been dipped in water marked '*non potable*'. Soon she fell severely ill, and was diagnosed with typhoid fever. She was in a critical state for six weeks, and, she says, 'I was left just a little bag of bones, like a concentration camp victim'. When she was well enough, she returned to London to her parents and made a good recovery.

Dora talks about mixed 'nuances in my painting, my French way of seeing things, but deeply intermingled with my Jewish birth'. She loves medieval tapestries, like *Lady with Unicorn* at the Musée Cluny, Limoges enamelware, the poetry of Baudelaire, Rimbaud, Verlaine and Prévert, the paintings of Douanier Rousseau, Rouault, Vuillard, Van Gogh, Gauguin, Monet, Renoir, Cézanne, Colette's writings, the works of the Ecole de Paris – Picasso, Matisse, Modigliani, Chagall, Soutine, Dufy. She also loves the French cinema.

In the gouache *The Artist in Paris* (Plate 44), Dora portrays herself on a bridge on the Seine, in the act of painting a gouache of this superlative vista. Her Parisian birthright is eminently clear. As well as any other, this work displays to the full the acute painterly sensitivity of a colourist whose work has many crepuscular, French overtones. The picture's three main colour elements – grey, green and yellow gold – are distributed and interlinked with skilful subtlety. A rich tonal poem of flaring, sinking, melding colours, suffusing river and sky, it fulfills Mallarmé's dictum that 'to suggest is to create, to name is to destroy'. Buildings, bridge and Eiffel tower, conjured up by fresh, loose, swift brushstrokes, are compact, substantial and deeply familiar structures, at the same time appearing on the verge of dream-like dissolution. Gold dropping from the air onto the leaden waters is beautifully multi-layered within a kind of wistfully (rather than wilfully) abstract conflagration.

Other French correspondences can also be observed in Dora's work. Her picnic and garden pictures have a certain perfume, an air of evanescence and a graceful yearning for the unattainable, in common with Jean-Antoine Watteau's *fêtes galantes*, painted in the early eighteenth century. She finds Rimbaud's espousal of a visionary *'dérèglement des sens'* ('a disorientation of the senses')[32] highly sympathetic. Dora's mark-making in gouache is sometimes close in spirit to what Georges Rouault called his own 'outrageous lyricism',[33] a broad, rapid, unpremeditated form of Expressionistic notation. The penmanship defining and containing her watercolour washes (often generously over-brimming their linear limits), and in her Indian ink drawings, is characterised by a boundless calligraphic quickness, a disciplined spontaneity, at once Zen-like and with some affinity to Matisse's draughtsmanship. The erotic sensuousness and plenitude of Dora's female nudes, and her ripe appreciation of unextraordinary domestic pleasures, find their parallels in Renoir and Colette. Colette once wrote, 'I am tasting all the joys for which I was created'.[34] This uninhibited delight in being alive here and now – far removed from hedonism – is close to the Jewish view, as expressed in the Talmud: 'A man is to give account in the Hereafter for any permissible pleasures from which he has abstained.'[35] At such a point of blessed detachment, Jewish and French nuances in Dora's paintings are perfectly wedded.

Dora is also inspired by the spirit of the painters of the Ecole de Paris. Tribal art, religious icons, child art, popular prints and great naive paintings by Henri Rousseau and the Russian-Georgian Niko Pirosmanashvili (in all a territory of art enjoyed and appreciated by Dora) were revelations for modernists like Picasso and Chagall early this century. Dora is often asked whether she is a naive painter herself. In a literal sense, perhaps she is. The roots of the word naive lie in the Latin word *'nativus'*, meaning inborn, natural, spontaneous (all of which aptly evoke Dora's talent). But the Douanier Rousseau himself, whose work is surely all of these things, was in his idiosyncratic way a cultured man who aspired to the status of the academia of his day. Dora's work certainly shows strong affinities with that of notable twentieth-century 'primitives' – Morris Hirshfield in America, Moshe Maurer in Britain,

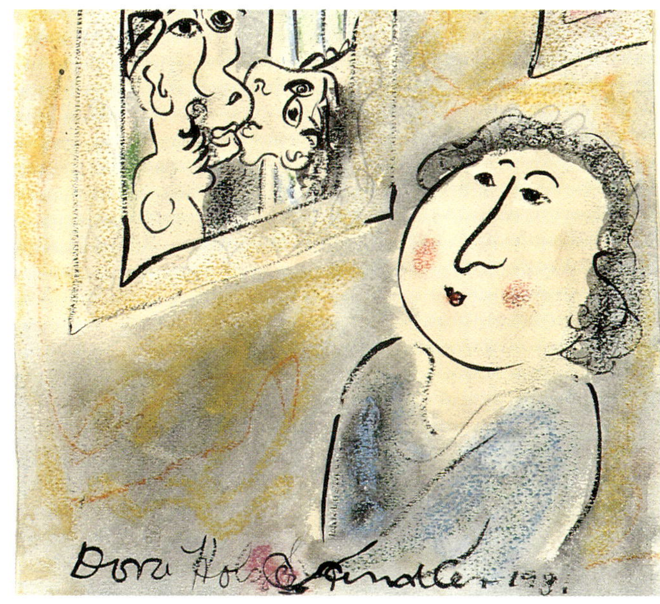

At the Picasso Exhibition, Hayward Gallery   1981
Indian ink and pastel on paper   27.9 x 34.3 cm (11 x 13½ in)

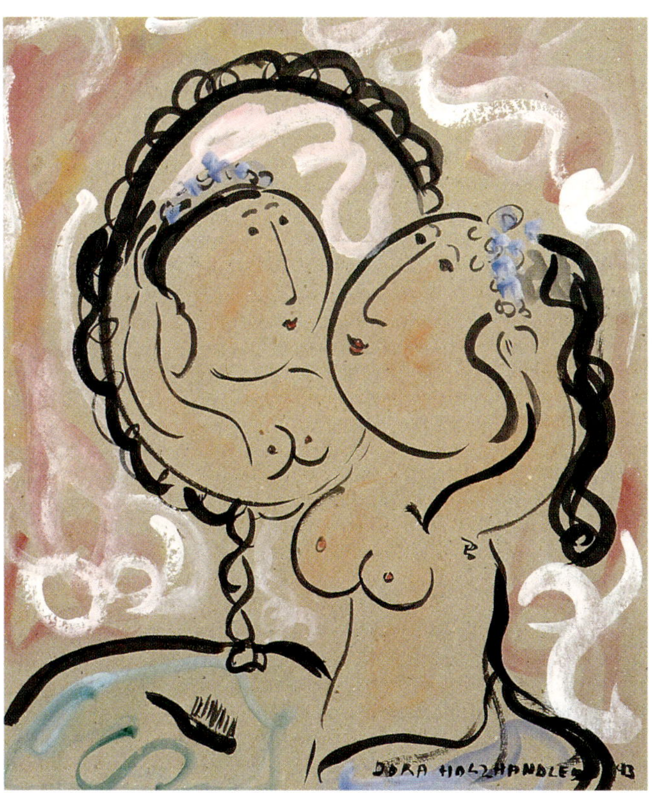

Lady at a Mirror   1993
Indian ink and gouache on card   34.3 x 29.2 cm (13½ x 11½ in)

Nikifor in Poland. Like them, she paints from the mind's eye perspective, not *en plein air* or from life; rarely does she make any preparatory sketches, not even for portraits. Morris Hirshfield had this to say about painting solely through the imagination: 'If I paint a tiger, can I have a tiger pose for me?'[36] – yet the tigers he portrayed so non-academically are tigerish to an unsurpassable degree. Similarly, Dora recreates – or remembers – the world in all its poetic immanence, its quintessence, its unposed suchness.

She calls the process of painting 'a very strange thing. You have the thought – I'll paint, say, a lion. If you do it too consciously, it doesn't look right. Somehow you have to be in a state of meditation, where the thinking is deeper. I read somewhere that Rousseau used to get frightened by his tigers and ran out of the room. That's how art is.' Certainly, the lions Dora paints have haunted looks of alarming sagacity. In common with the great naive painters mentioned above, all of them deeply religious, for Dora 'there is no distinction between what a thing "is" and what it "signifies"'.[37] Each of these artists has, with single-minded intuition, resurrected his or her very own pre-Renaissance perspective on the world. However, Dora could not be described as a naive painter in quite the way, for example, that the American Grandma Moses or the English Margaret Baird are, both of whom were untutored, and started painting delightfully direct and unaffected works when in their seventies. Perhaps a new art-historical category needs to be invented for artists like Dora who are, paradoxically, naive and not naive (without ever being *faux*-naive), knowledgeable but never knowing, whose sophistication comes from a childlike source fathomlessly within.

Some time after her return to her parents in London in 1947, Dora was accepted as a student at the Anglo-French Art Centre in London's St John's Wood. (Soon afterwards, she found a tiny room to rent above a ballet school in Heath Street, Hampstead.) The students there organised sketch clubs, displaying works for criticism by visiting artists and academics. At one, a small painting she did of anemonies was much admired by Victor Pasmore. After she had been at the Anglo-French for about a year, she met George Swinford, who had just enrolled there following his National Service. It was November 1949, Dora was twenty-one and George was twenty. 'Our meeting was very right and auspicious. We had neither of us had much under-

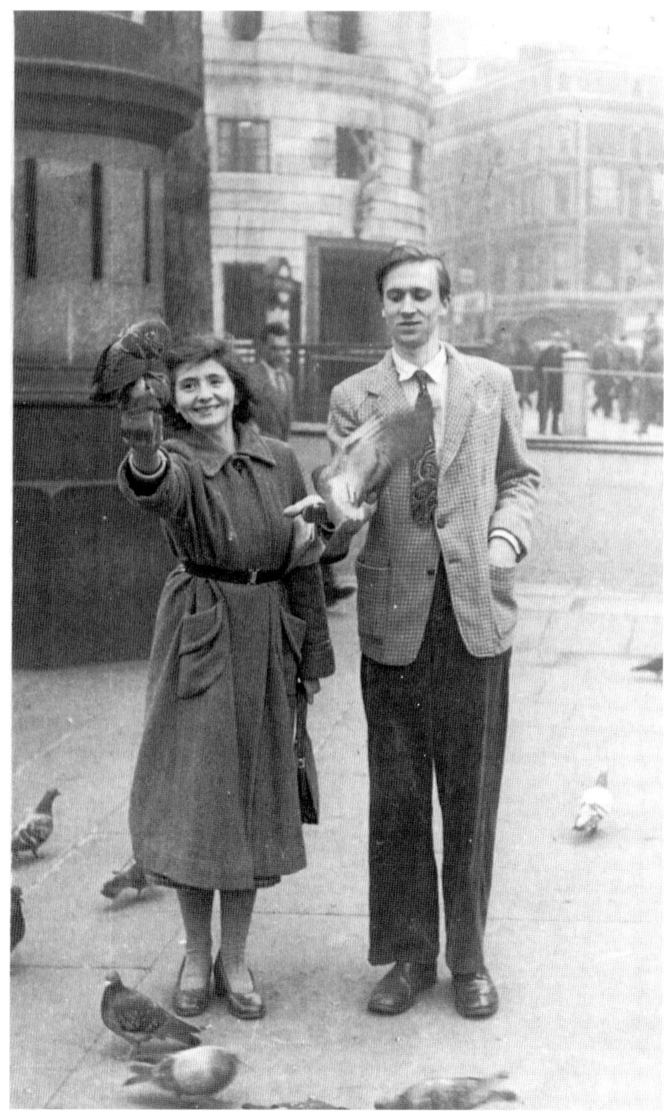

Dora and husband George 1953

standing or sympathy from our families, and for both of us the discovery of the world of art had been an undreamt-of happiness. We have always talked to each other about art and religion, our long loving conversation has lasted forty-seven years.' They were married in Kensington Registry Office in September 1950, and their first daughter, Amalie, was born the following year. From time to time, the young family paid visits to Dora's parents in the East End. 'My parents made us feel welcome, and my father had overcome his Jewish taboo feelings about my marrying a Gentile very well and always greeted George shaking hands and bringing out presents for Amalie … she would sit on her grand-father's knee playing with his watch chain, and my mother served the inevitable chicken soup. George

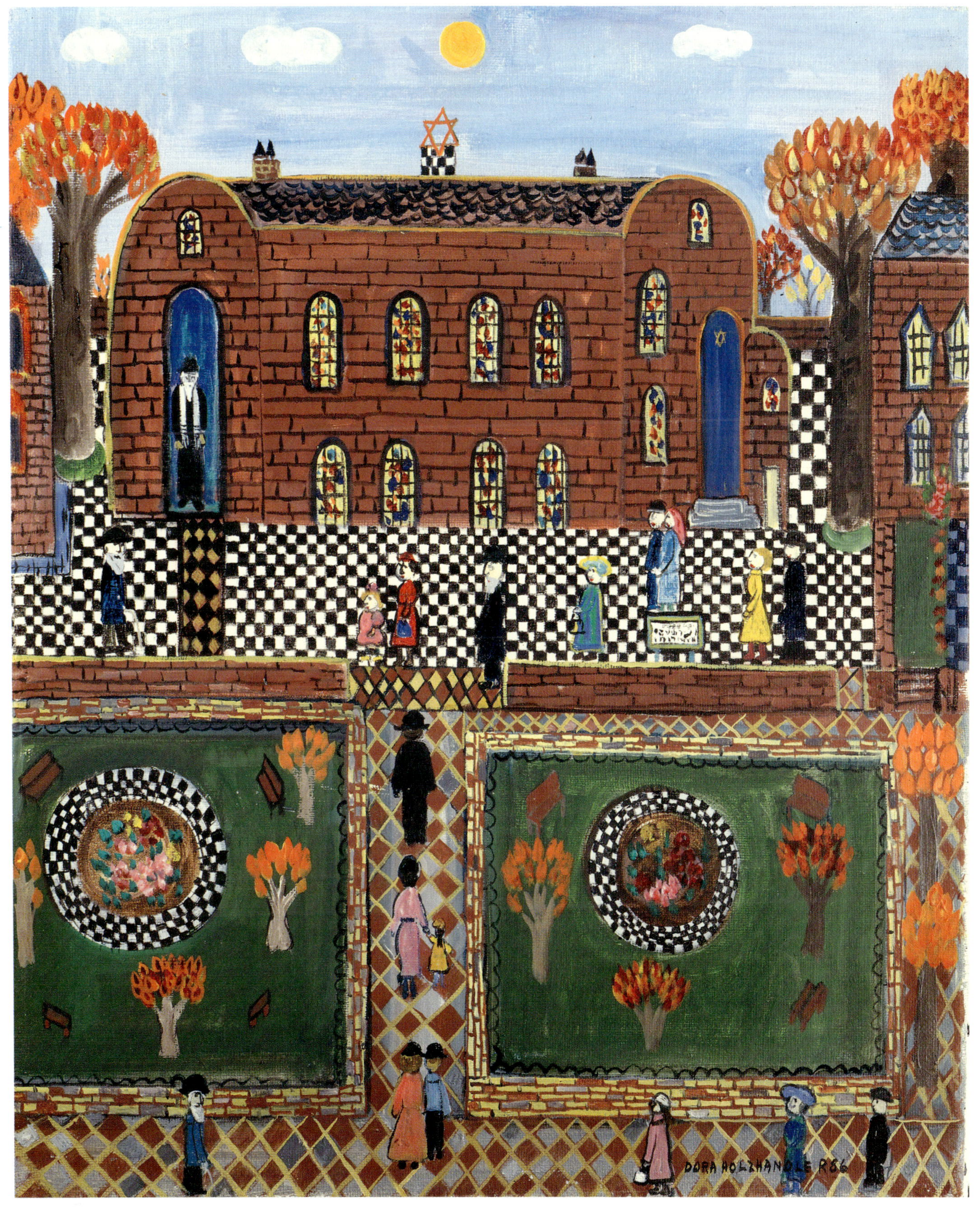

Plate 45
Childhood Memories of the Synagogue   1986   Oil on canvas   55.9 x 40.6 cm (22 x 16 in)

loved this Jewish ambience.'

When, in 1954, her father Sehia died of a heart attack, Dora 'was very upset and cried for several days. I had not realised how much I loved my father – the heart has its reasons.' It was arranged that Dora and George would take over the family flat at the top of a Georgian house in Dalston; Dora's mother went to live with her sister. Stripping away the brown paint, 'we painted everything white, and with rugs and Indian bedspreads and pictures, made our first real home'. George worked as a jewellery maker, and Dora painted her pictures. She describes this period as a rebirth. 'On Sundays, they'd have weddings at the synagogue opposite, and I'd look at them out of the window. It was like beginning again, as it were, with one's roots, which is always very good and strengthening.'

It was at about this time that Dora began to study Buddhism, 'which made me more of a mystic and a conscious student of religion. I was always interested in Judaism and painted many Jewish subjects, but studying it from a more esoteric point of view helped my understanding. In a way, Buddhism has brought me back to Judaism. Buddhism says to seekers that it's only a raft to reach the other shore, and then to be discarded; it's not to do with worshipping Buddha or being clinging. It educates the mind to be non-grasping, happy and accepting. Now, as a Buddhist, I can really enjoy being Jewish. There's a paradox there!'

In *Childhood Memories of the Synagogue* (Plate 45), the congregation, as it assembles, is composed of an ordinary variety of Orthodox people. As always, Dora faultlessly observes the social milieu: the women's hats, clothes and accessories (pink headscarf, fashion-statement blue hat, smart pink coat, the necessary handbags) belong both to the 1930s and to contemporary Jewish Orthodox life (whose sartorial fashions partly reflect and partly resist those of the wider world). The background figure of the rabbi, greeting them at the door, is the key; this slender, upright, authoritatively gentle man is naturally (not naturalistically) shown as greater in stature than his congregants so foreshortened in fore- and middle ground. He wears a *tallith*, the fringed prayer shawl. In ancient times, a single thread on one of the tassels was dyed an azure blue. In the Talmud, there is the following meditation:

The tassel is blue;
The blue is the colour of the sea;
The sea is the colour of the sky;

And the sky is the colour of the Throne of Glory.[38]

This is the blue which frames the rabbi in the synagogue doorway.

The stained-glass windows in this picture, and in *Going to Synagogue in Winter* (Plate 46), are glazed and leaded through a maelstrom of brushstrokes that evoke the uplifting, condensed translucency of that medium, a magic defined by Abbot Suger (who designed windows at Saint Denis, outside Paris, in the twelfth century) as the power to transform 'that which is material to that which is immaterial'.[39] It is indeed this kind of transformative power, based in an awareness (as Buddhists acknowledge) that 'form is empty, emptiness is form',[40] that underpins all Dora's paintings.

The wider historical dimension to Dora's pictures, rooted in her childhood Paris and then London, is a heart-rending one. Britain was not immune to the threat of Fascism and anti-Semitism that shadowed the 1930s. On 4 October 1936, Oswald Mosley and his 4,000 Blackshirt thugs attempted to march through London's East End; in the Battle of Cable Street, 100,000 local people effectively barred the way. Seeing Dora's painted synagogues, with their windows of delicate, otherworldly beauty, whose infinite radii encompass community and cosmos, ineluctably calls to mind, through an insistent and tragic train of thought, the terrible destruction in the events of *Kristallnacht* on 9 November 1938, when synagogues throughout Germany and Austria went up in flames, portending the still greater conflagration of the Holocaust.

Dora's pictures rooted in childhood eschew nostalgic literalism; presented timelessly in the here and now, they are often clothed in three-centuries-old Chassidic garb – as remembered from her 1930s childhood – whose roots lie in the even earlier traditions of what Milton called 'The gowned *Rabbies*'.[41] (Sartorially, her pictures can be quite up to date too: one depicts a little girl in a Snoopy tee-shirt (Plate 51); the cartoon canine has come scamperingly alive, possessing also the rough compactness of a neolithic carving.) She talks about the painterly process – remembering the present – in this way: 'When you paint a picture, you have to start thinking in terms of patterns that work and things like that. But the beginning of a picture, the moment of inspiration, is reliving the actual moment, really. In that way, a person never changes. When I paint something I've seen fifty years ago, it's the same moment recreated. The moment is the truth.'

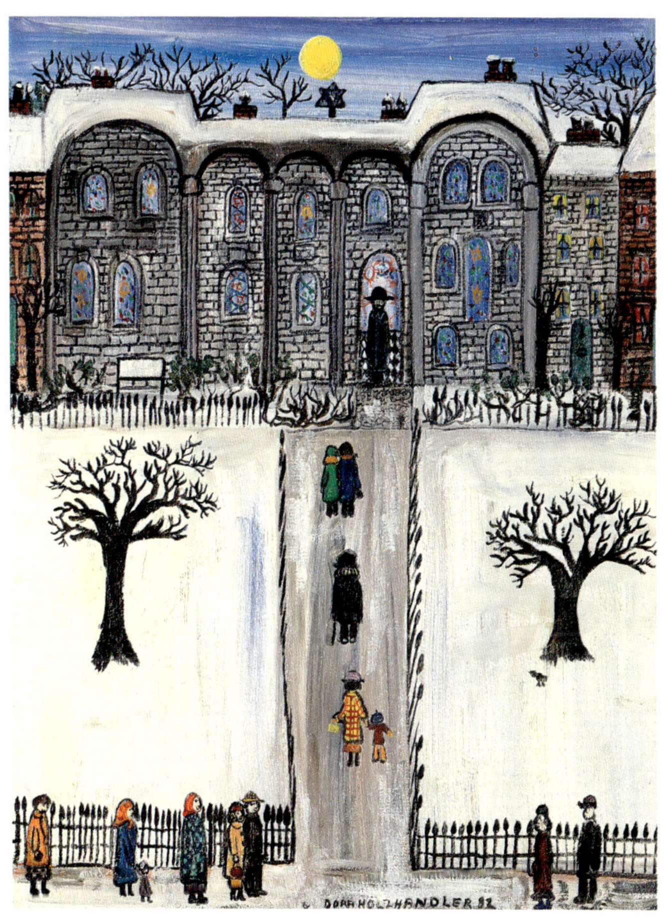

Plate 46
Going to Synagogue in Winter   1982   Oil on canvas
55.9 x 40.6 cm (22 x 16 in)

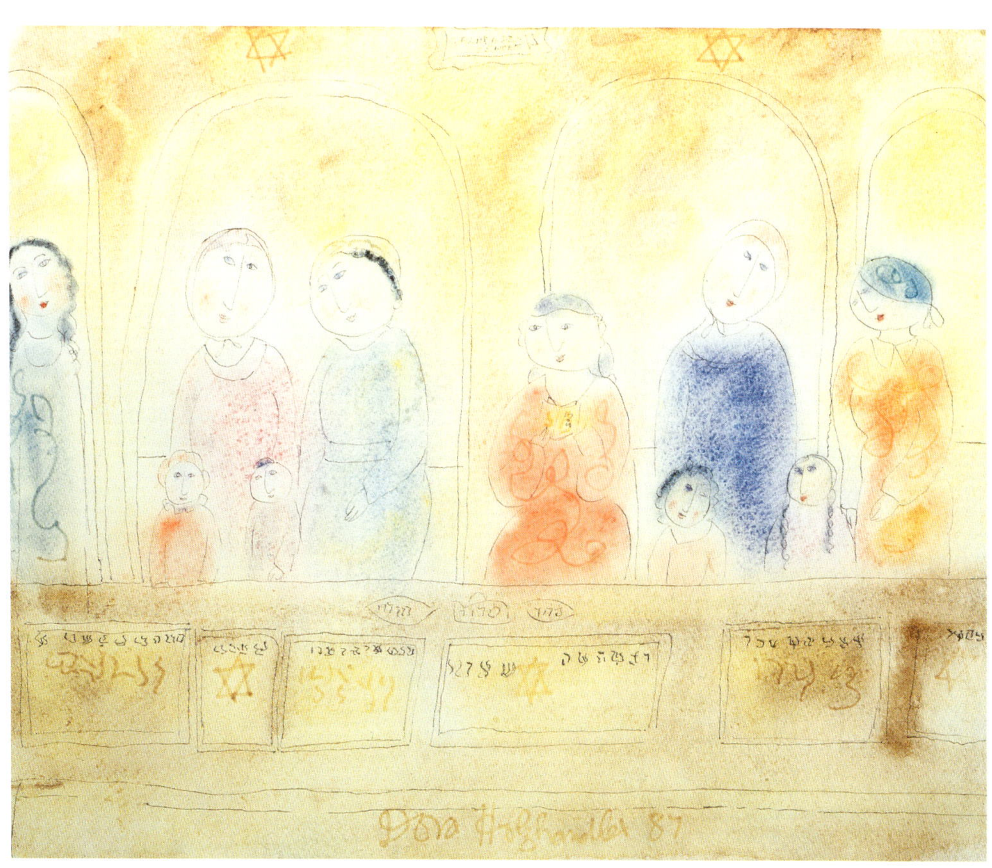

Plate 47
In the Synagogue, Morocco
1987   Watercolour on paper
30.5 x 45.7 cm (12 x 18 in)

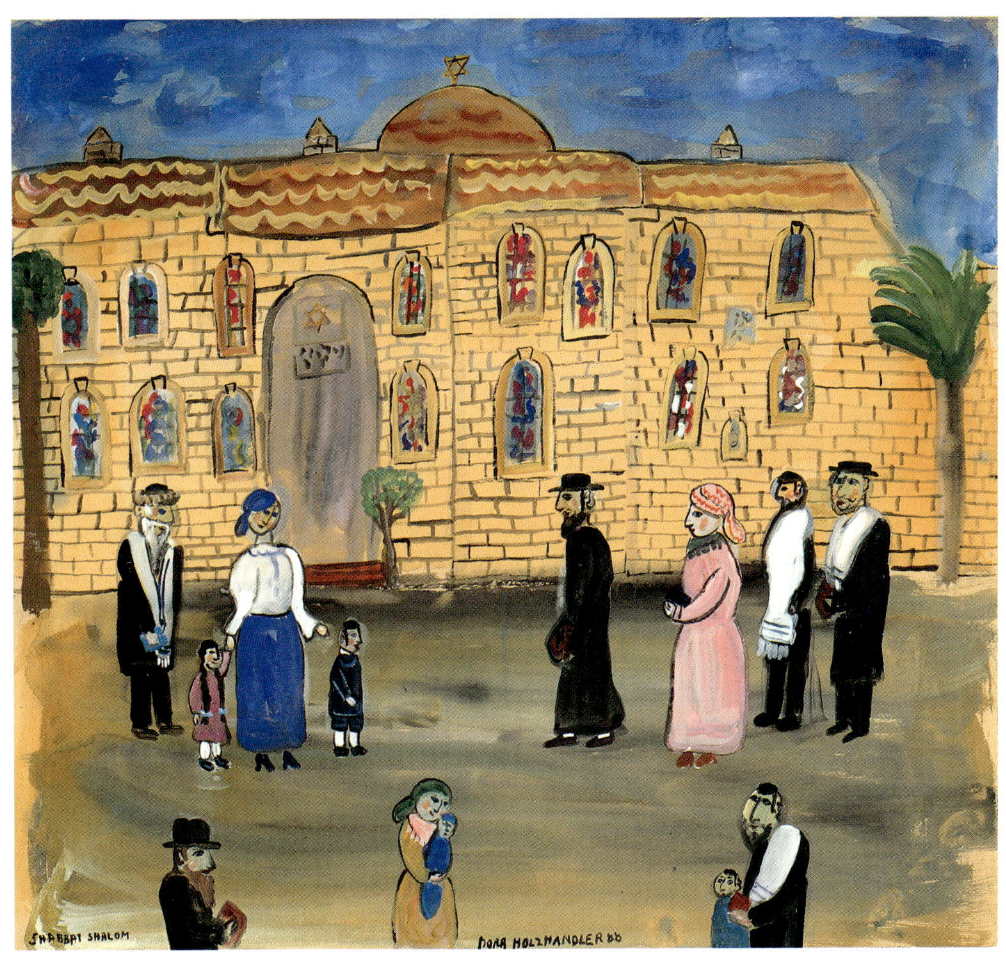

Plate 48
Shabbat Shalom: Sabbath in Jerusalem 1988
Gouache on paper
50.8 x 54.6 cm (20 x 21$^{1}/_{2}$ in)

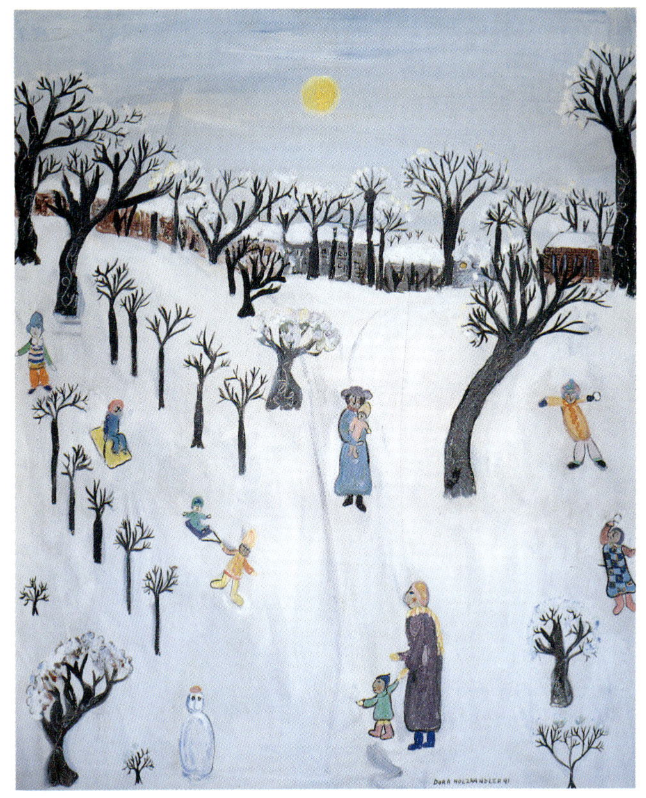

Plate 49
The Park in Winter 1991
Oil on canvas
61 x 50.8 cm (24 x 20 in)

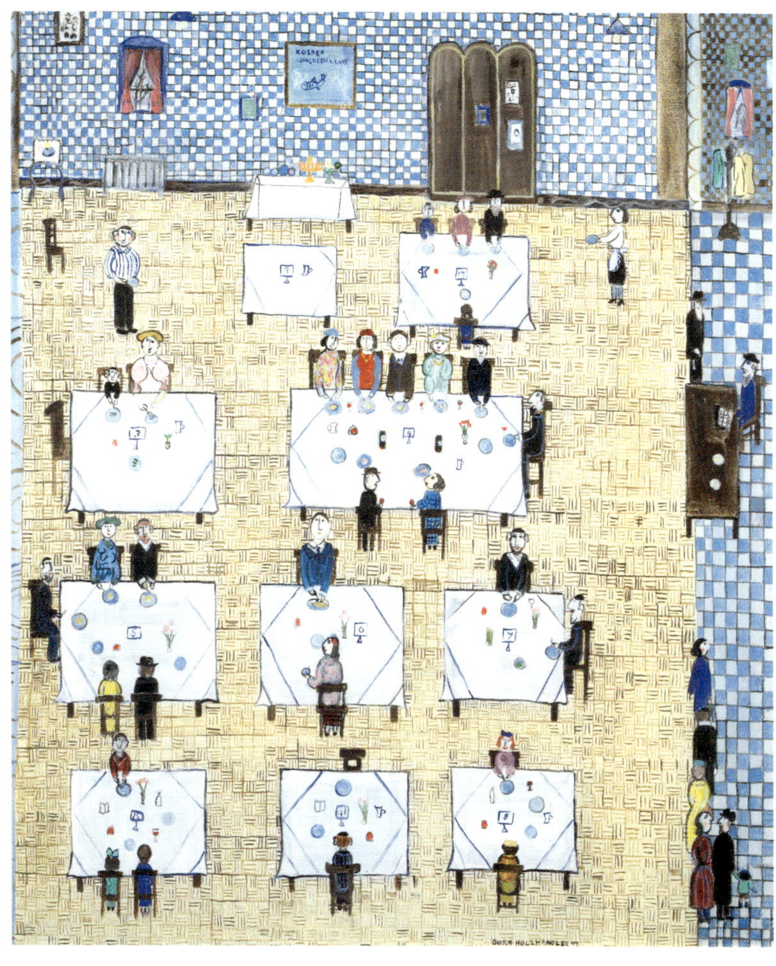

Plate 50
The Kosher Luncheon Club   1992
Oil on canvas   58.4 x 50.8 cm (23 x 20 in)

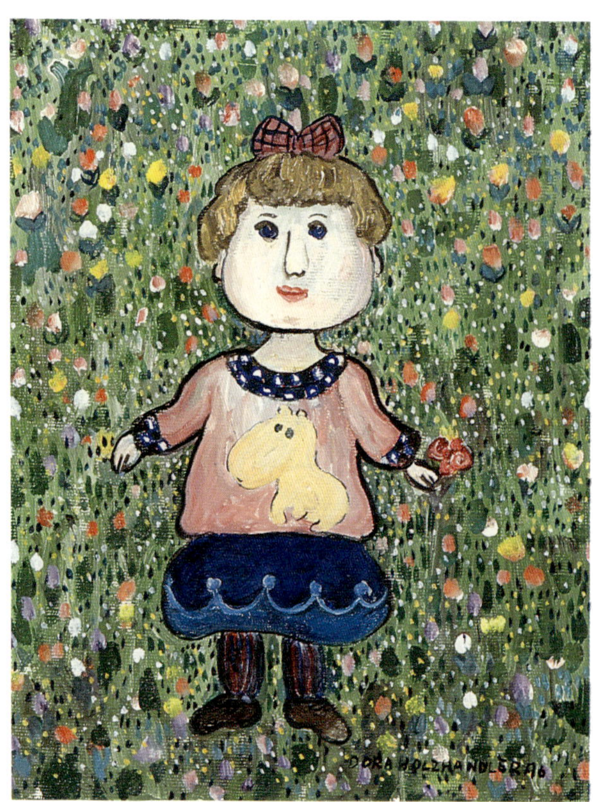

Plate 51
Little Girl with Snoopy Tee-shirt
1996   Oil on canvas
25.4 x 20.3 cm (10 x 8 in)

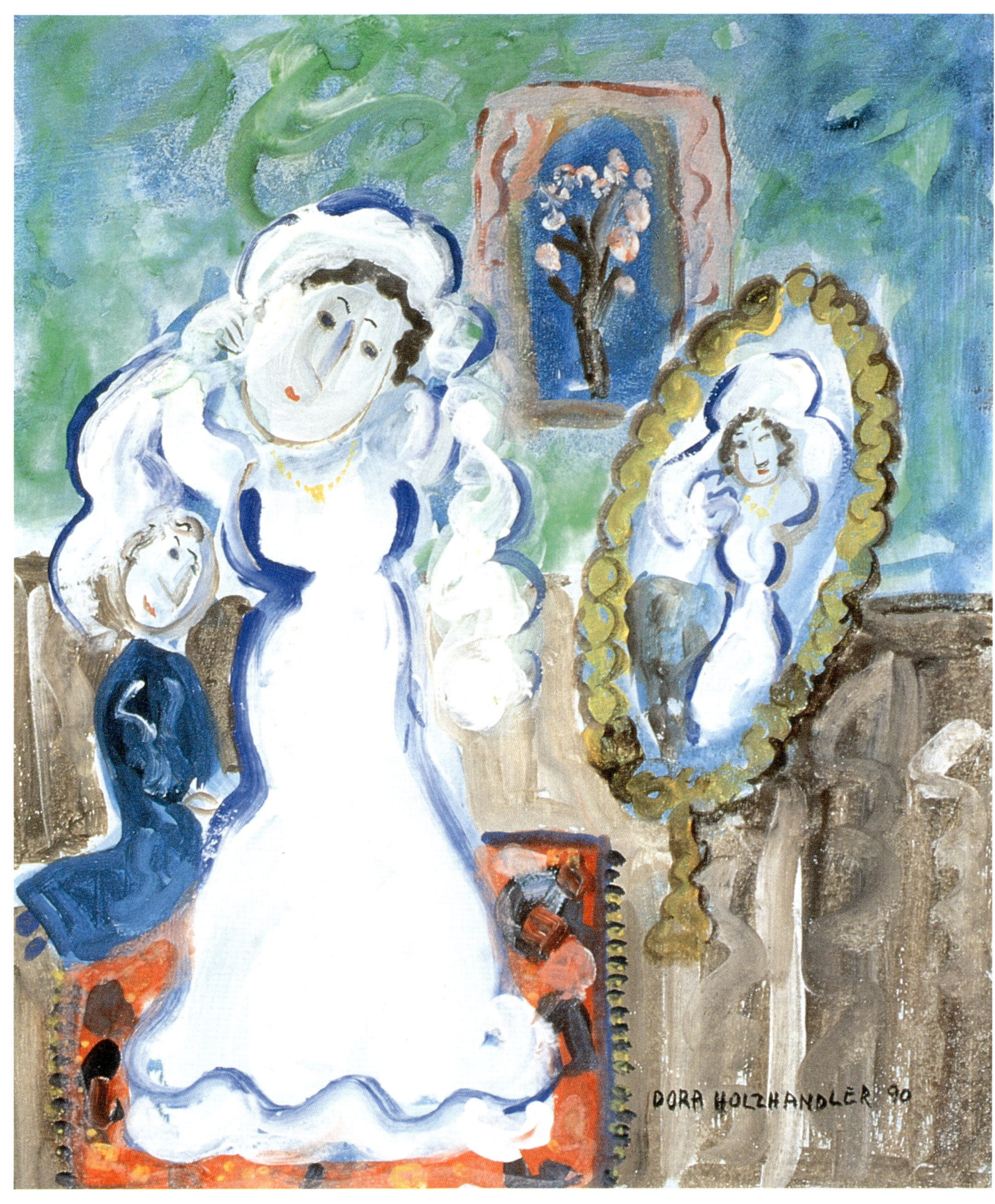

Plate 59
The Bridal Dress   1990   Gouache on paper   20.3 x 15.2 cm (8 x 6 in)

74 DORA HOLZHANDLER

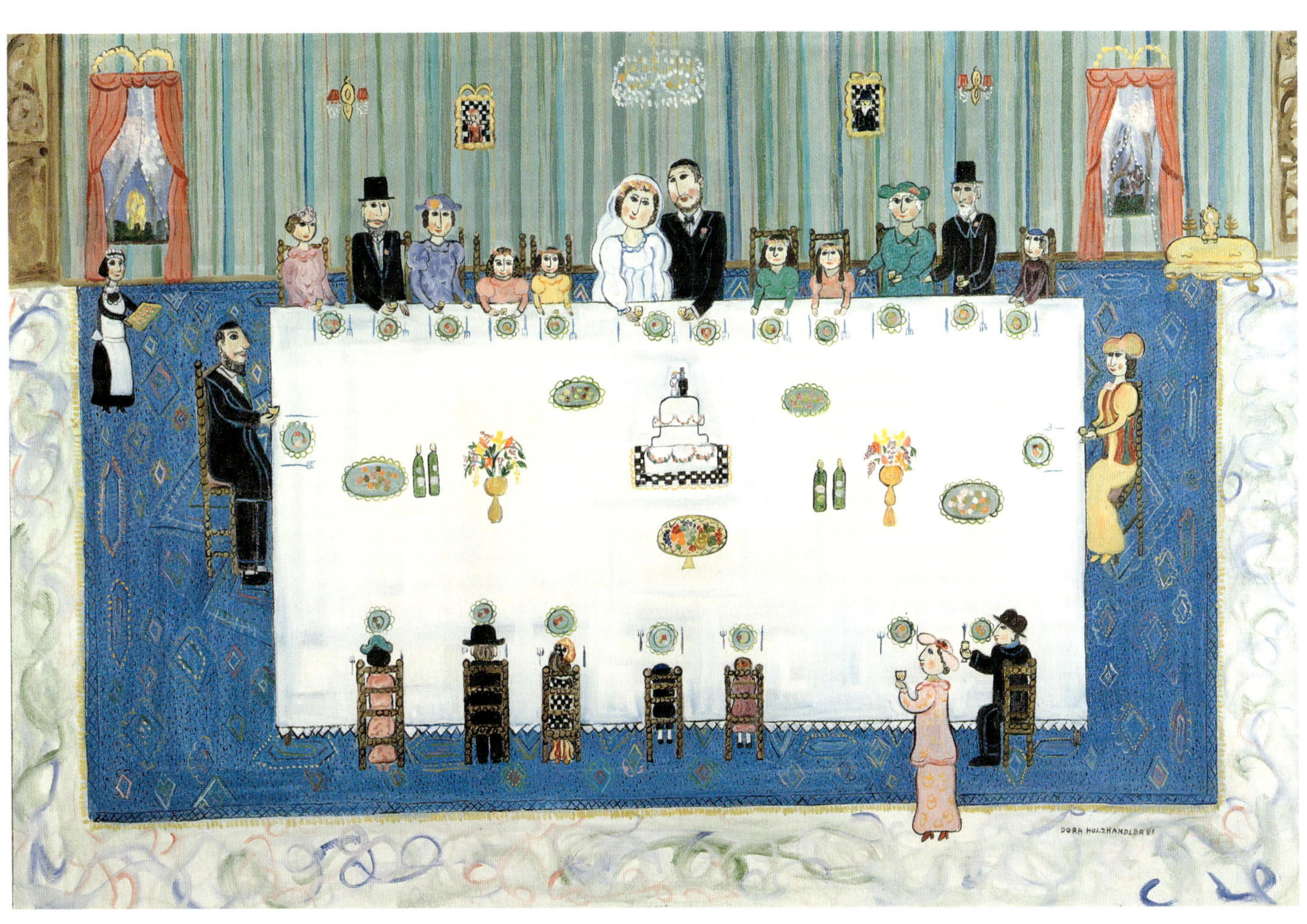

Plate 60
A Toast at the Wedding   1988   Oil on canvas   71 x 106.7 cm (28 x 42 in)

pure no-thingness – the whiteness of the bridal gown and rabbi's *tallith* and clouds of unknowing above.

Other wedding pictures show celebrants moving in sparkling harmony to a fiddler's tune. Music and dance as forms of spiritual celebration have a notable precedent in Judaism. In the Second Book of Samuel, King David is described as dancing 'for joy before the Lord without restraint to the sound of singing, of harps and lutes, of tambourines and castanets and cymbals'.[45] Dora feels temperamentally drawn to Chassidism, a mystical Jewish movement founded by Rabbi Israel Baal Shem Tov Besht (1700-60),[46] to which the destitute Jews of the Ukraine and Poland turned with joy following the dreadful period of Cossack persecutions (in which perhaps a quarter of a million Jews died). Chassidism rejects highbrow asceticism in favour of redeeming the present moment through ecstatic prayer (*hithlahabuth*), and through mindfulness towards all activities – eating, drinking, dancing, love-making and, not least, work.[47] (In so many respects, Chassidim and Zen Buddhists have arrived at startlingly similar insights and conclusions.)

Right up to the Holocaust, Chassidic spiritual leaders, known as *caddiks* (the 'just' or 'righteous'), held spiritual courts in towns throughout Poland, at Góra Kalwaria, Czortków, Husiatyń, Kock and elsewhere. Dora says, 'The fantastic thing about the Jewish mind is its questioning, those secret conversations with an invisible God: "I don't believe in you, or on the other hand I do believe in you." That mixes in very well with the Buddhist point of view. The sayings of Baal Shem Tov are very near to Zen Buddhism. In a way, both seem like nonsense, but are in fact fantastic cosmic humour.' Zennishly, Dora herself asks, 'Why be a rabbi? Why not?'.

The Chassidic cast of mind – its passionately sincere celebration of life even amid abject or unpromising circumstances, its delight in paradox and 'fantastic cosmic humour' as a way to truth – has certainly left its mark on twentieth-century Jewish art, literature and philosophy. Isaac Bashevis Singer and Marc Chagall were its free-thinking heirs. It was Chagall's departure for Paris in 1910 (there, he later said, 'the canvases of Cézanne, Seurat, Renoir or Van Gogh, the Fauvism of Matisse amazed me'[48]) which liberated him to depict his native, provincial Jewish Vitebsk with such original, radical fervour. Dora first encountered a book on Chagall as a student at the Anglo-French Art Centre. She says she finds him 'not so much an influence as

a similar sort of soul. I mean, he loves lovers, I love lovers.'

She is sometimes grouped and compared with Chagall – and in family and cultural background and subject-matter there are parallels between them as well as a certain acknowledged 'similarity of soul' – but there are also limits to how useful the comparison is. It was in the few years either side of the Russian Revolution that Russian Jewish avant-gardists, notably Chagall, El Lissitzky and Nathan Altman, were proudly resurrecting Jewish folklorism in a modernist idiom. The schematic geometry of Chagall's early Parisian pictures owes a good deal to both the discoveries of Russian Constructivism and French Cubism. His figures hallucinatorily defy gravity and waking reason. Dora talks about Chagall's 'floating' subject matter which 'then goes onto another level, almost like surrealism, whereas I always keep my feet on the ground'.

Chagall's lovers partake in an ecstasy of surreal acrobatics; Dora's devoted couples remain whole and grounded, even her transcendently soaring dancers (on closer analysis) are seen to have their feet on – or barely above – the ground. Unlike Chagall, Dora never geometrises or schematises the human form itself, though she consistently introduces abstract patterning into clothes and environment. (In this respect, she is closer to the *intimiste* pattern-making of Vuillard and Bonnard's interiors than to Cubism.) The lovers in her *Wedding Night* (Plate 61) are not free-floating; actually, they are literally embedded in their surroundings. Viewed from an aerial perspective, their reclining posture looks vertical, so that it may appear they are recumbent *and* upright, rooted yet hovering gently above the surface. The generously diverse orientation of sheets, quilts, coverlets, cushions, pillows and pyjama bottoms, has set in motion whole fields of energy, each a flowing, myriad-petalled vortex of its own ('the world's whirling diamond'[49]), embracing contours of the lovers' forms. Pillows of a spinning, radial construction like a rose window are crowns or auras around their heads. Among a little gallery of symbols on the walls is a portrait of an angel, representing the *Shechinah*. Pellucid veils are everywhere: shimmering in the bride's right hand, on side-table and dressing-table, and as a curtain half-revealing the night sky. At the heart of *Wedding Night* is an inexhaustible sweetness – the mystery of naked reality veiled beyond ordinary understanding.

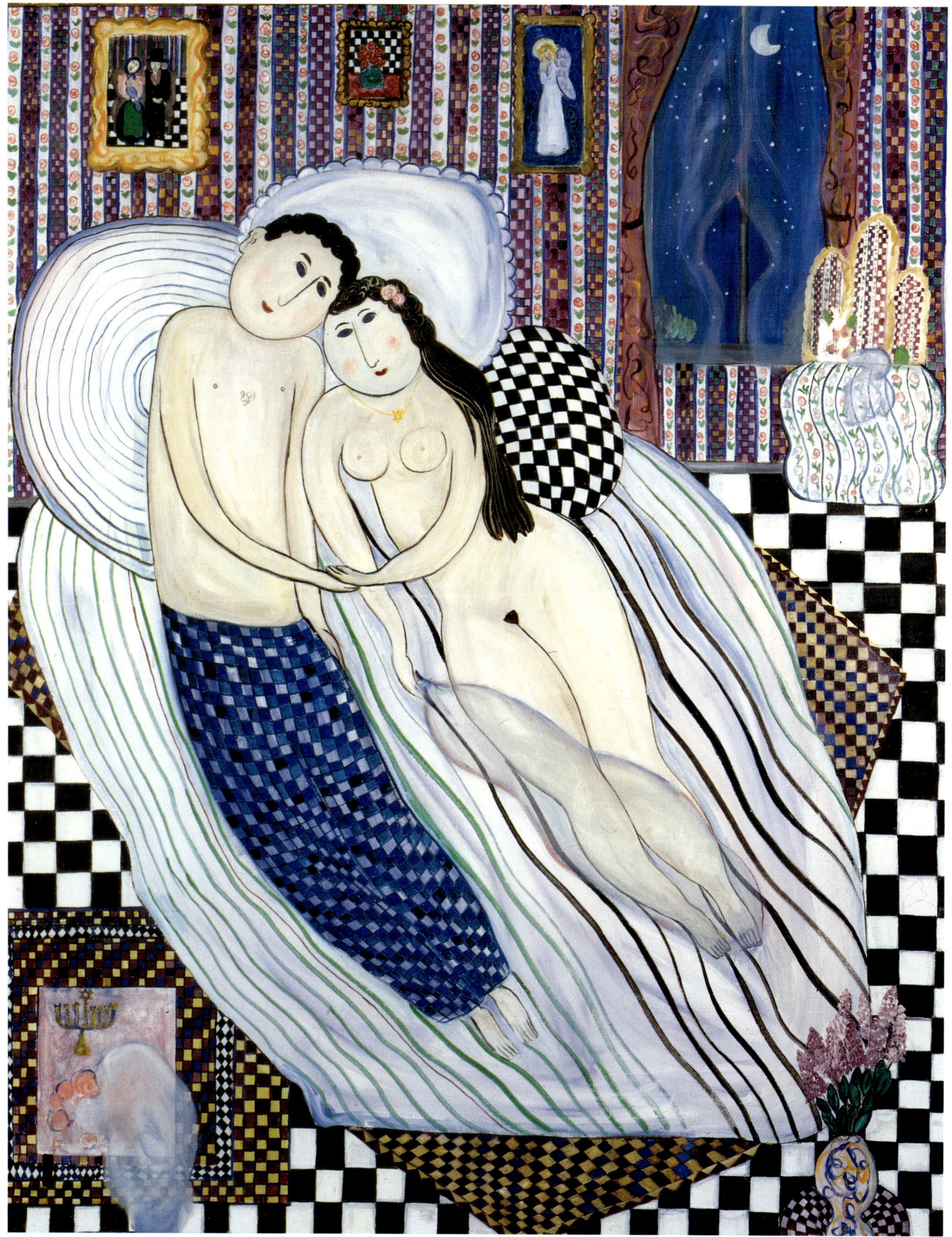

Plate 61
Wedding Night 1989 Oil on canvas 129.5 x 102.9 cm (51 x 40½ in)
Courtesy Gallery of Modern Art, Glasgow Museums

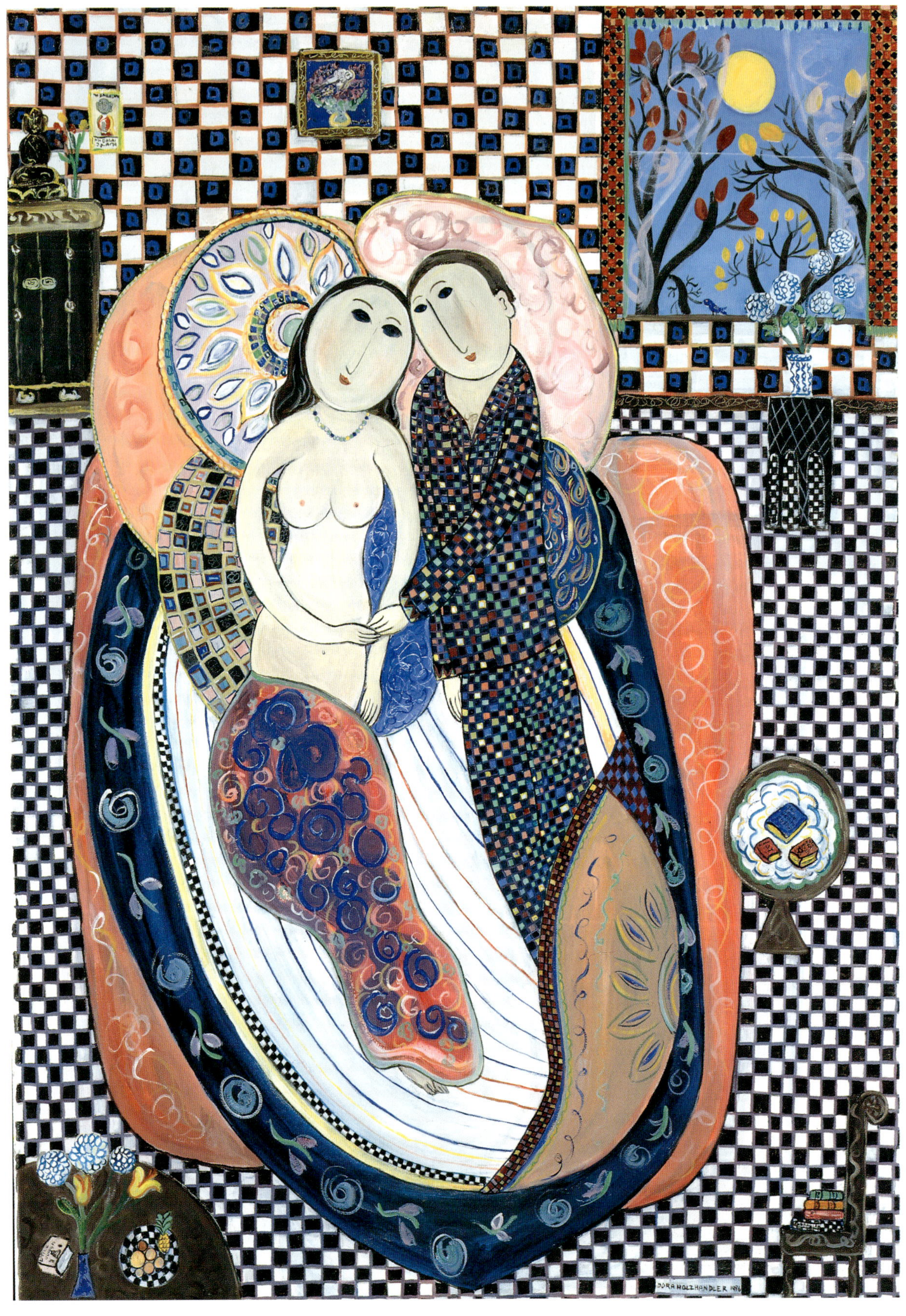

Plate 62
Lovers in Autumn 1996   Oil on canvas   99 x 71 cm (39 x 28 in)

Musical analogy is useful in helping us appreciate such compositions. In polyphony, separate musical parts (each with an individual, independent melody) combine simultaneously to conjure up an overall harmony. So it is in *Wedding Night* (Plate 61) and *Lovers in Autumn* (Plate 62). The latter's fertility of design, detail and reference is astounding. Its basic forms are the square (nearly ubiquitous in the background design) and the orb, seen in the sun, the lovers' round faces, the woman's breasts, fruit, flowers, floral motifs, and in a round side-table (curiously resembling both an egg and a tree – two essential emblems of life) supporting books on Buddhism and Kabbalah. The wall is patterned in what seem to be reiterated *alephs*, in a kind of exuberantly deliberated yet near-automatic script.[50] The man's pyjamas form a complex Op Art mosaic. The woman wears a kind of sarong decorated profusely with flowers. Pillows are, variously, pink, lilac, cerulean blue, checkered and of a sunburst motif. Further layers of pattern and colour (sheets, blankets and rugs) are precisely constructed over a checkerboard floor. On the walls are a portrait of the Dalai Lama and a Chagall picture of lovers floating above a vase of flowers. A little blue bird on the window-sill observes all.

Here, as in Dora's other highly complex, polyphonic compositions, it is as though innumerable, independent melodies are being played at once, creating a continuous, extravagant outpouring of contrapuntal themes. From the picture's epicentre, where the lovers' hands meet, emanates 'a remarkable stillness and serenity of soul',[51] transposing the picture's multitudinousness to a single, sonorous 'no-sound' in a transcendent key. (Similarly, for Dora, the messages of Jewish and Buddhist mysticism are seen ultimately to meet at a point beyond words.)

In Judaism, no essential split is predicated between mind, body and spirit; their source is seen as one. Therefore, the traditional Jewish attitude towards sexual intimacy has been (on the whole) a healthy one. The great Spanish Talmudic scholar Moses Nachmanides (d. 1270), whose writings helped spread Kabbalism in Spain a few decades before the publication of the Zohar, wrote: 'Sexual intercourse between a man and a woman is both unsoiled and sacred ... God made everything and didn't make anything unattractive or disgusting ... The male is the unknown of wisdom and the female is the unknown of understanding and the unblemished act of sex contains the unknown of knowledge.'[52] This attitude is virtually identical to

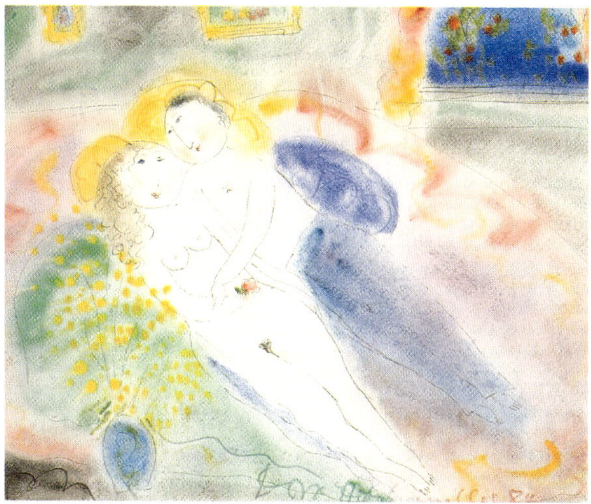

Plate 63
Lovers with Mimosa 1984 Watercolour on paper
27.9 x 33 cm (11 x 13 in)

that which informs the Tantric tradition in Hinduism and Buddhism. Dora recognises this affinity, and in one painting of lovers has represented on the wall an ancient Hindu relief sculpture of a couple enjoying sexual intercourse. She says, 'I find naked ladies very easy to paint'. It is noticeable that, on occasion (as in her portrayals of the statue of Liberté in La Place de la République or the dancers at Paris's Folies-Bergères), they are akin to temple statues of Hindu goddesses, undulating with waves of ecstatic energy or *kundalini*.

Dora has found watercolour a perfect medium to evoke lovers' abandon or egolessness.[53] In *Lovers with Mimosa* (Plate 63), the white paper brings light to every element of the composition. The lovers' faces and bodies radiate the spendid 'no-thingness' that comes from unmarked, virgin paper. In this medium, Dora achieves molten intensities of colour. The sun is seen not only in the profound blue, orange-starred sky; it also infuses the room's interior, in gilded frames, a vase of yellow mimosa, and pillows, like golden crowns or auras, which support the lovers' heads. Areas of grey and black wash form a sombre counterpoint to all this spreading sumptuousness of colour and lucidity. With characteristically succinct, pared-down penmanship, a few strokes deftly describe the woman's pubic hair, hair on the man's chest, the couple's feet and, in the woman's right hand, a rose, which, at the very heart of the picture, is the life-blood of the lovers' mutual enlightenment. (Interestingly, in the Kabbalah, the centre of the rose is described as the sun, its petals as nature's manifold harmony.)

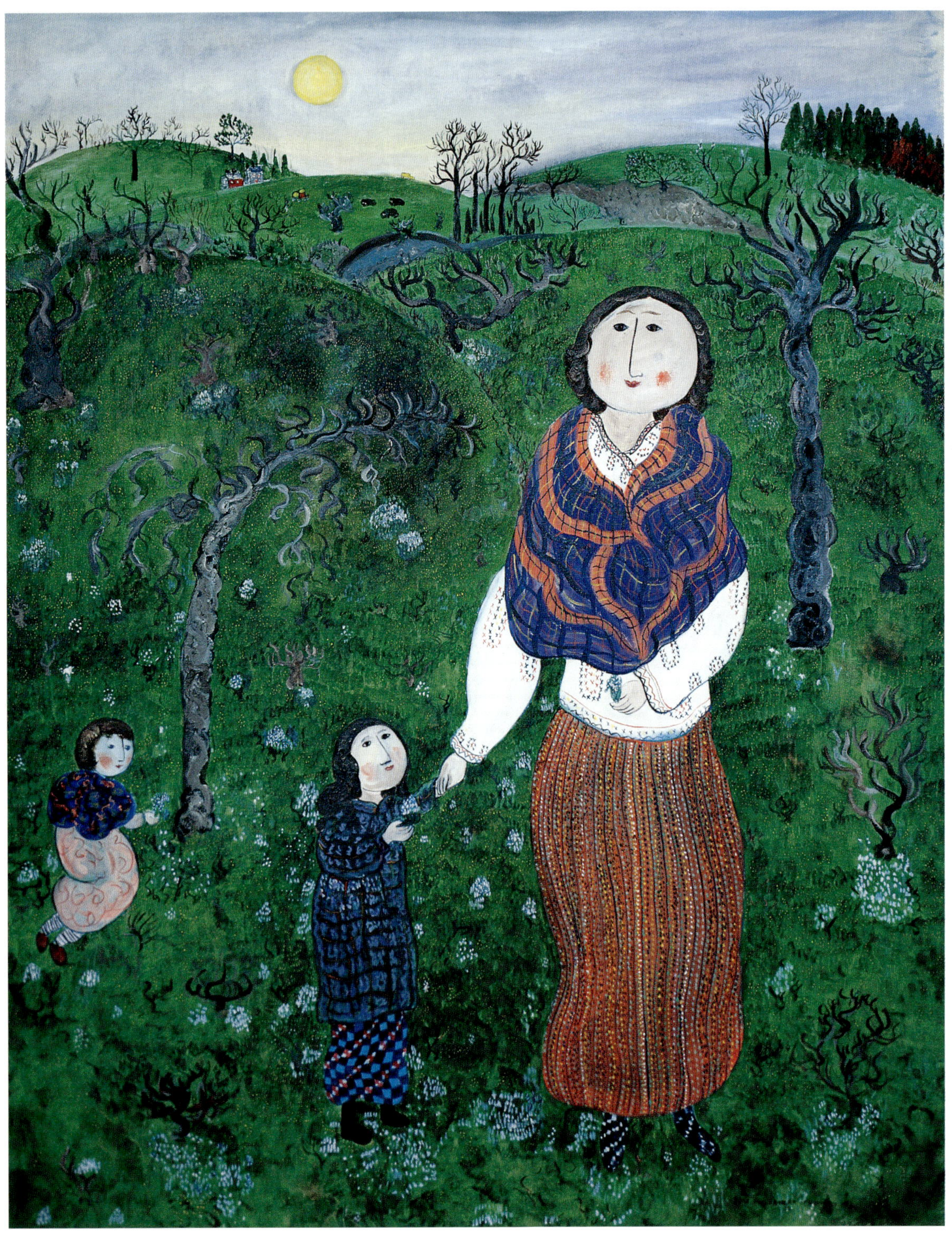

Plate 64
Hermione and Tara, Snowdrops at Allanton   *c.*1974   Oil on canvas   101.6 x 91.4 cm (40 x 36 in)

Exactly What Was Felt

'So that's the way it is,' the rabbi thought. 'Well, now everything is clear.'
ISAAC BASHEVIS SINGER[54]

In the early 1950s, Dora exhibited at the Beaux Arts Gallery in London, run by Helen Lessore. The dealers at that time could not make up their mind how naive (or not naive) an artist Dora was – each, amusingly enough, had his or her own preconceptions. 'Mrs Lessore encouraged me but she didn't like me to finish my pictures. The last picture I brought to her I did finish, and she said, "You're no good for me. You're primitive. Go to Arthur Jeffries," then the leading London dealer in naive art. I went there and he said, "You don't have enough finish for this gallery".' Her first one-person show of importance was at the Chenil Galleries in Chelsea in 1960. The critic Eric Newton came along and, with his usual perspicacity, later described the artist as 'a temperamental primitive'.[55]

From the mid-1960s onwards, Dora and George travelled more widely. Their base was a flat in London's Earl's Court. Towards the end of the decade, they made several visits to Samye Ling, a new Buddhist monastery founded by Chögyam Trungpa, the Tibetan Lama, in what Dora calls the 'empty and enchanted hills of Eskdalemuir', which they continue to visit to this day. They bought a chapel fifteen miles from Samye Ling at Tushielaw Kirk, which they planned to convert into a home and studio. However, they only settled there briefly in 1971, and then moved temporarily into a fine Edinburgh flat. Amalie and her husband Allan Sinclair purchased a large Georgian house (actually a Christian retreat earlier this century) at Allanton near Dumfries. So it was, from late 1971 until 1975, that Dora and George lived with their children and grandchildren in this house with its two dozen rooms and a romantic tower, all 'set in twenty acres of landscaped gardens, including a beautiful walled garden covered in roses and flowers and wild fruits. If nothing else,' Dora says, 'the children played in paradise.' (See Plate 64)

At Allanton, Dora had several large studios; it was there that she also discovered the potential of water-colour. This was a settled, productive period for her.

Reviewing one of her London exhibitions at the Langton Gallery at this time, the Duchess of St Albans wrote in *Art and Antiques*: 'I had the good fortune to be there when the artist and her daughter floated in like a couple of Chagall figures, decked out in flowers and beads and jewel-like embroidered gowns, on one of their rare visits from Scotland.'[56] Sadly, the Scottish house had to be sold in 1975, and for many months afterwards, Dora, George and Hermione led an itinerant existence, living in Nice, Cambridge, and in Launceston and St Ives in Cornwall. They spent the winter of 1975 living in a St Ives studio, Crab Rock, situated on a rocky outcrop overlooking the sea. Deeply disheartened following the loss of the family home at Allanton (another loss of Eden), Dora felt inspired by the example of the St Ives primitive Alfred Wallis – the simplicity of his life and the directness of his vision – to appreciate anew her own gifts as an artist. Wallis, she says, 'is a case of a real artist who, when he sat down and painted, would remember a fisherman or whatever, and exactly what he felt would come into the picture'. Ever since, St Ives has been a regular retreat for Dora; its quite continental sharpness of light, spectacular natural situation and the inspiration of Wallis continue to attract her.

In 1976, Dora, George and Hermione moved back to London, staying for eighteen months in a 'big family room with rose-patterned wallpaper' at a hotel owned by friends in Earl's Court Square. It was while they were living there that Dora's mother, who had been living in a small country cottage, fell seriously ill. Up to then, Dora had found her mother in some ways hard to deal with, but visiting her every other day in hospital outside London just before she died, 'I had nothing but compassion and love in my heart, and arranged for the rabbi to see her. I could hold her hand and tell her with great love and conviction that there was nothing for her to be afraid of.' It so happened that one evening during that time, there was a short feature, 'Naive Paintings of a Buddhist Lady', on Arena, the BBC arts programme, made to coincide with Dora's latest exhibition. Ruchla saw 'there on the screen my painting of the big Japanese Buddha in the Victoria and Albert Museum in spring, and a picture of the Thai Temple in Wimble-

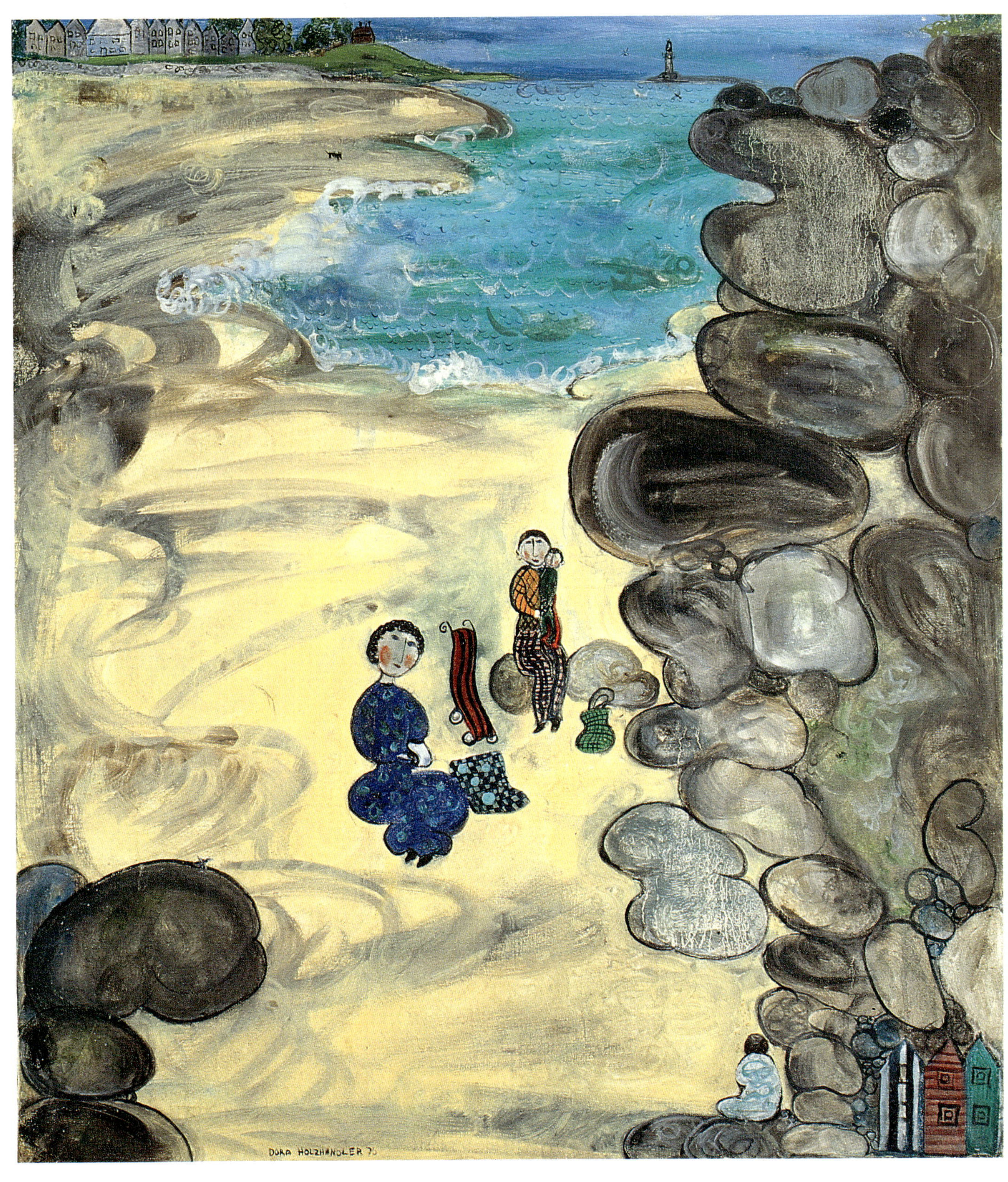

Plate 65
Porthmeor Beach, St Ives 1976 Oil on canvas 71 x 61 cm (28 x 24 in)

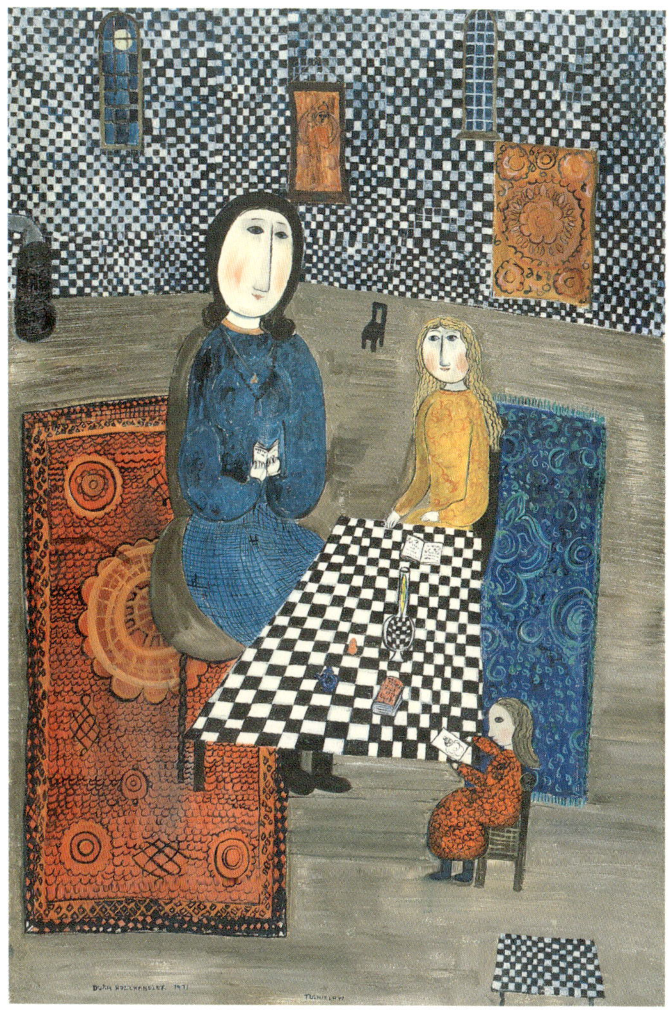

Plate 66
Meditation at Tushielaw, Scotland   1971   Oil on canvas
76.2 x 50.8 cm (30 x 20 in)

don with the orange-robed monks. And the nurses said my mother had been very happy and proud of me. I also brought with me to the hospital a criticism about my work from the *Jewish Chronicle*, with a reproduction of my painting of the Sabbath Meal.' Soon afterwards, Dora and George moved to their present home in Holland Park.

In 1981, Dora, George and Hermione made a revelatory trip to India and Thailand. Dora has painted many pictures on Buddhist subjects, for example, *Lady Reading a Sutra*, and a family meditation session in Scotland showing Dora, Hepzibah and Hermione (Plate 66). She has also painted her teachers, notably Chögyam Trungpa (who later also became Allen Ginsberg's teacher in California), the Dalai Lama of Tibet (a figure for whom she has the utmost admiration and respect), and Sogyal Rinpoche (author of *The Tibetan Book of Living and Dying*[57]) – portraits of irrepressibly tender gravity and humour. (Their orange robes are mirrored by golden suns, lighted candles, gilded Buddhas and burnished autumn leaves.) Each face that

Dora depicts is uniquely universal; an intrinsic shapeliness about them is reminiscent both of heads in Oriental prints and of the stylised, archaised features of portraits by, notably, Modigliani and Picasso. Seeing the 1971 picture of meditation in Scotland supplies a clue to the origins and development of the archetypally rounded and pear-shaped countenances in Dora's paintings. The full moon seen through the windows is echoed in the full, pale faces of the mother and her two daughters. Similarly, in daylight pictures, forms of radiant visages are often repeated in the full disc of the sun seen above or glimpsed through a window. The Oriental parallel is worth pursuing further. The famous Chinese Zen Master Ummon, when asked about his health, would invariably answer, 'Sun-faced Buddha and moon-faced Buddha' (whether he was well or ill, no matter).[58] The imperturbable composure in Dora's portrayals is that of people viewed with an open, loving regard, their enlightened or Buddha nature made as plain as the moon or sun shining in the clear sky above.

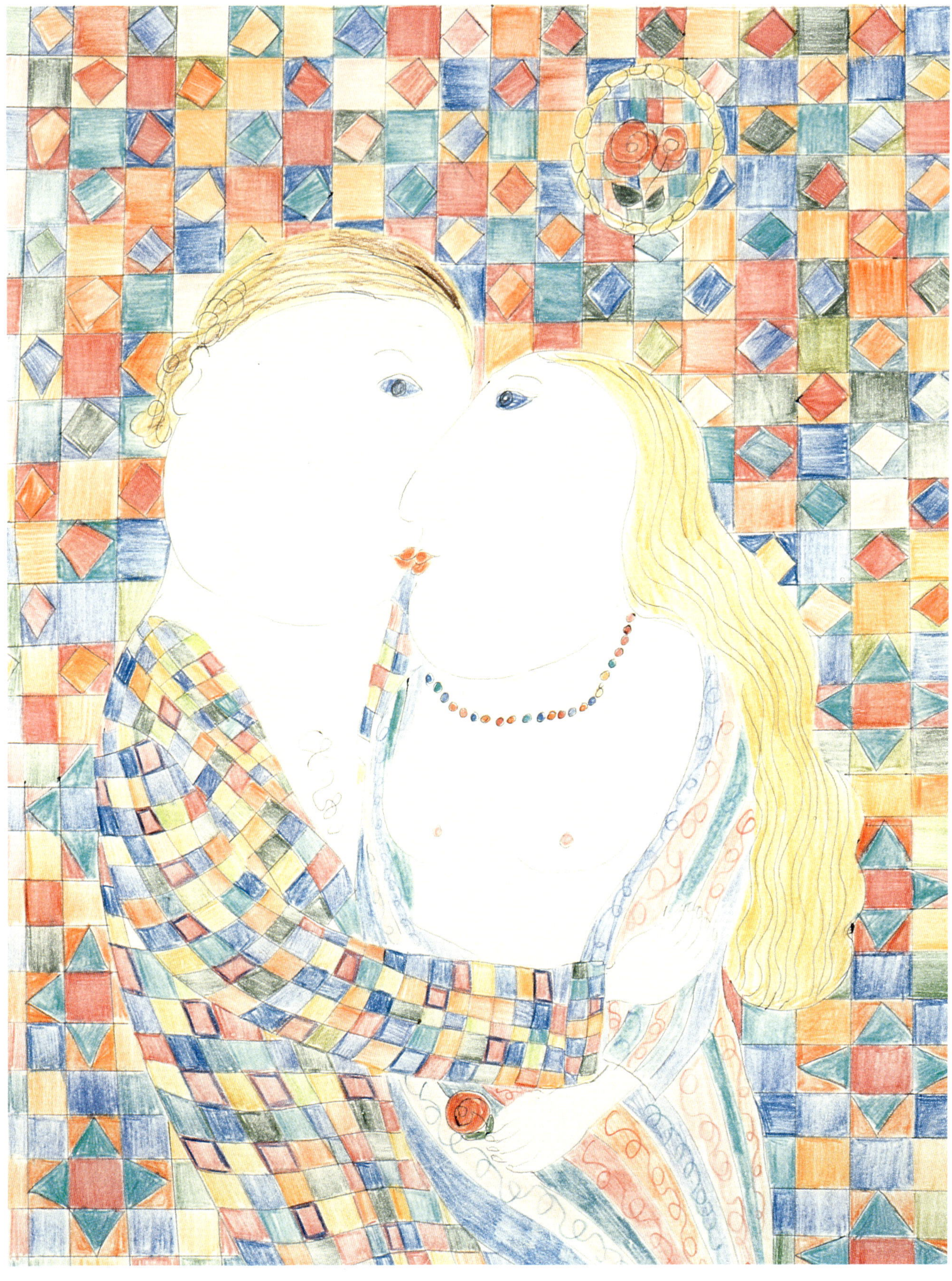

Plate 67
The Kiss   1995   Crayon on paper   40.6 x 30.5 cm (16 x 12 in)

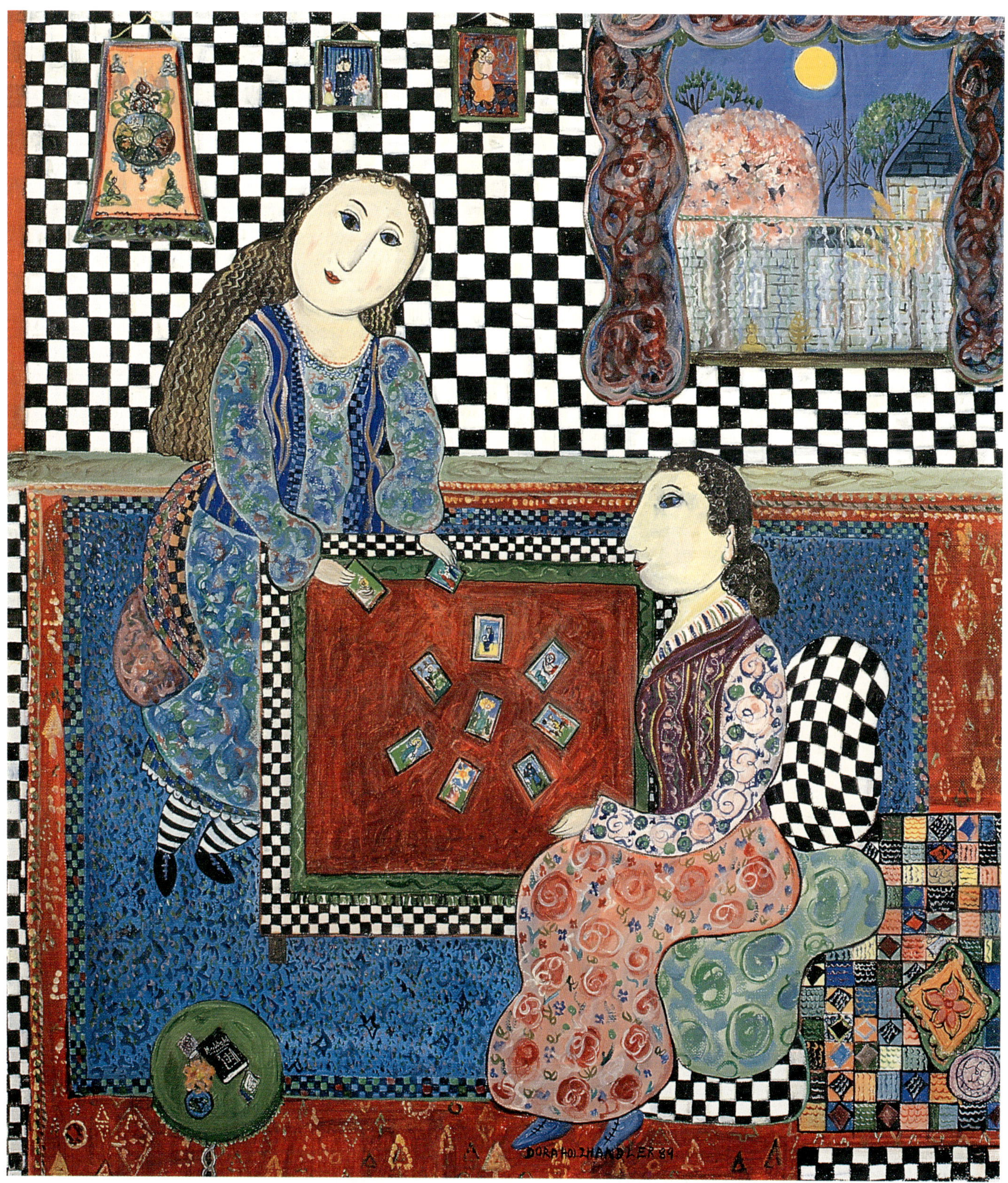

Plate 68
Tarot   1989   Oil on canvas   71 x 61 cm (28 x 24 in)

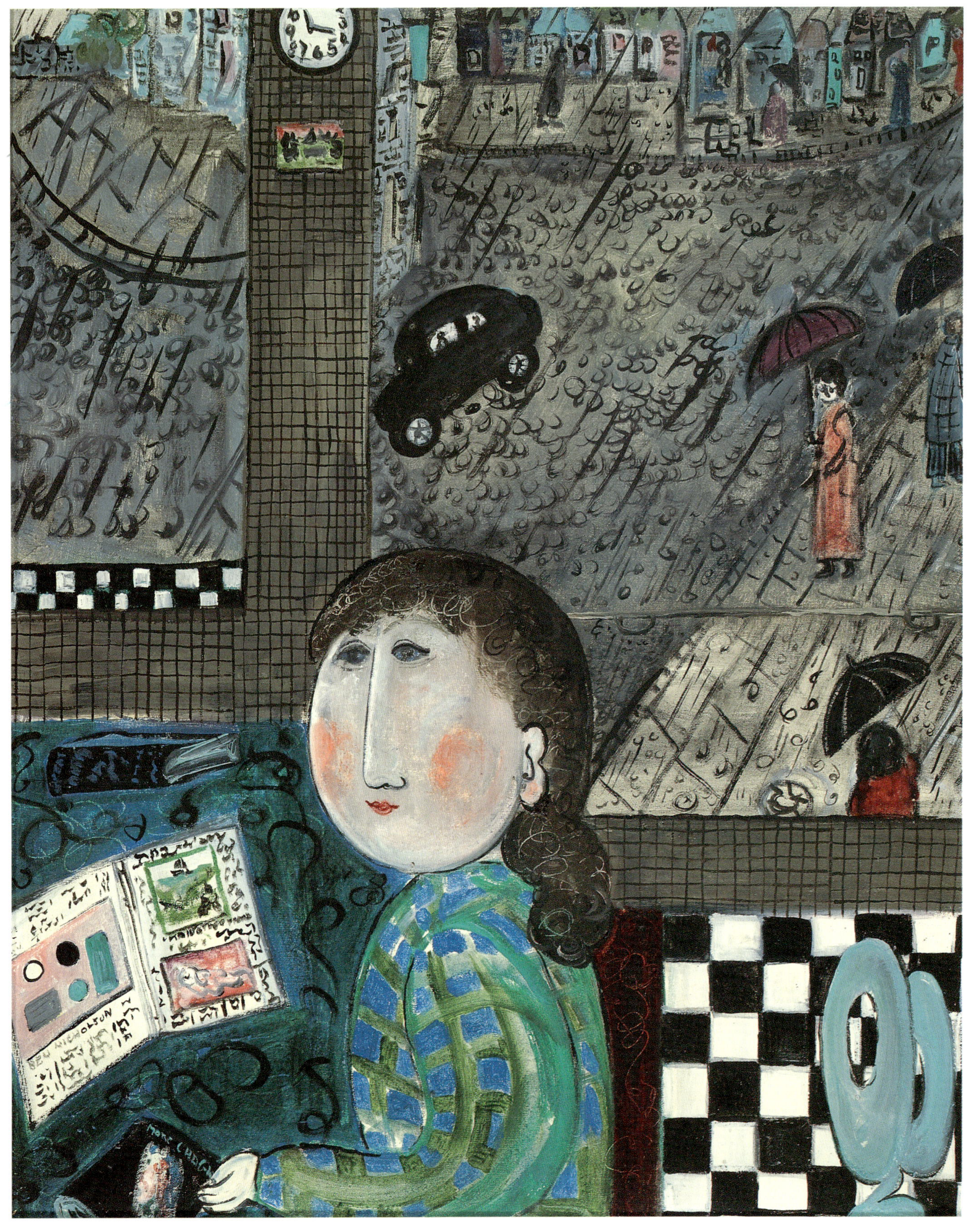

Plate 69
Library in St Ives 1976 Oil on canvas 61 x 50.8 cm (24 x 20 in)

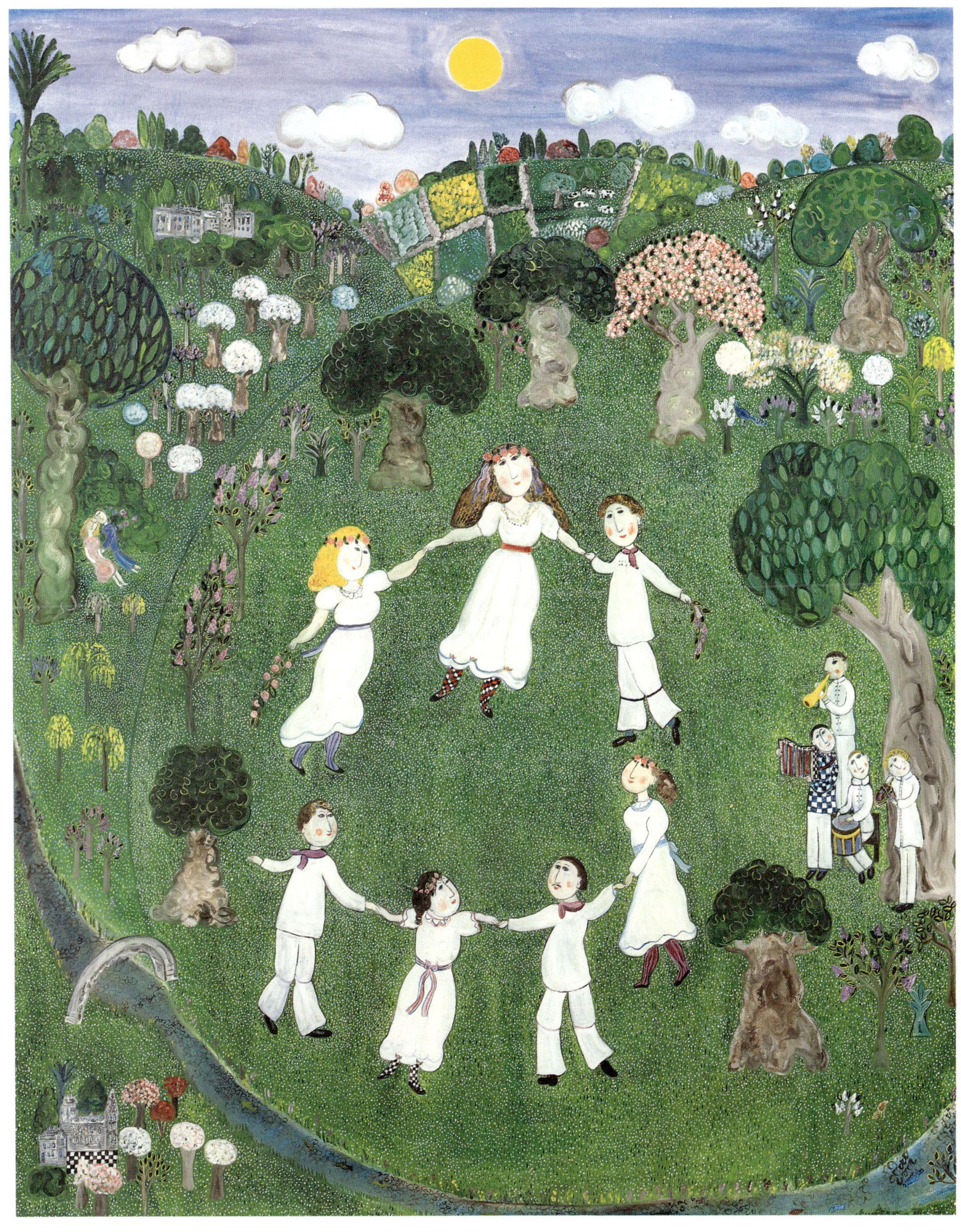

Plate 70
Cornish Floral Dancers   1984   Oil on canvas   162.6 x 129.5 cm (64 x 51 in)

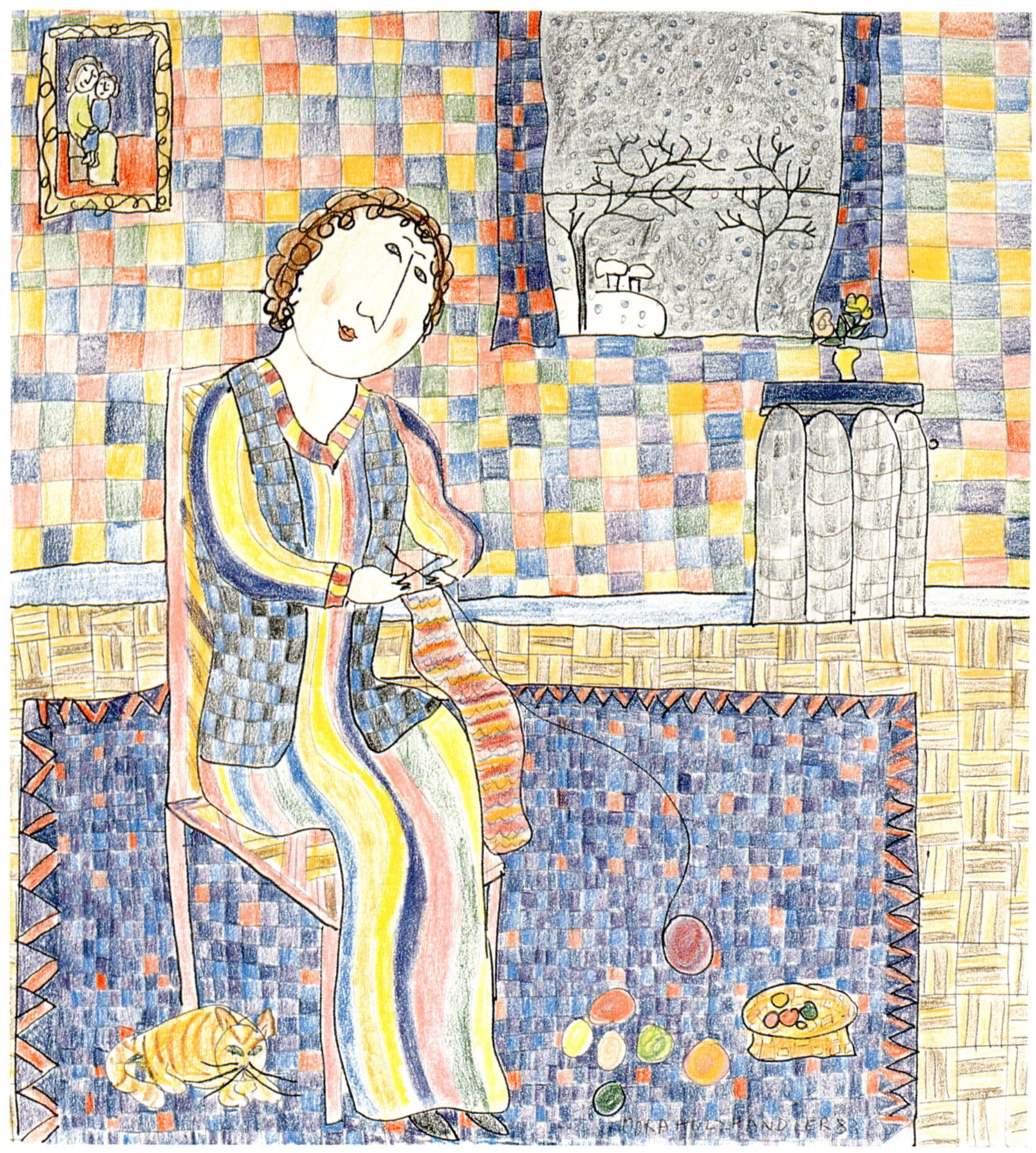

Plate 71
Lady Knitting   1983   Coloured pencil on paper   40.6 x 30.5 cm (16 x 12 in)

Plate 72
Crossing the River   1975   Oil on canvas   61 x 50.8 cm (24 x 20 in)

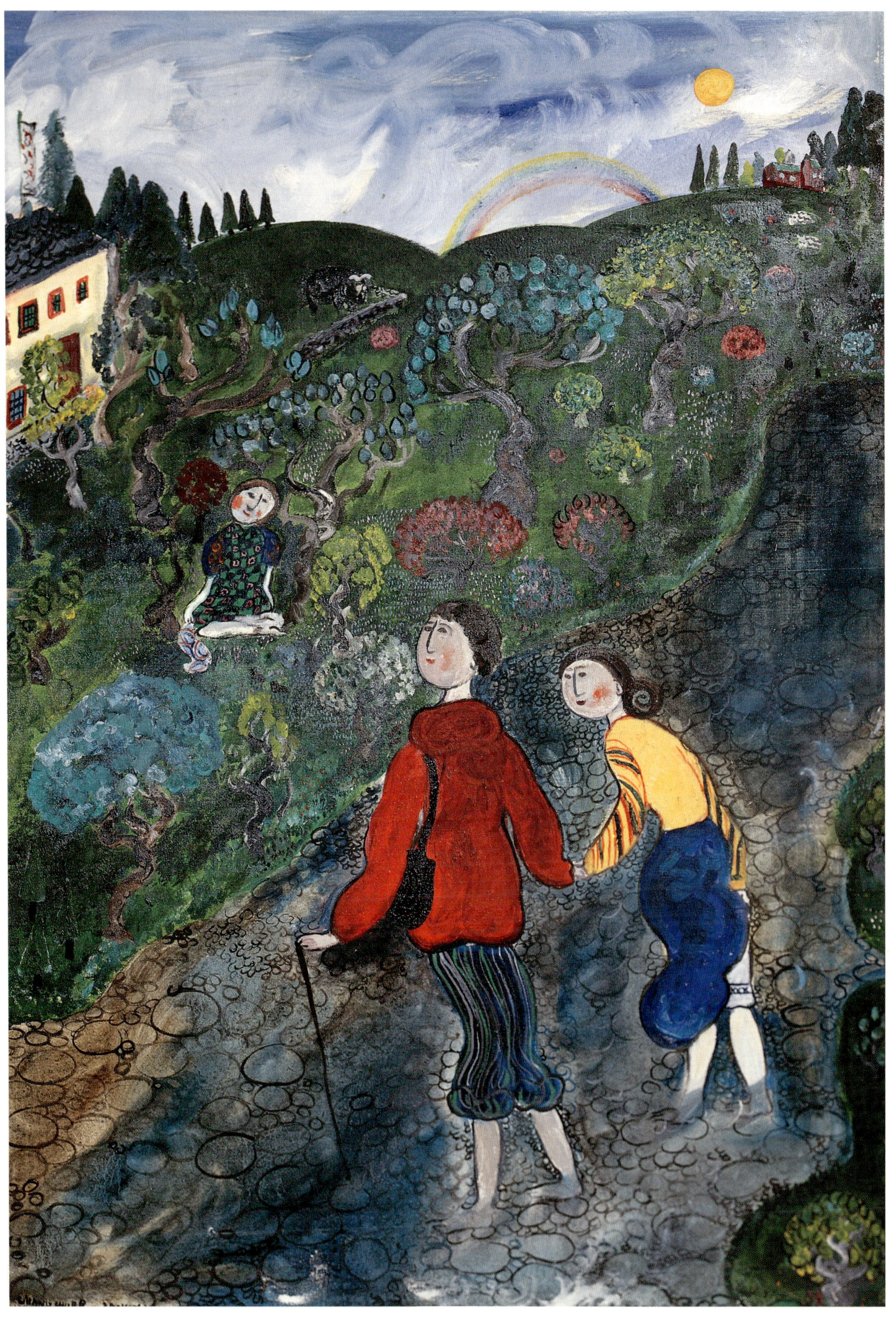

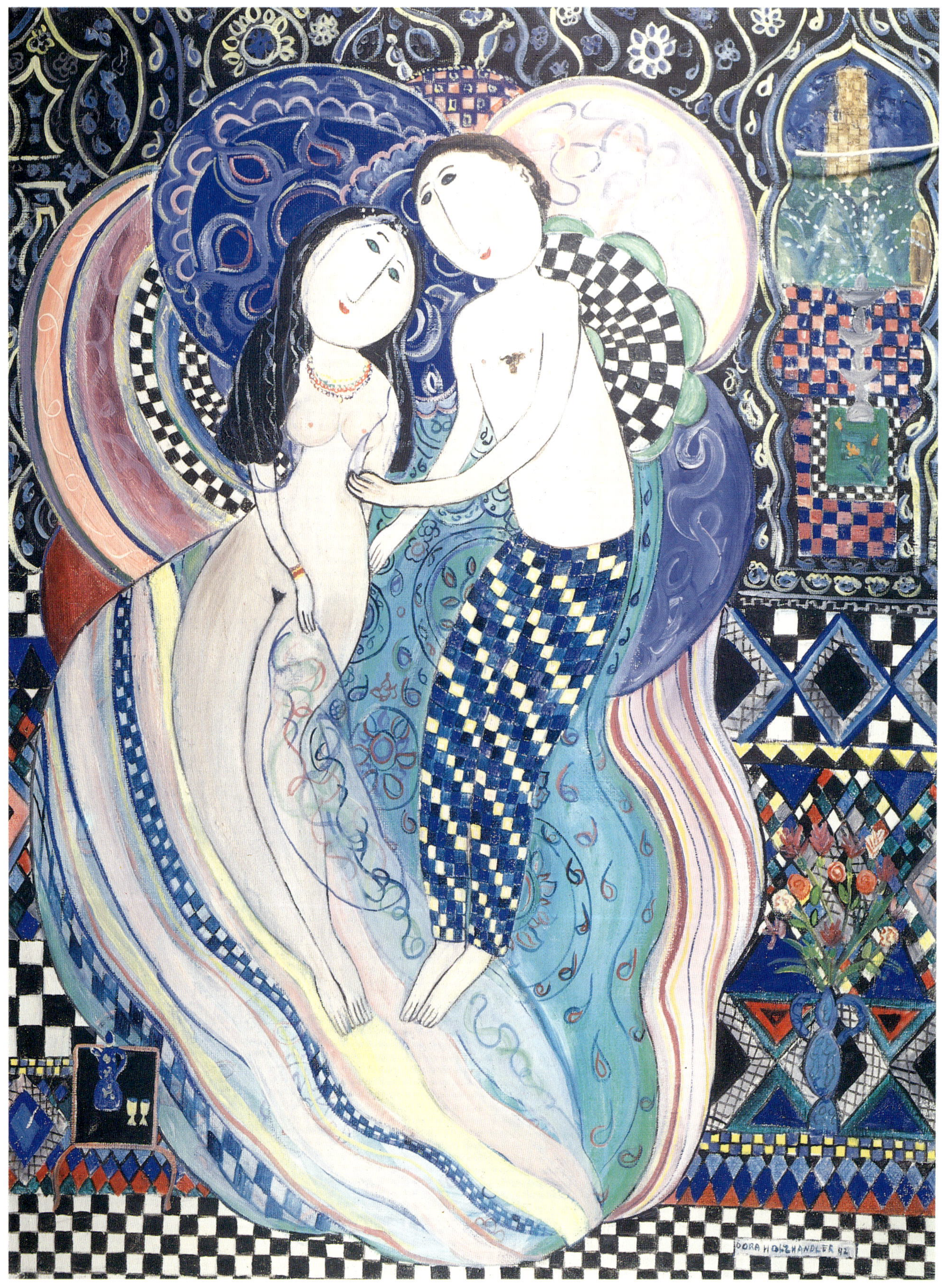

Plate 73
Moroccan Lovers   1992   Oil on canvas   61 x 50.8 cm (24 x 20 in)

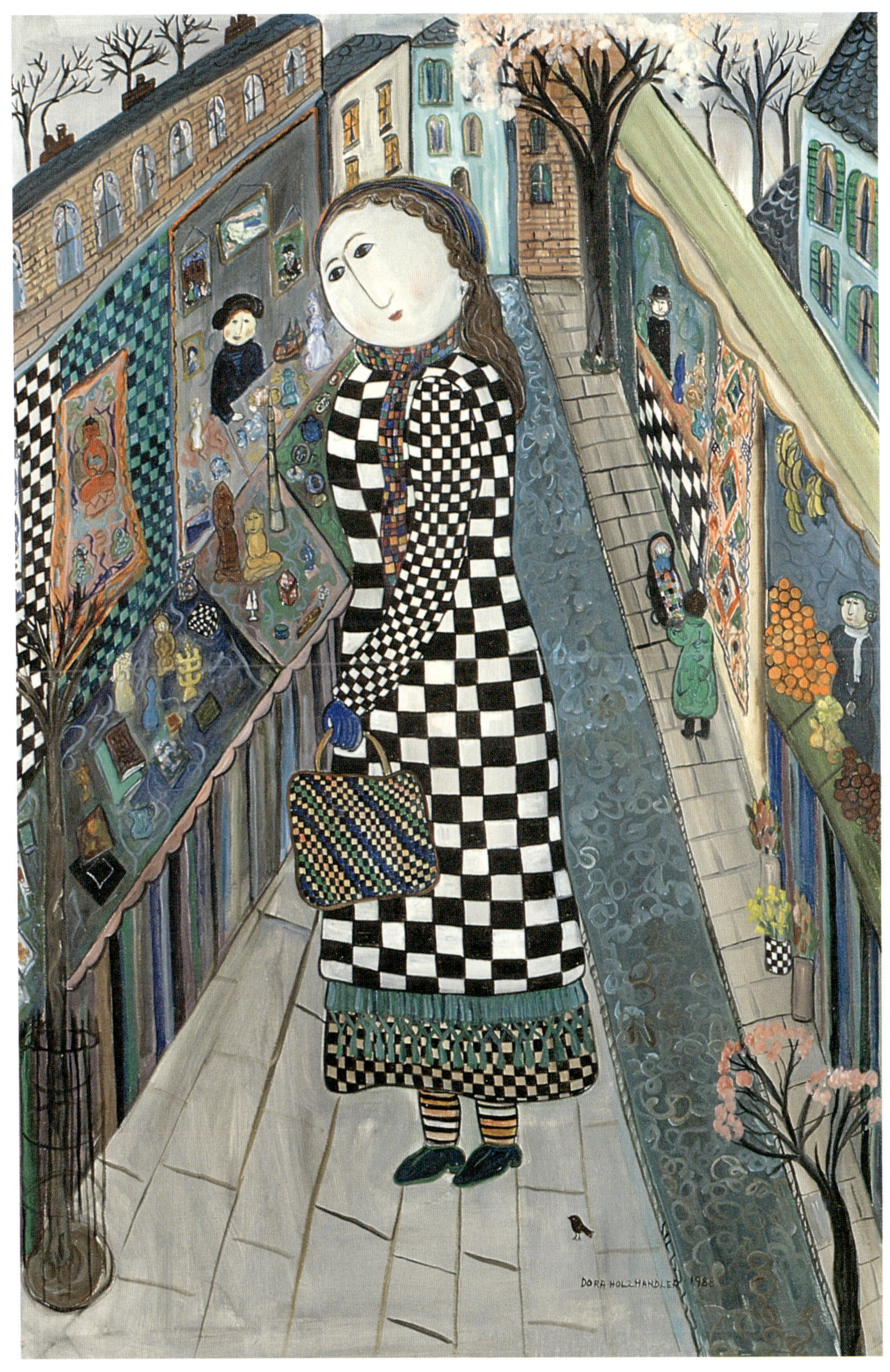

Plate 74
Portobello Road Antiques   1988   Oil on canvas   119.4 x 78.7 cm (47 x 31 in)

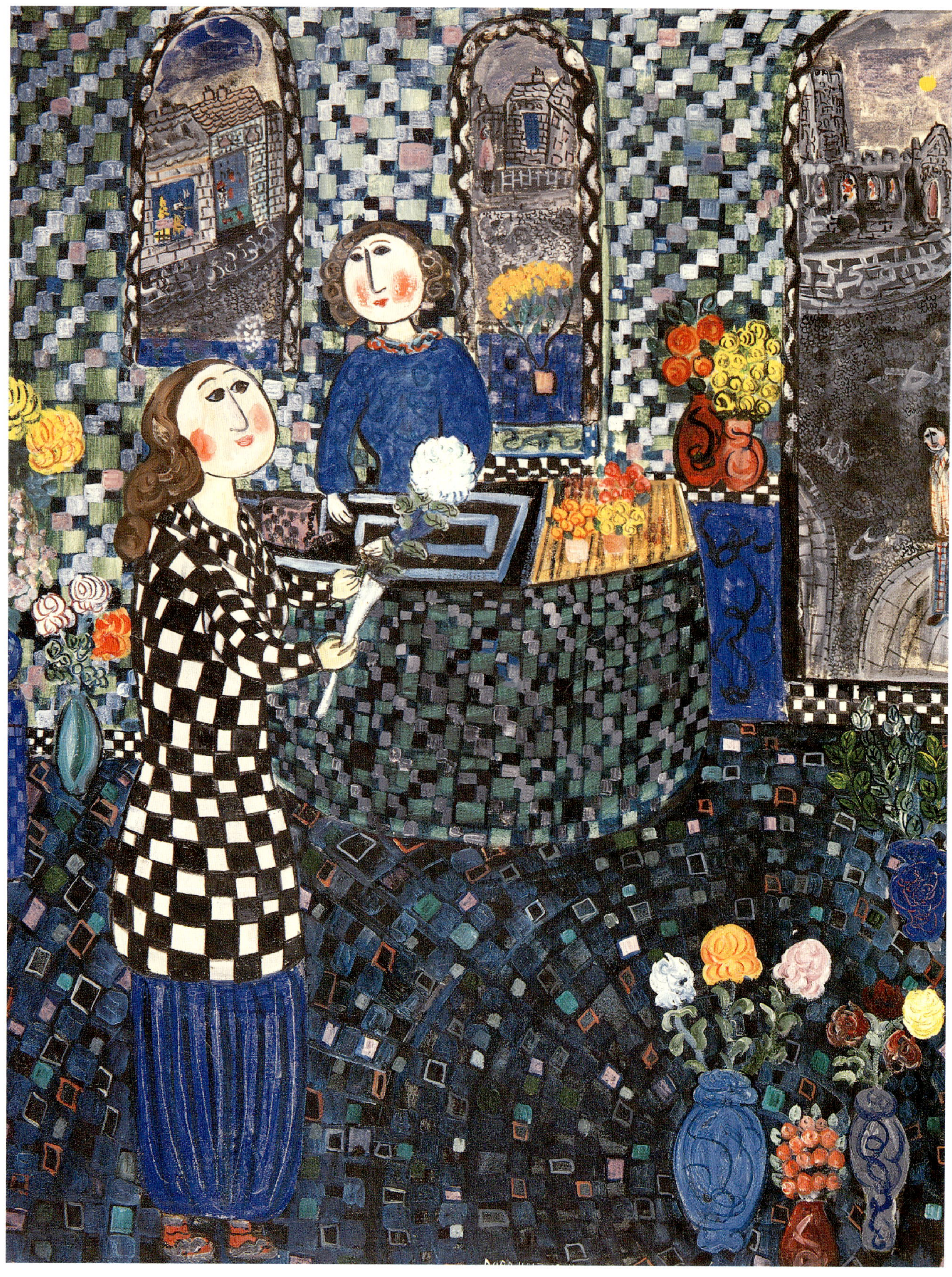

Plate 75
The Flower Shop, Launceston, Cornwall   1975   Oil on canvas   66 x 50.8 cm (26 x 20 in)

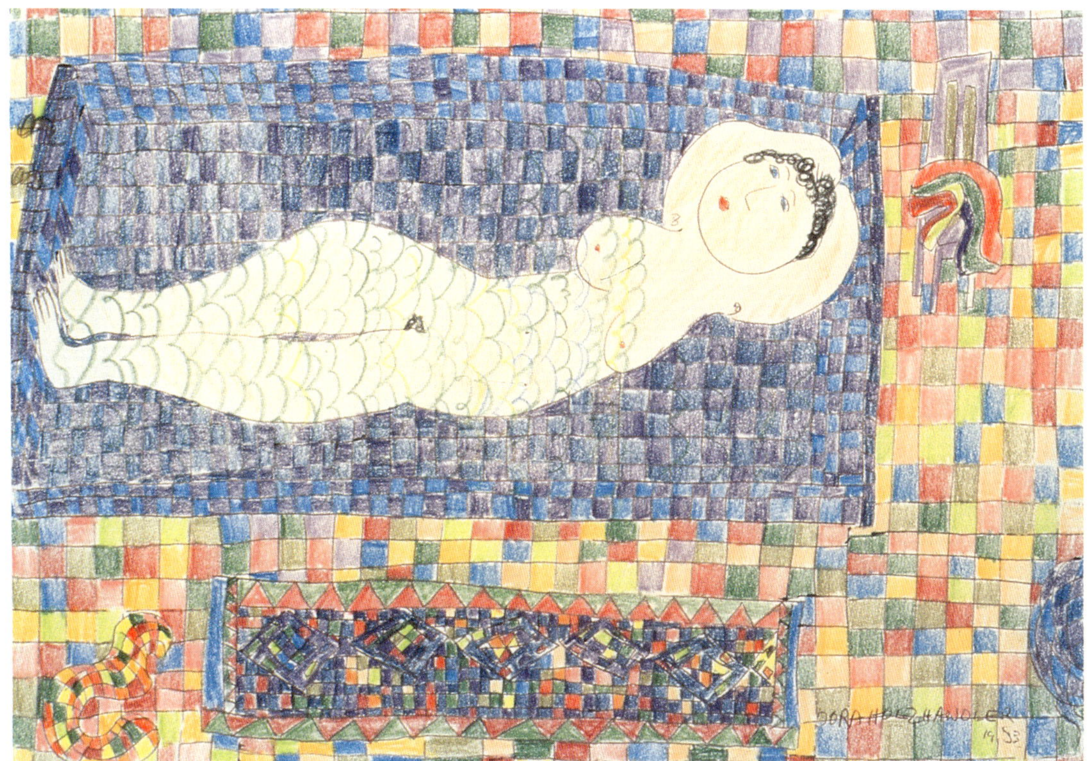

Plate 76
Lady in Bath 1983
Coloured pencil on paper
25.4 x 36.6 cm (10 x 14 in)

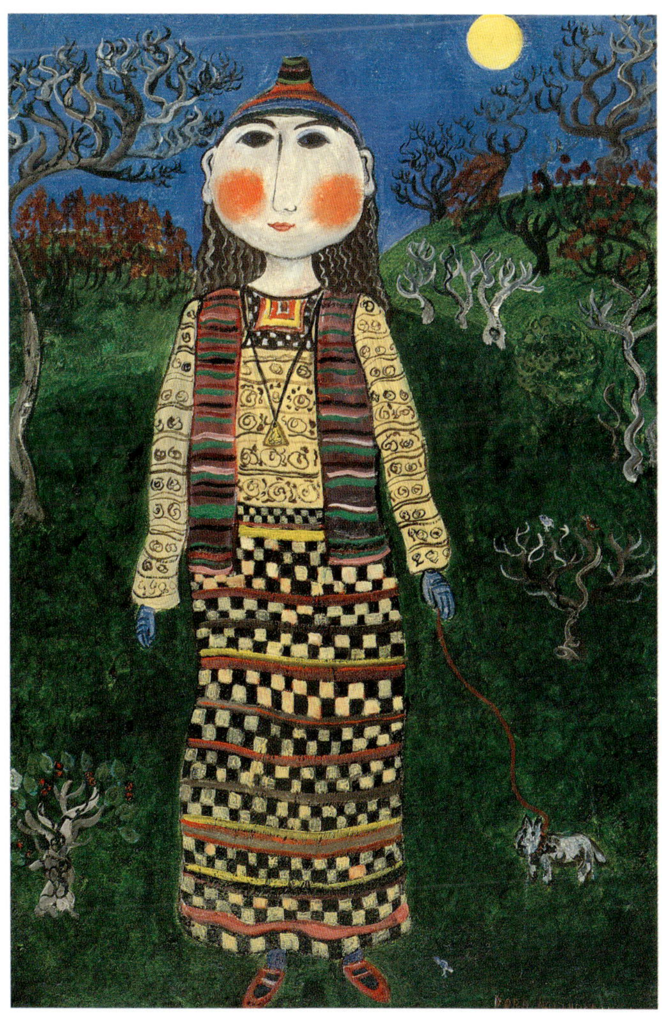

Plate 77
Young Girl in Scotland 1974
Oil on canvas
50.8 x 40.6 cm (20 x 16 in)

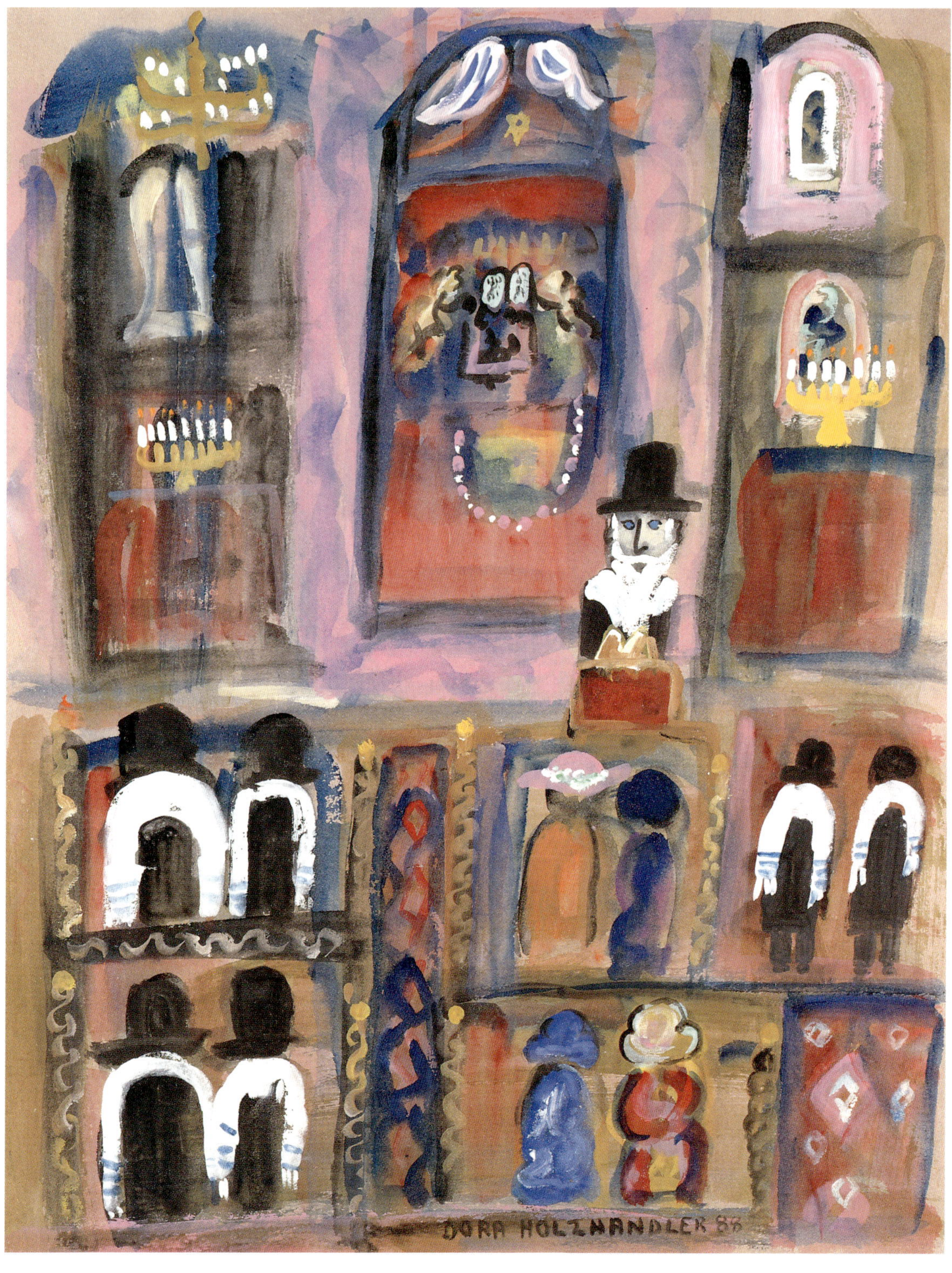

Plate 78
Synagogue in Jerusalem   1988   Gouache on paper   50.8 x 39.4 cm (20 x 15½ in)

All in the Face

For the masters of the inner wisdom, the features of the face are not those which appear outwardly but those within formed by intense forces … When one looks on the face of such a man, one is moved to love him.
THE ZOHAR[59]

In 1987, Dora and George visited Israel for the first time, staying in Eilat and Jerusalem. In works painted on her return to London, she says, 'what I want to convey is the feeling that Israel is what I've always imagined, or rather experienced'. She is right to stress that 'art is not travelogue. The inner world is important.' For an artist, interior exploration is what matters; thus, 'there is no way I can be an anecdotal artist – going to Jerusalem is like sitting in this chair'. In Israel, she re-encountered her own archetypes, her childhood, herself.

Gouache's flowing non-linearity, she discovered, was especially suited to evoking the Jewish world. 'When I was working towards an exhibition of Jewish subjects in 1986, I found that it worked very well. That's how I remember it all: my parents' house had dark brown and green paint and dark chenille table-cloths, and that's very much the atmosphere in the background of the gouaches.'

Gouache, she has also found, works very well in picturing synagogue interiors. Rhythms of the swaying cantor, congregational incantations of praise and thanksgiving, the burning darkness of mystical awareness, are evoked through a sweeping tonal flood and fire of dark, velvety blues and reds streaked with waves and flashes of white and gold. In *Yom Kippur in the Synagogue* (Plate 79) (this most sacred day in the Jewish calendar, one of fasting and penitence), the men are attired in white shrouds – in the artist's words, 'symbols of purity and reminders of the Day of Judgement when men and women will meet God face to face'. The figures have become almost abstract as sculpted bodies of pure, white light, defined by vigorous binding lines of sombre ruggedness.

For many, Yom Kippur is also a day when they remember the millions of innocent victims of the Holocaust. On Yom Kippur in 1995, George and Dora attended a service at the West London Reform Synagogue, movingly led by Slovakian-born Rabbi Hugo Gryn (who died in August 1996), an Auschwitz survivor himself who had lost his father and younger brother in the death camps. For Dora, as for countless others, Rabbi Gryn was a man of real integrity who worked tirelessly for understanding between people of different faiths and beliefs. As we have seen, Dora herself lost her grandfather Zaida, her half-sister Marcelle and other relatives in the Holocaust. On the subject, she has this to say: 'Every Jew has a broken heart, at least every Jew of my generation. I'm not bitter. But the consciousness has been affected by the sufferings of the pogroms and the Holocaust. I did a picture of a concentration camp once – my grandfather amid barbed wire and heaps of bodies and a setting of a very blood-red sun – but I haven't done a lot.'

Before 1986, she seldom depicted rabbis. Working newly in gouache, she felt able, she says, to make 'the icon of the rabbi's face. Through that I could say things that I couldn't say through just, for instance, a self-portrait. As soon as there's the beard and the *tallith* and the *yamulke* [the skullcap], the thing is there. If the face is painted by an intelligent Jewish mind, the one that paints becomes the face that is painted. It's a little creation, a universe.' No one has depicted rabbis before in quite this way. Rabbis depicted by twentieth-century Jewish painters like Chagall, Mane Katz and Jacob Kramer all possess powerful hieratic and rhapsodic qualities, but none has quite this same searchingly intimate look – one of amazing, open-hearted sweetness within the steadfast embrace of the All. In art, Dora says, 'it's all in the face'.

As already remarked, in the Zohar the candlestick is recognised as an important mystical symbol, its flame as an essential aid to meditation. In *Rabbi Lighting a Candle* (Plate 81), whiteness of the subject's visage, hair, hands, *tallith* and the wax candle itself (each slightly tinged with grey or blue or green) elucidates the circumambient, eddying darkness. The Zohar says that 'Above the white light [from a candle] and surrounding it is still another light scarcely perceptible, symbolical of the supreme essence'.[60] It is this 'scarcely

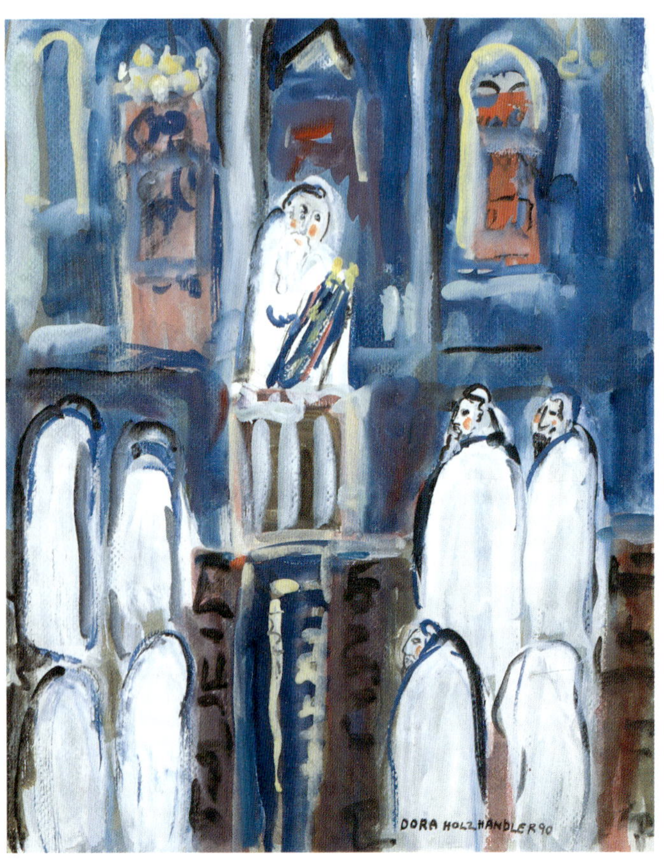

Plate 79
Yom Kippur in the Synagogue   1990   Gouache on paper
38.1 x 30.5 cm (15 x 12 in)

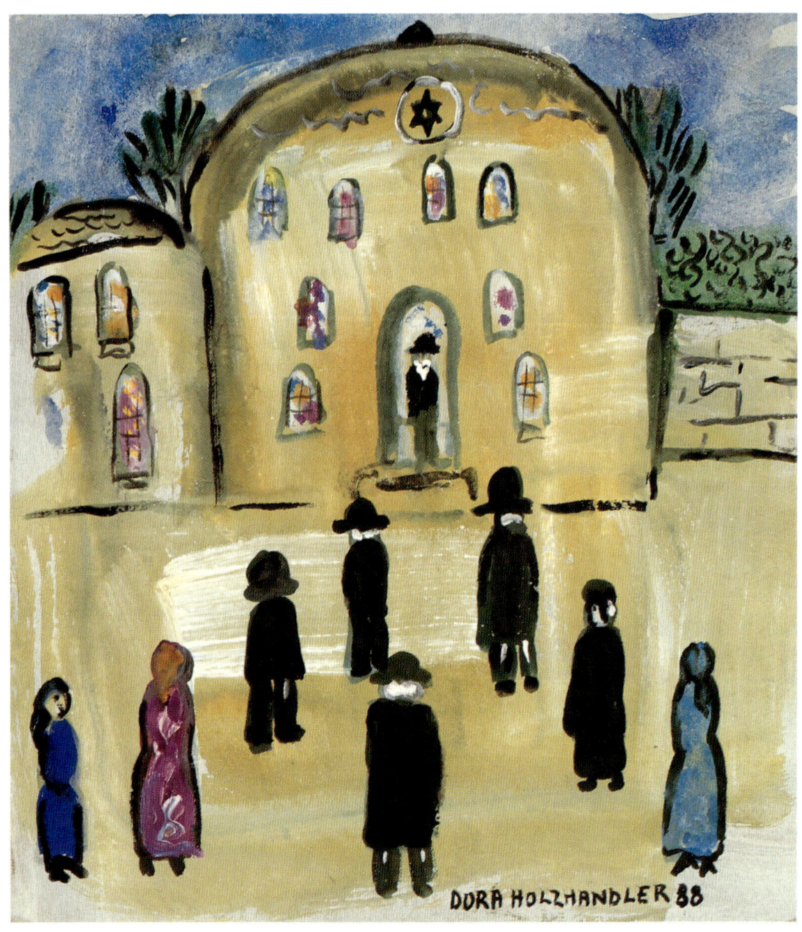

Plate 80
Yom Kippur, Jerusalem   1988   Gouache on paper
26.7 x 23.5 cm (10½ x 9¼ in)

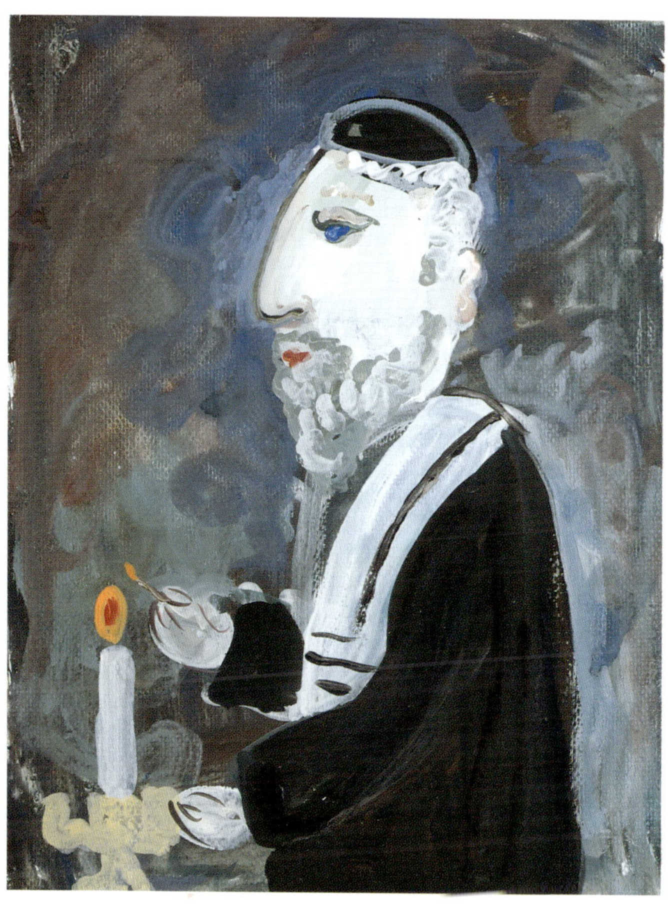

Plate 81
Rabbi Lighting a Candle   1987   Gouache on paper
25.4 x 20.3 cm (10 x 8 in)

perceptible light' that illumines the rabbi's counten-ance here. Contemplating this picture may light a candle of recognition within ourselves, so that we identify his face, luminous with cosmic kindness, awe and humour, as the face (so mystics describe it) we wore before we were born.

Lemon Tea (Rabbi and Wife) (Plate 82) was inspired by a description of a couple in a Singer short story. As in Dora's pictures of young couples on their wedding night, so here a pair of candles are a burning symbol of the unending devotion of the elderly rabbi and his wife – to each other and to the life of the spirit. At the com-position's core is an asymmetric, triangular section, its points defined, in turn, by the pair of candlesticks, the Holy Book in the rabbi's hands, and the glass of lemon tea in his wife's. Each of these three elements seems to reflect and reinforce the others (and, in turn, their over-all triangular shape is echoed in the patterned carpet), carrying the subtly interwoven message that homely, personal love (its glowing symbol a glass of lemon tea) and spiritual wisdom (its no less burnished symbol a gilt-edged book) form a supreme partnership as inti-mately wedded as the pair of Sabbath candles – and the rabbinical couple themselves. Tall, twisting houses (their white fronts underlaid and sensuously scumbled by deliquescent blues, pinks, greens and browns) like those seen through the window, occur in other pictures, such as *Rabbi in Village* (Plate 83). The latter was painted in 1986, 'when I stayed in a village near Mahon in Menorca, and the streets there reminded me of the little medieval streets of a Jewish shtetl, though I've never actually seen one'.

The traditional Hebrew class ('*cheder*') is a recurring subject. Her oil painting *Aleph* (Plate 86) has the sub-limely muted pitch and hue of her works in gouache. The little boy chalks *aleph* on his little blackboard: in Kabbalah, *aleph* is a symbol of the divine Nothingness from which all the other letters of Creation flow. The picture on the wall might be a circle of infinity on a blackboard or even a window view of the moon's aurora in the night sky. The contrast between the bowed, greenish-visaged, long-sorrowing rabbi, and his pupil, pale and pert, is as moving as that in her pictures of maternal love; perhaps here is also a reflection of Dora's own brief childhood relationship with Zaida, her de-vout, story-telling grandfather.

'If I want to paint a rabbi with pupils,' Dora says, 'I imagine darkness, a little candlelight.' The setting of *Hebrew Class* (Plate 87) – based on the Yiddish song

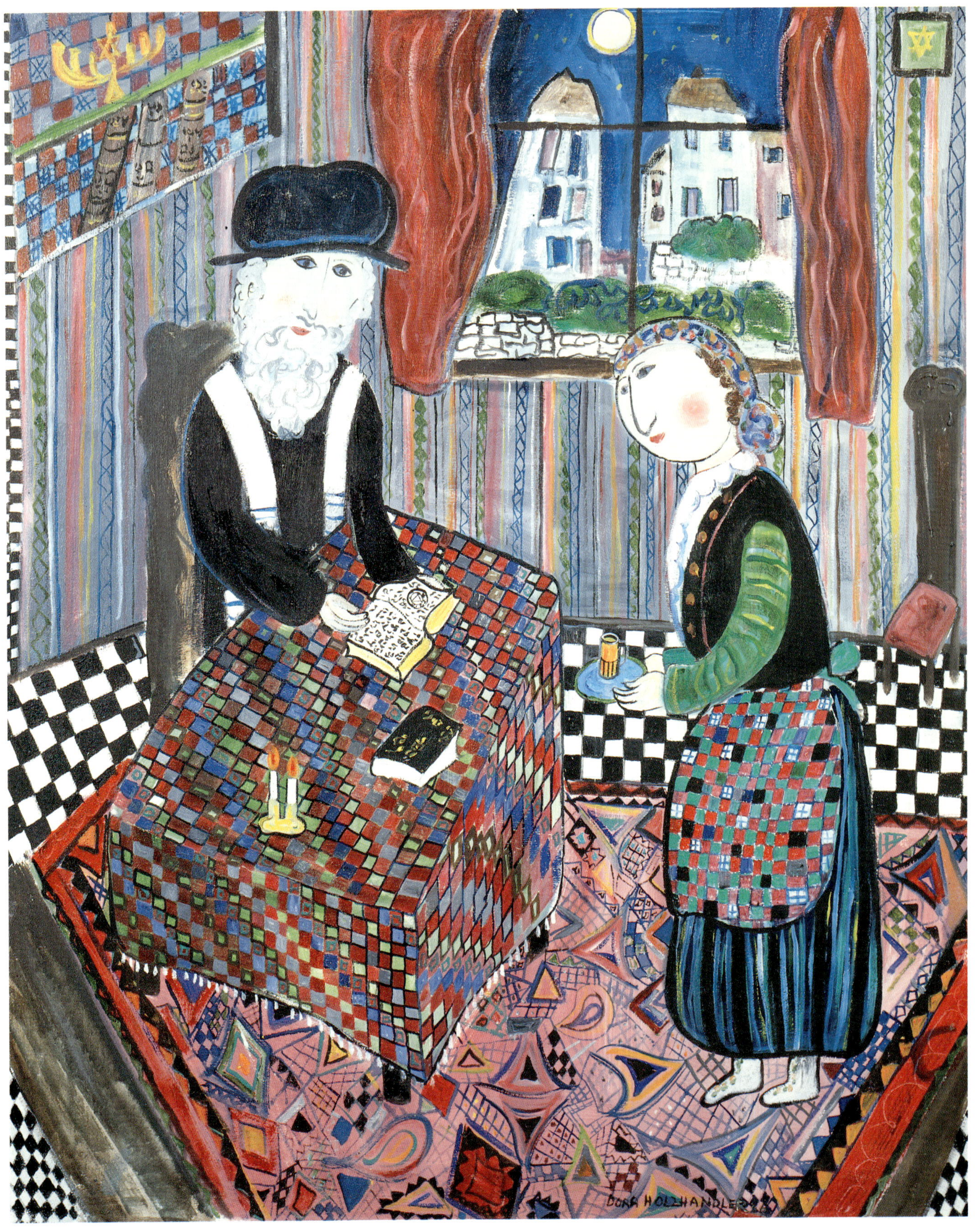

Plate 82
Lemon Tea (Rabbi and Wife)   1987   Oil on canvas   71 x 61 cm (28 x 24 in)

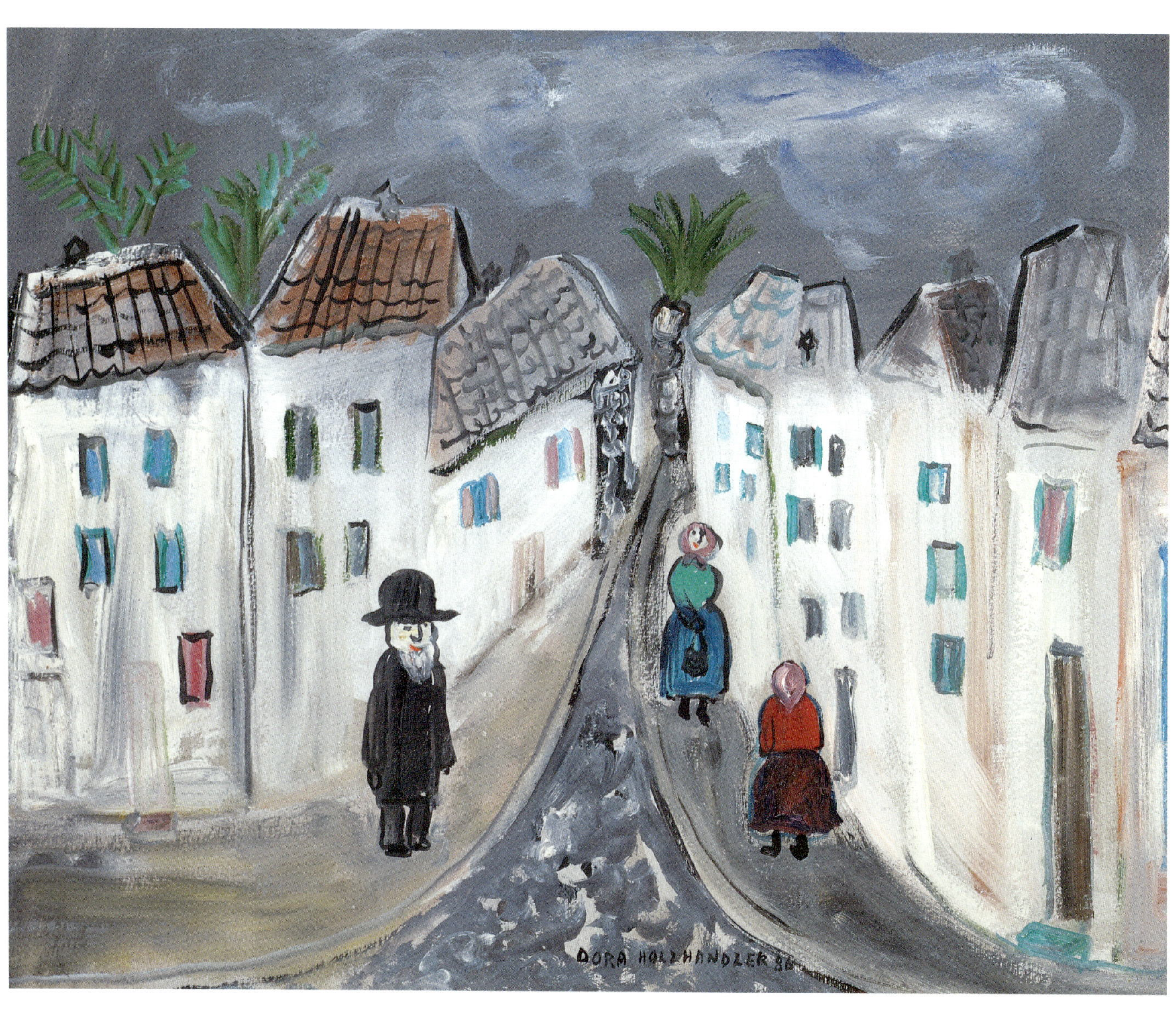

Plate 83
Rabbi in Village   1986   Oil on paper   30.5 x 35.6 cm (12 x 14 in)

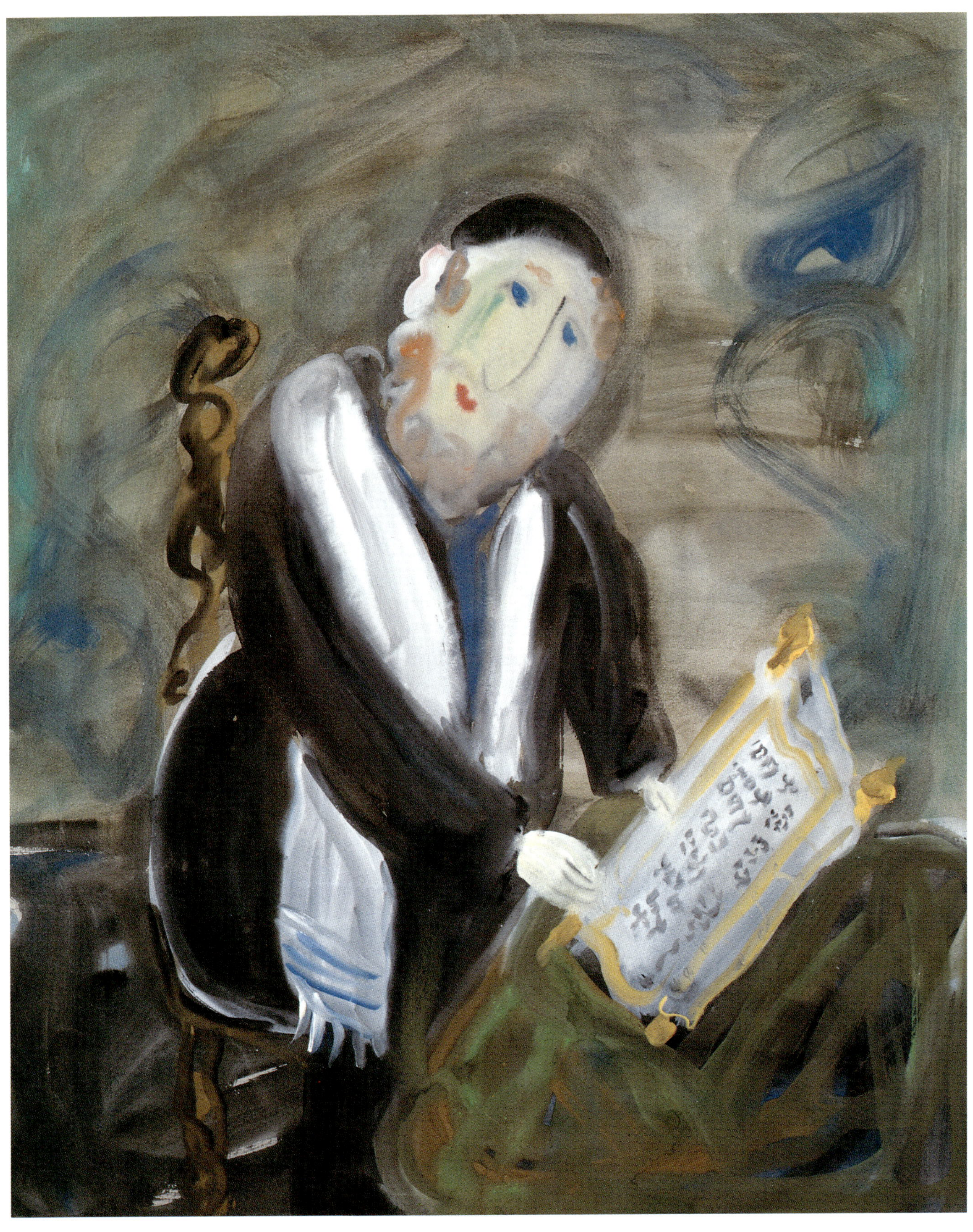

Plate 84
Rabbi   1987   Gouache on paper   25.4 x 22.9cm (10 x 9 in)

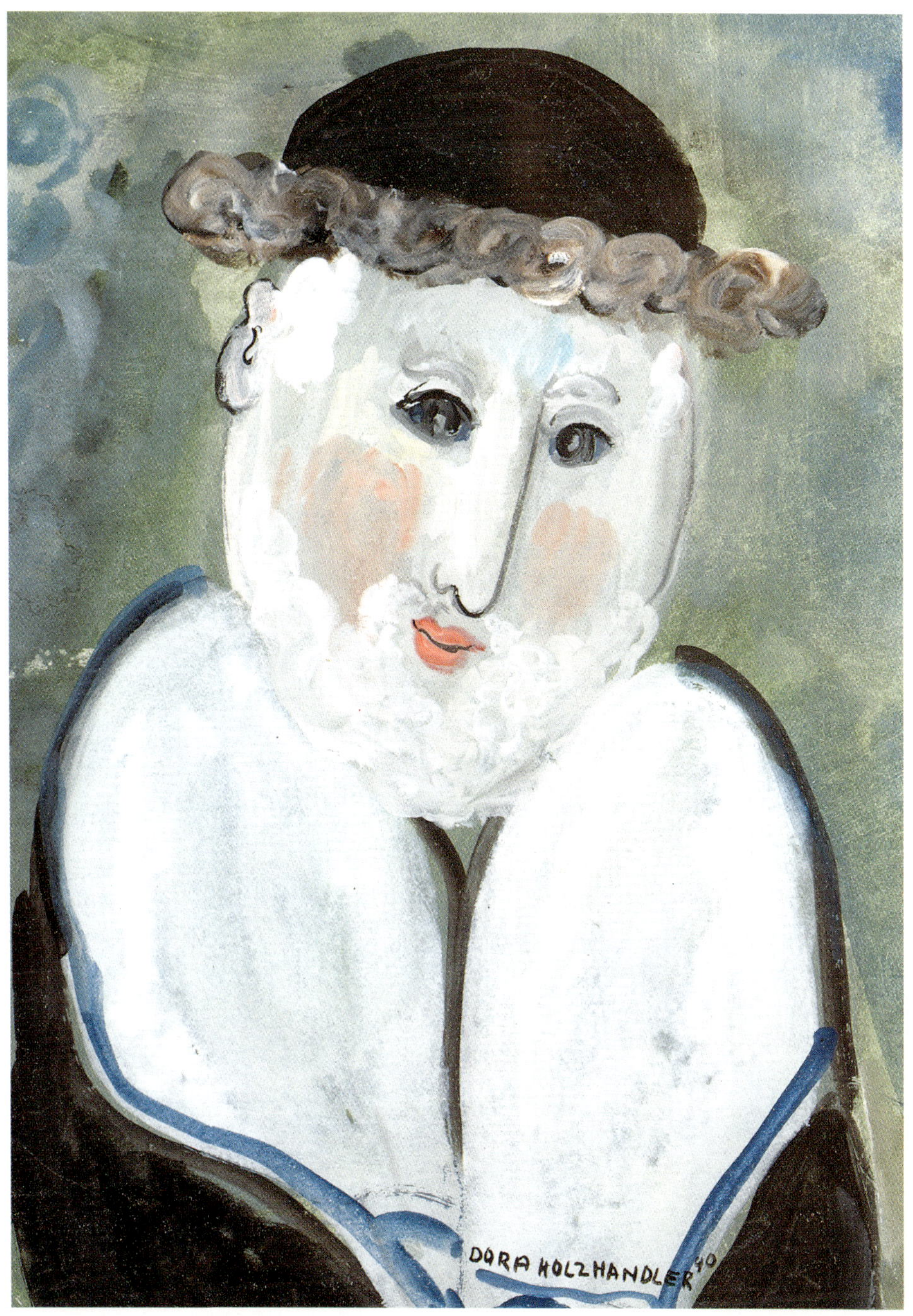

Plate 85
Rabbi with Fur-brimmed Hat   1990
Gouache on paper
27.9 x 20.3 cm (11 x 8 in)

'*Oyfn Pripetshik*' ('At the Fireplace')[61] – is what appears to be a windowless wooden attic room (most shtetl buildings were made of wood). It is necessarily a poor, dark, simple scene but far from being claustrophobically dingy. Dora identifies this kind of 'rather brilliant but sombre' atmosphere with 'the mood of the Jewish soul that Rembrandt or Soutine captured'. The room's basic furnishings scintillate with light from the *Menorah* and the corner, wood-burning stove. Bare, wood-planked walls and eaves are patterned with (yet unadorned by) a 'rather brilliant but sombre' autumnal palette. The composition resembles that of Dora's religious meal pictures. 'Tiny and delightful' like a little doll, each little boy is seen also as a living presence of unique preciousness – unlike a doll, of course, utterly irreplaceable. Within the tragic context of twentieth-century Jewish history, Dora's timeless shtetl-like creations move us in a way that is both poignantly commemorative and lovingly redemptive in character.

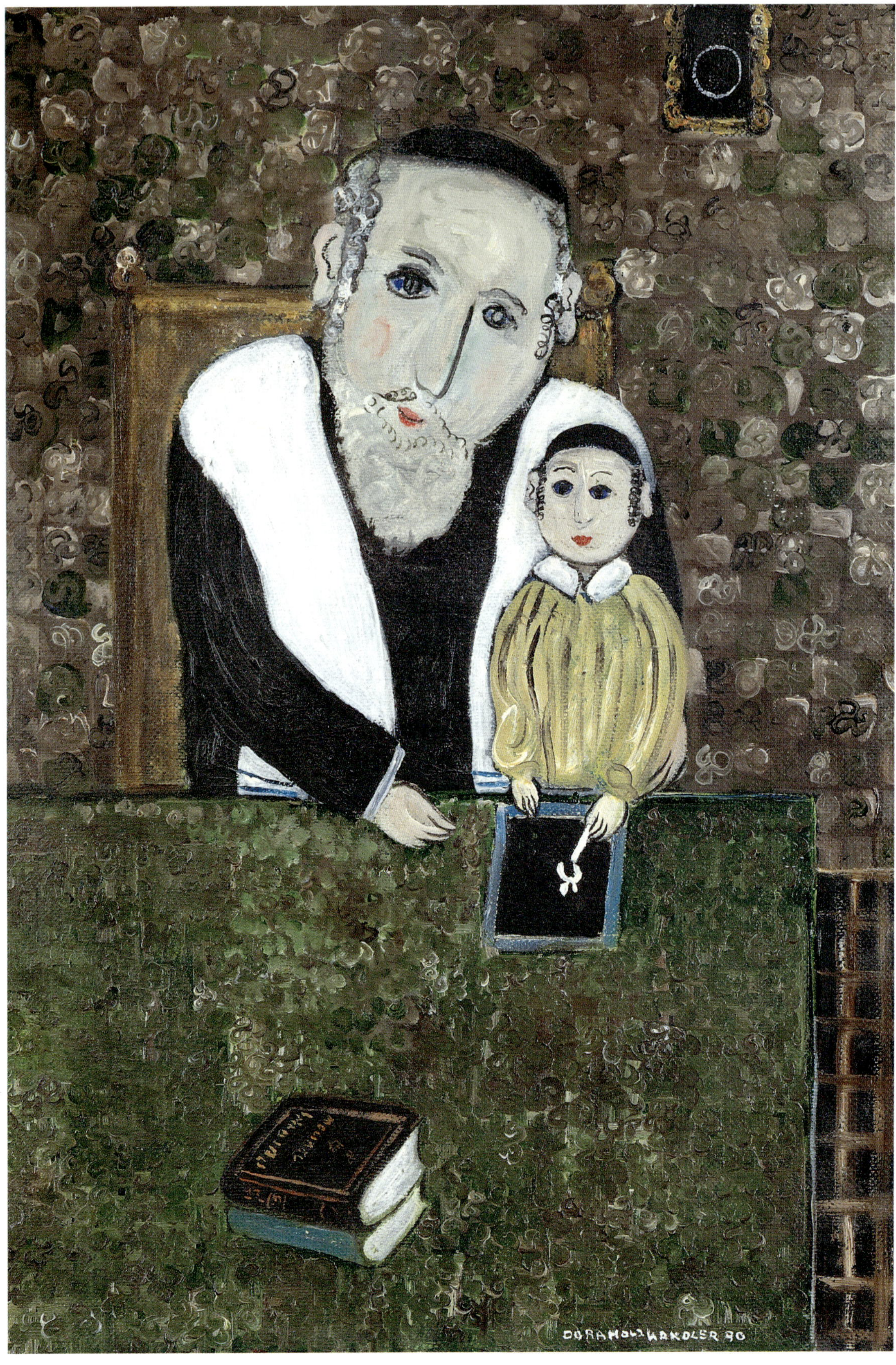

Plate 86
Aleph   1990   Oil on canvas   50.8 x 40.6 cm (20 x 16 in)

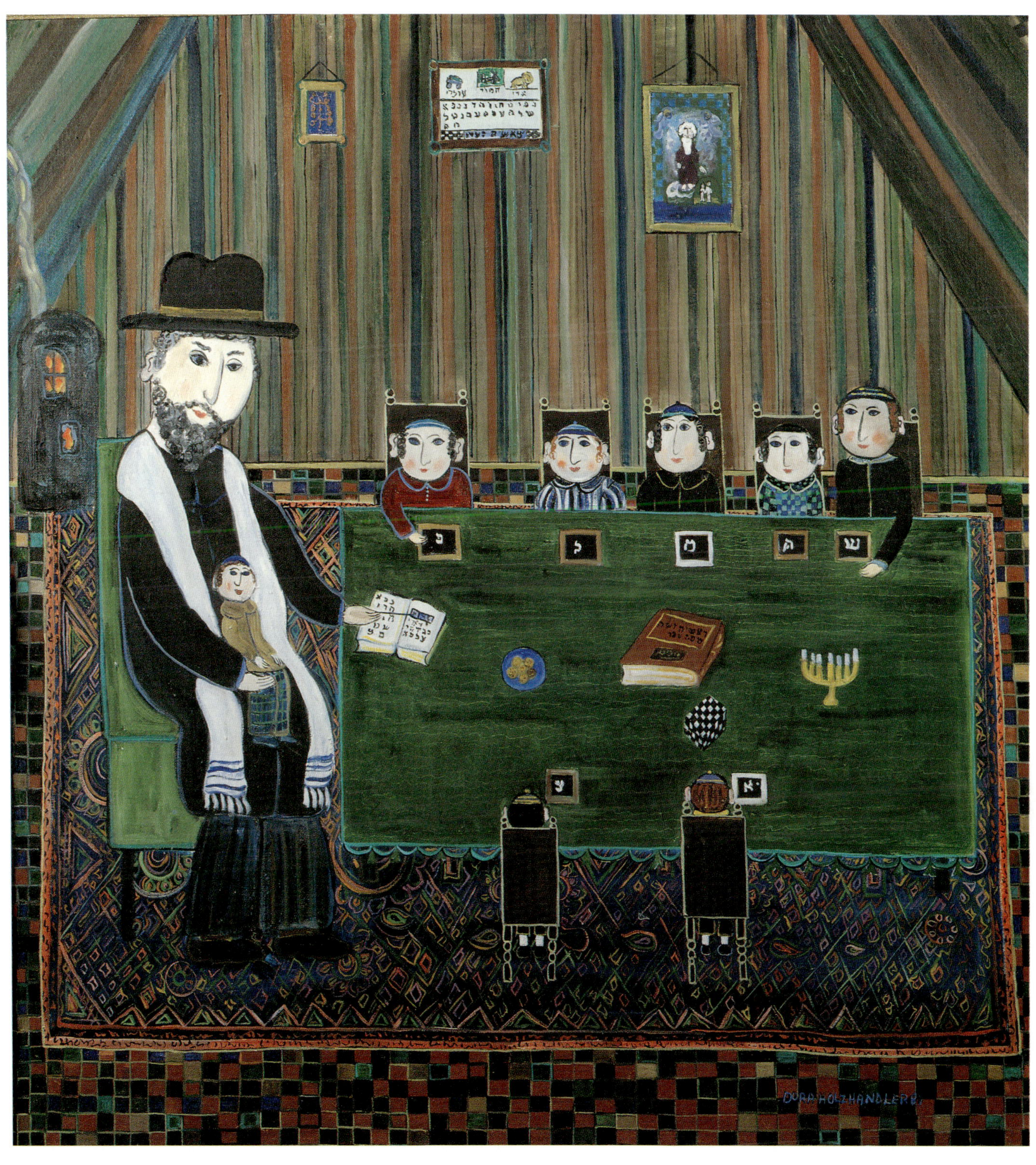

Plate 87
Hebrew Class   1987   Oil on canvas   91.4 x 86.4 cm (36 x 34 in)

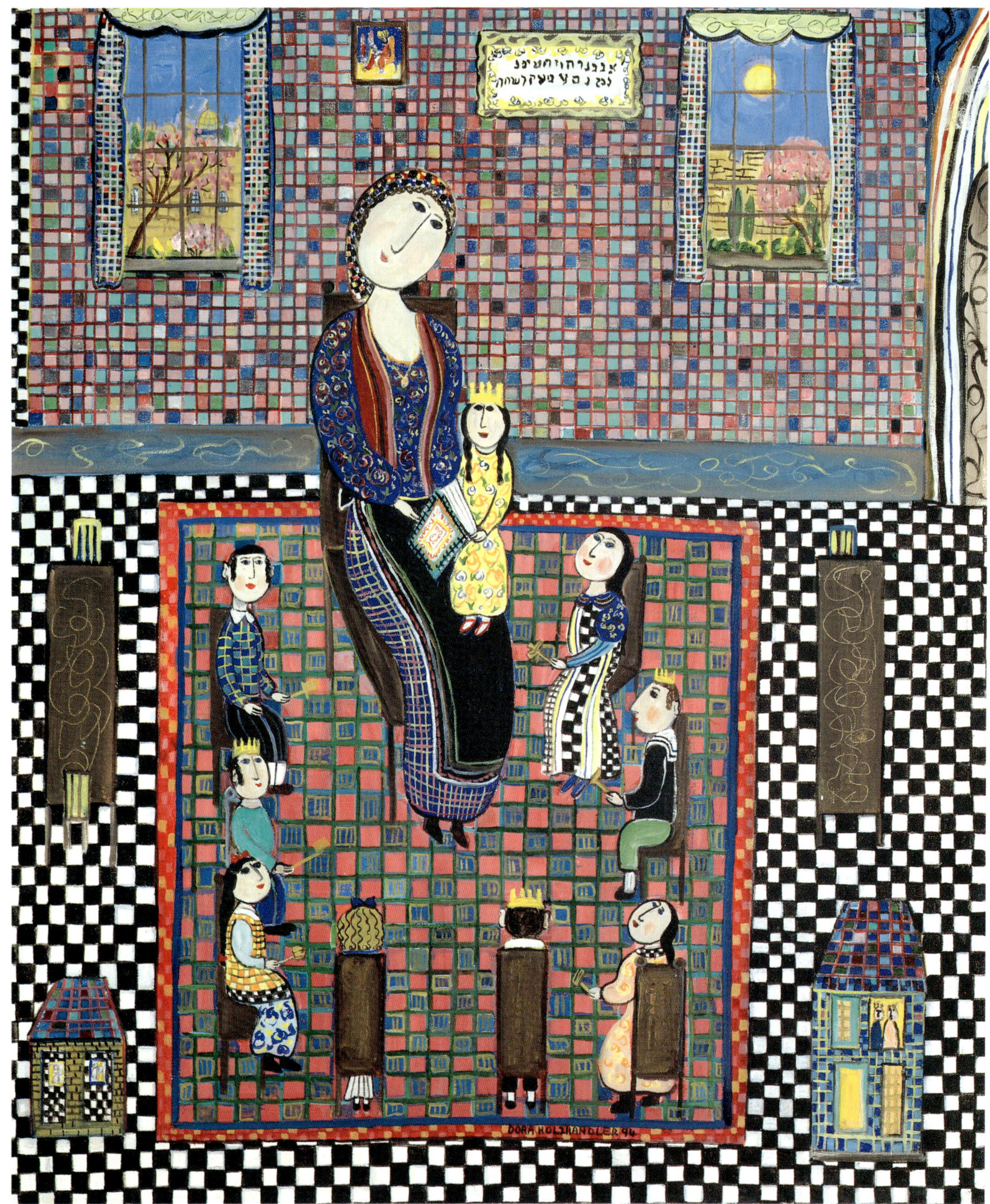

Plate 88
The Story of Esther   1994   Oil on canvas   54.6 x 41.9 cm (21$\frac{1}{2}$ x 16$\frac{1}{2}$ in)

On one of the *cheder* walls is a framed representation (perhaps unique in Dora's work) of God as a substantial, white-bearded Jehovah standing over Adam and Eve in Paradise, who appear as 'tiny and delightful' living dolls He has created. Judaism has always shown a highly ambiguous attitude towards the making of religious pictures. On the one hand, Jewish manuscripts through the ages have been illuminated with wonderful figurative forms; on the other, the Mosaic ban against making graven images (which would certainly include any divine representation) has been a powerful taboo force. 'In Buddhism and Christianity,' says Dora, 'the images of Christ and of Buddha very instantly bring religion to people, so I wonder why Jews don't have icons really, because it's a very good way of explaining religion.'

Within *The Story of Esther* (Plate 88), a tiny wall icon helps explain the biblical tale, commemorated at the Festival of Purim. It shows Queen Esther in (ultimately successful) supplication to her husband, the Persian King Ahaesuerus, to spare her fellow Jews from the genocidal plans of the chief courtier Haman. The seated pupils in the main composition hold ritual rattles ('*groggers*'), which they shake whenever the villain of the piece, Haman, is mentioned by the story-telling schoolteacher. The central apex point is where the fingers of the modestly scarfed teacher and her royally crowned pupil meet in a mutual grasp of the Holy Book. In two little dolls-houses in the classroom's near corners, the ancient figures of Esther and Ahaesuerus come blissfully to life.

Brilliancy crowns Jerusalem's stone seen through the classroom windows. Arriving in Jerusalem for the first time in 1987, approaching it by a walk through 'a garden with almond and pepper trees', Dora found the golden walls 'unimaginably beautiful'. Being there was 'like experiencing the Bible in depth. That's the extraordinary thing about Jerusalem: you don't have to think about it, because you're in it. Churches, mosques and synagogues ...' The semi-veiled window view in *Shabbat Shalom (Lovers in Jerusalem)* (Plate 89) of the pink-gold cityscape under a glinting, Prussian-blue sky is a miniaturist *tour de force*, comparable in pale, architectonic translucency with David Bomberg's more academically scrutinised Jerusalem overviews dating from the Anglo-Jewish artist's visit in 1923.[62]

Jerusalem's Western or Wailing Wall – all that remains of the ancient Temple – is the setting for a series of studies in gouache of rabbis at prayer. Against the Wall's near abstract plane in thin, pale amber and grey wash, figures in black and white (with the odd beard of red-gold) stand out in subtly dynamic relief. In *Simchat Torah at the Wailing Wall* (Plate 90), dancing rabbis jubilantly pass the Scrolls of the Law from one to another, as is customary at this Festival, which celebrates the divine giving of the Torah to the Jewish people. It is illuminating to note in the context of this painting that 'according to the Midrash the primeval Torah was written ... as "black fire on white fire"'.[63] The men here do suggest an appearance of dancing letters or hieroglyphs or even birds in flight, yet their fervently gentle humanity remains paramount.

In her portrait of *Rabbi at Wailing Wall* (Plate 91), each multi-layered brushstroke uncovers hidden layers of meaning. His white and silvery bearded locks trickling like winding rivulets of incandescence into a blue-black lake, as well as being expertly rendered as physical marks of age, have the quite abstract appearance of mystical ciphers, as if each lock and curl was a message from the Zohar. The rabbi's pinkish-grey complexion appears almost as a concentrated human version or extension of the Wall's ancient fabric.

The generous stature Dora gives to Orthodox women, generally subject to severe religious rules, indicates her perspective on their true worth and central place in the scheme of things. The woman shopper in *Montefiore Market, Jerusalem: Friday Afternoon* (Plate 92) is indisputably the focal figure. 'Montefiore Market,' she says, 'is the Ridley Road Market of my Dalston childhood to the *nth* degree. On Friday night, everyone goes around saying "Shabbat Shalom", and market people pray in a tiny synagogue in the middle of it.' The tiny synagogue is simply another stall – each market stall, in turn, resembling a synagogue Ark – its gold-braided curtains withdrawn. Fruits, meats and other goods laid out with model-like objectivity on little counters also present an ardent, inner vision of sensuously abstracted patterns and forms which inform the contemplative eye, the maternal heart, the praying mind. In the suffused clarity of early dusk (rendered here with delicate acuity), distinctions between mundane and supra-mundane, ancient and modern (indeed all our accustomed perspectives) dissolve, so that even the funny, little, smoked salmon-pink buses are seen as wondrous realities, each one of its wheels no bigger than a single orange (a mini-sun) on a pavement stall.

Over the past twenty years, Dora has continued to devote her energies to one-person shows. Stanley

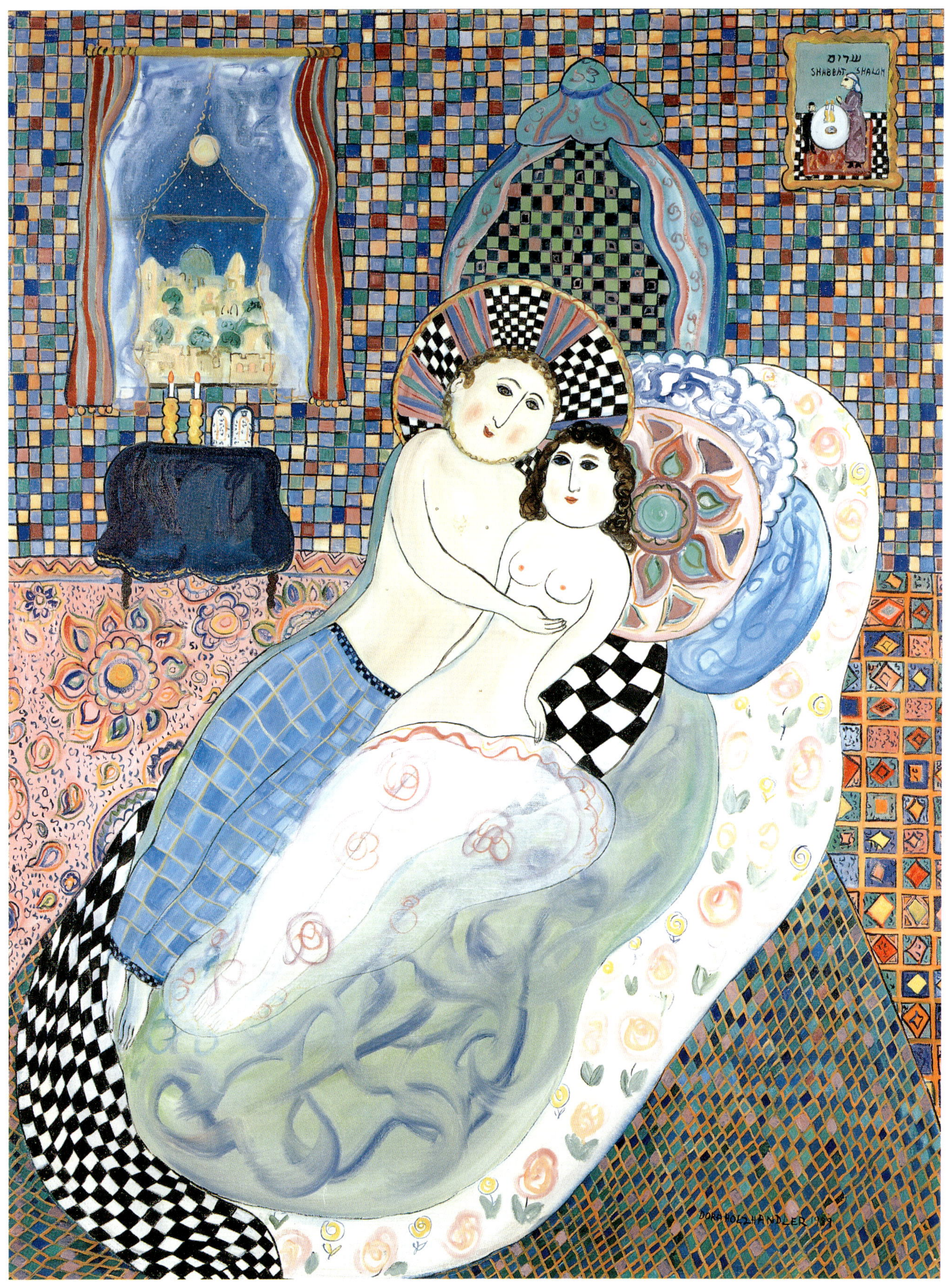

Plate 89
Shabbat Shalom (Lovers in Jerusalem)   1989   Oil on canvas   111.8 x 86.4 cm (44 x 34 in)

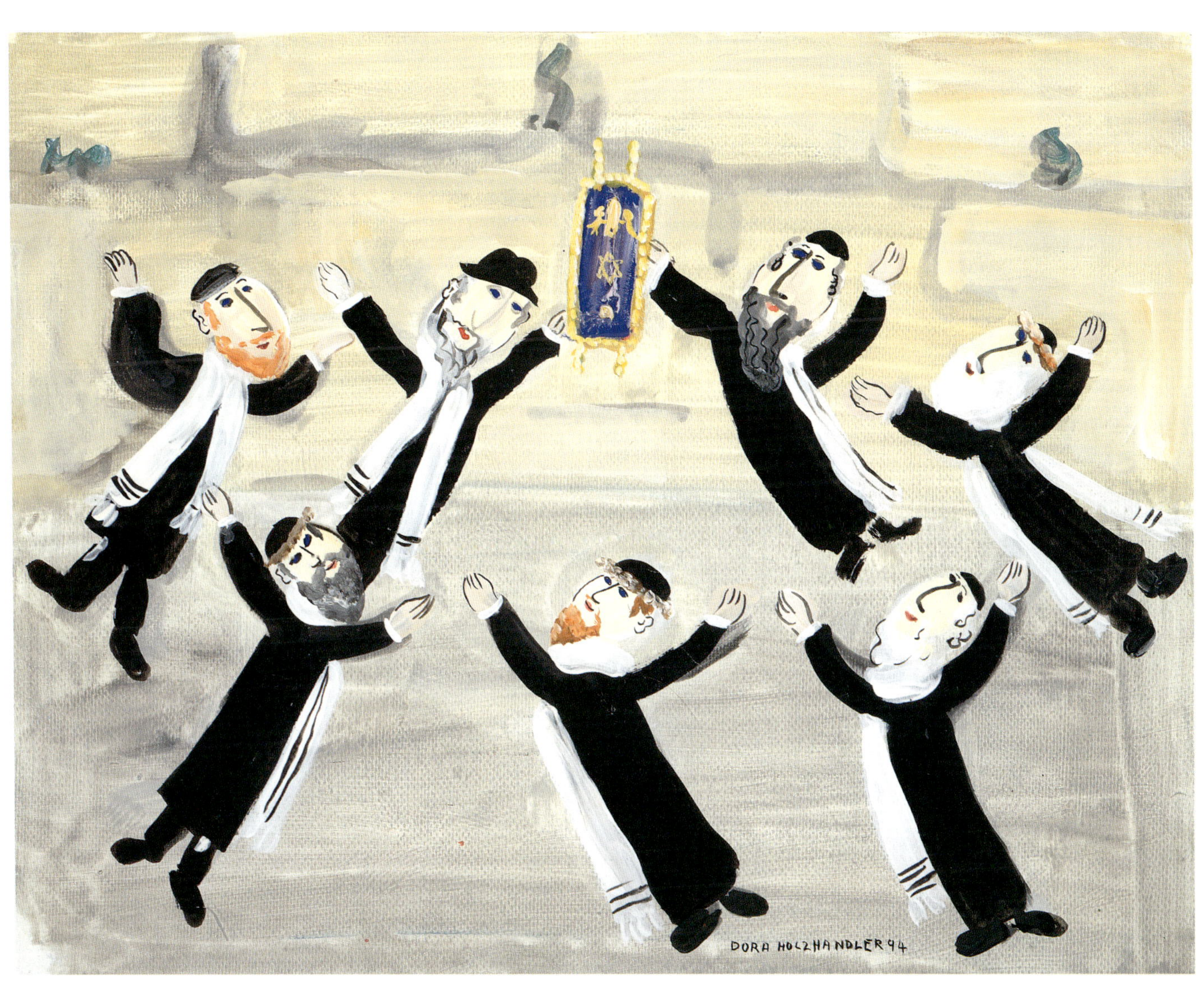

Plate 90
Simchat Torah at the Wailing Wall   1994   Gouache on paper   35.6 x 49.5 cm (14 x 19½ in)

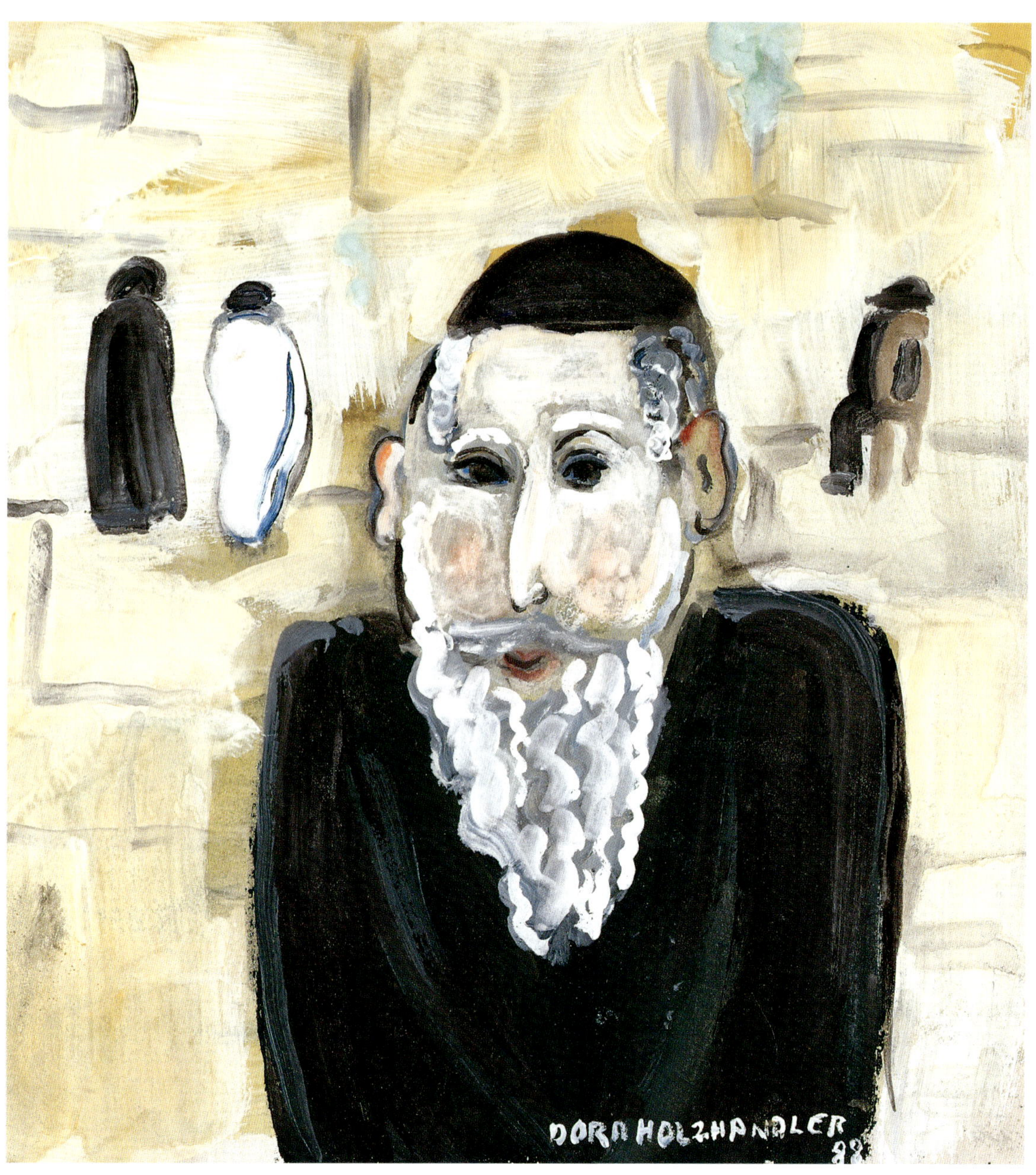

Plate 91
Rabbi at Wailing Wall   1988   Gouache on paper   27.9 x 26.7 cm (11 x 10$\frac{1}{2}$ in)

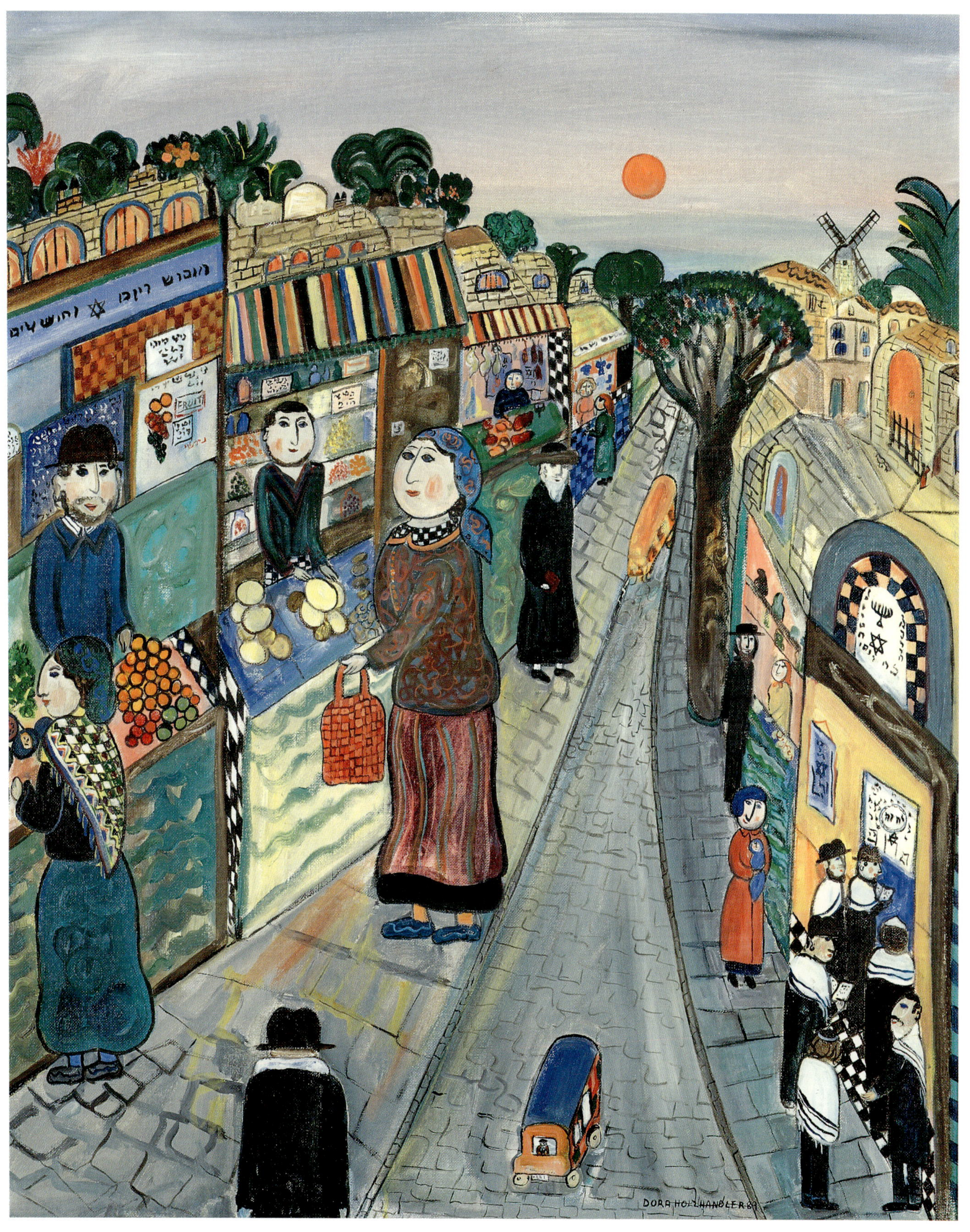

Plate 92
Montefiore Market, Jerusalem: Friday Afternoon   1989   Oil on board   78.7 x 64.8 cm (31 x 25½ in)

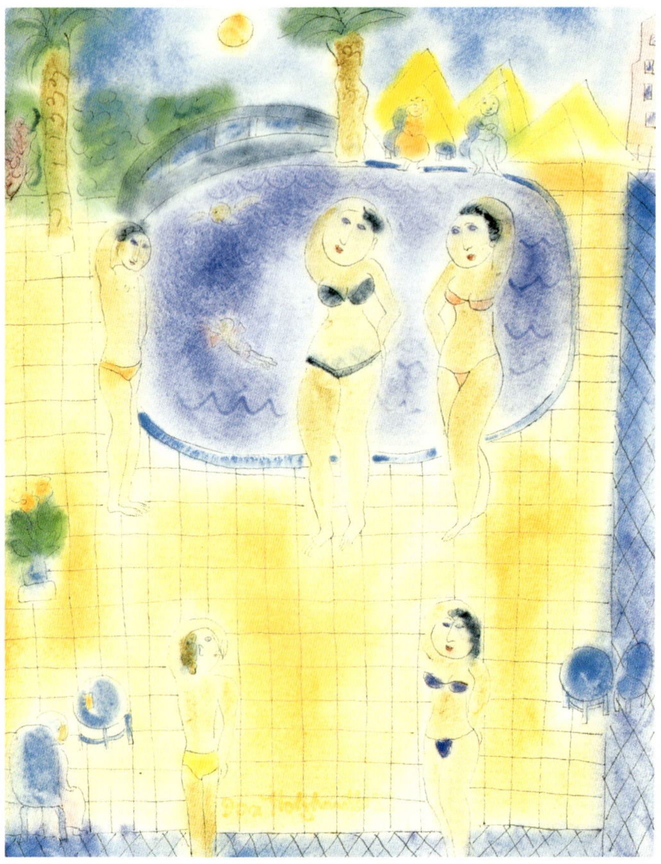

Plate 93
Aerobics at the King Solomon Hotel, Eilat   1988
Watercolour on paper   41.3 x 31.7 cm (16¼ x 12½ in)

Harries's Rona Gallery in London has held a series of exhibitions based on her childhood in Paris and London and her visit to Israel. In early 1985, a one-person exhibition was shown at Andras Kalman's Crane Kalman Gallery in London, and at the Graham Modern Gallery in New York towards the end of the year. There have also been regular one-person shows at Beaux Arts in Bath, and exhibitions of works on paper at the Holland Gallery near her home. In 1992, the Sternberg Centre, a Jewish cultural centre in north London, held a major exhibition of her works in its elegant Georgian manor house setting. The following year she had a special display as Guest Artist at the big, annual naive art exhibition *Naivistit Iittalassa* in Finland. A Scottish connection has latterly proved to be of singular significance. She had a one-person show at the Festival of Jewish Culture, part of 'Glasgow '90', and her painting *Sabbath Candles* was selected for the St Mungo Museum of Religious Life and Art in Glasgow, which opened in 1993. The picture is in fitting, multi-cultural company, hanging near to William Blake's portraits of Adam and Eve, Dürer's engravings of Stations of the Cross, a Hindu bronze of a dancing Shiva, and a medieval wooden *Pietà*. The view from this room in the gallery embraces a Zen Buddhist garden, Glasgow Cathedral and darksome monuments of the hillside Necropolis. An exhibition, *L'Chaim! To Life!: The Jewish Year in the Art of Dora Holzhandler*, was held at the St Mungo Museum in 1994 (and at the Manchester Jewish Museum the following year). 'Scotland has turned up in my life so often,' she says, 'without my even looking for it! I am so happy to be represented at St Mungo's – to be part of an artistic dialogue between all religions.'

When her painting *Wedding Night* (Plate 61) was acquired by the Gallery of Modern Art, which opened in Glasgow in 1996, the critic John Russell Taylor wrote in *The Times*: 'Dora Holzhandler is a senior artist, shamefully neglected, and if Glasgow is able to repair that and similar omissions from the current canon, then it has to be doing something right.'[64] It seems a fortuitous coincidence that *Wedding Night* has so many affinities with the work of the great Glasgow-based artist Charles Rennie Mackintosh. Mackintosh died in the year Dora was born but his 'emerging new vocabulary of forms'[65] – based on motifs of the square, flowers (notably the rose), archaic Celtic designs and microscopic visions – shares many intuitive resonances with Dora's own 'symbol consciousness'. Dora's painting

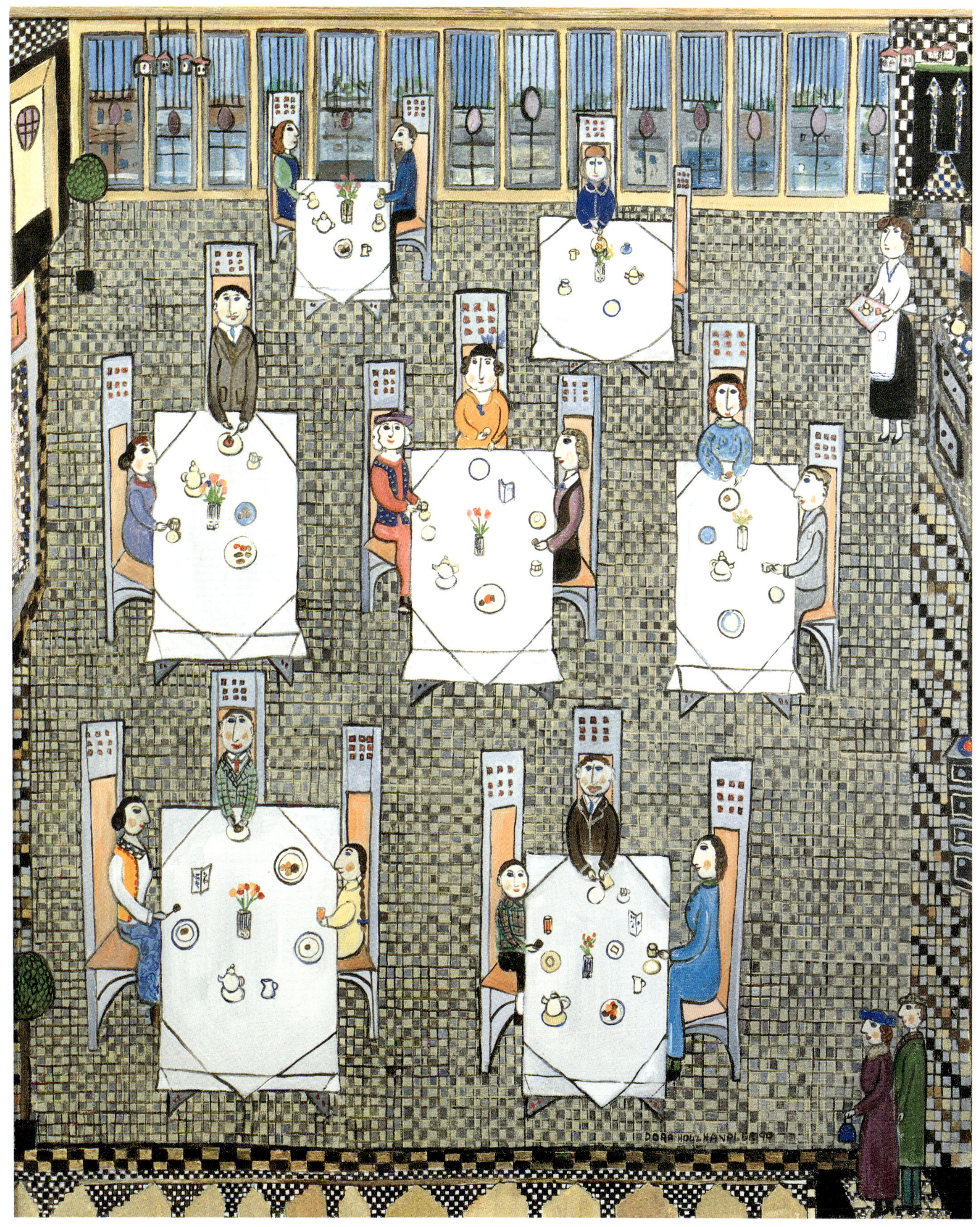

Plate 94
The Willow Tea Rooms, Glasgow   1990   Oil on canvas   61 x 50.8 cm (24 x 20 in)

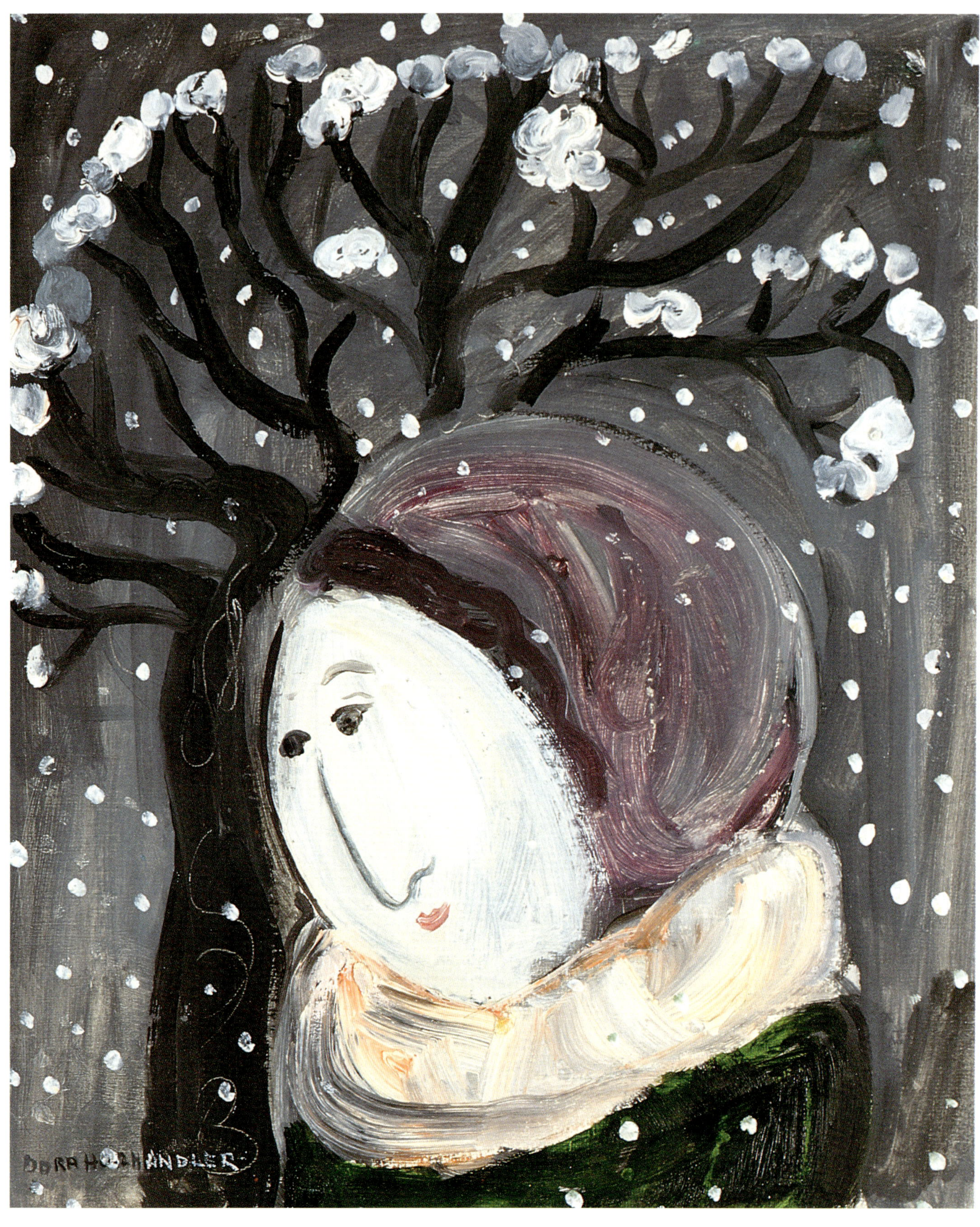

Plate 95
Self Portrait   1985   Oil on board   25.4 x 20.3 cm (10 x 8 in)

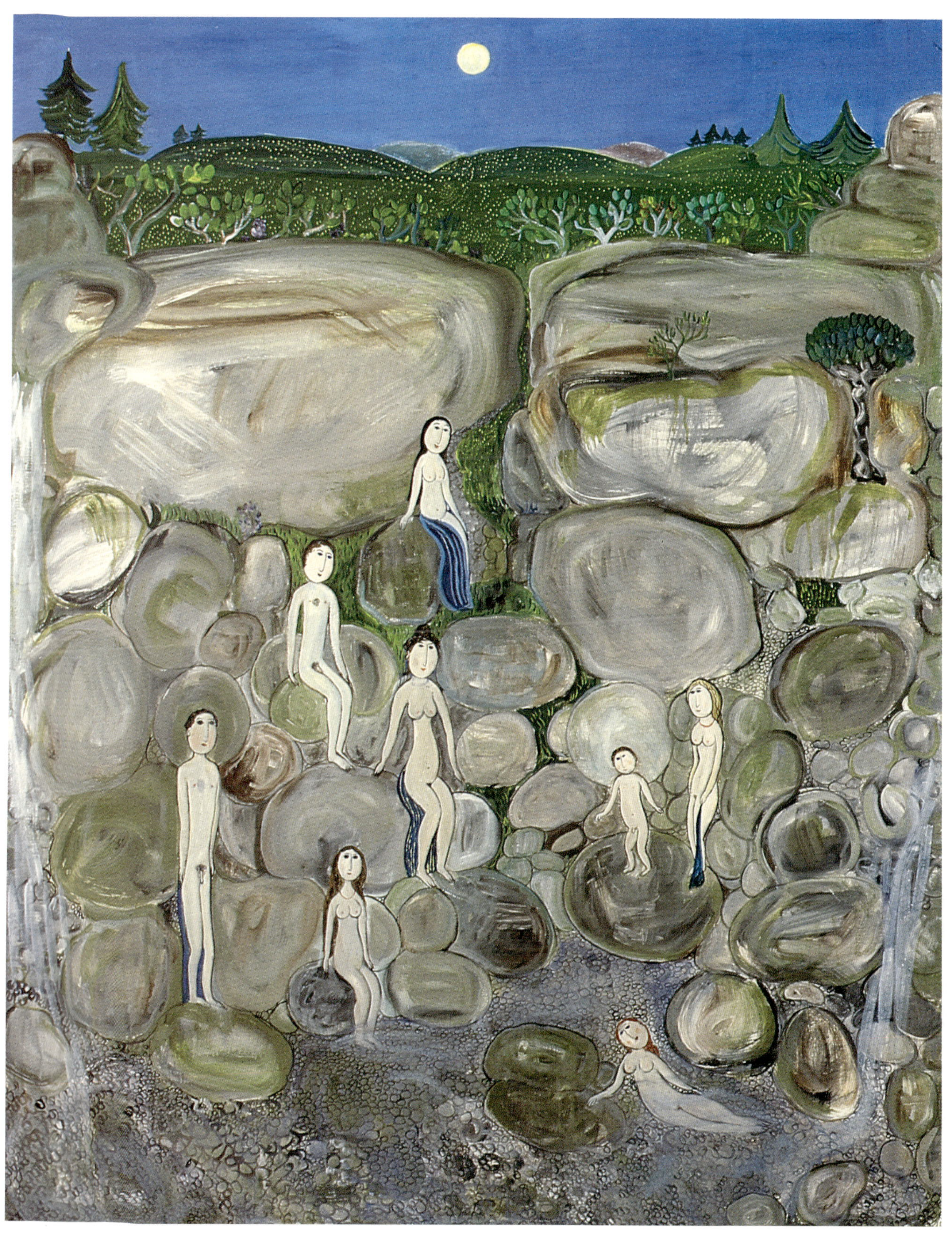

Plate 96
Garwood Gorge, Eskdalemuir, Scotland 1996 Oil on canvas 121.9 x 96.5 cm (48 x 38 in)

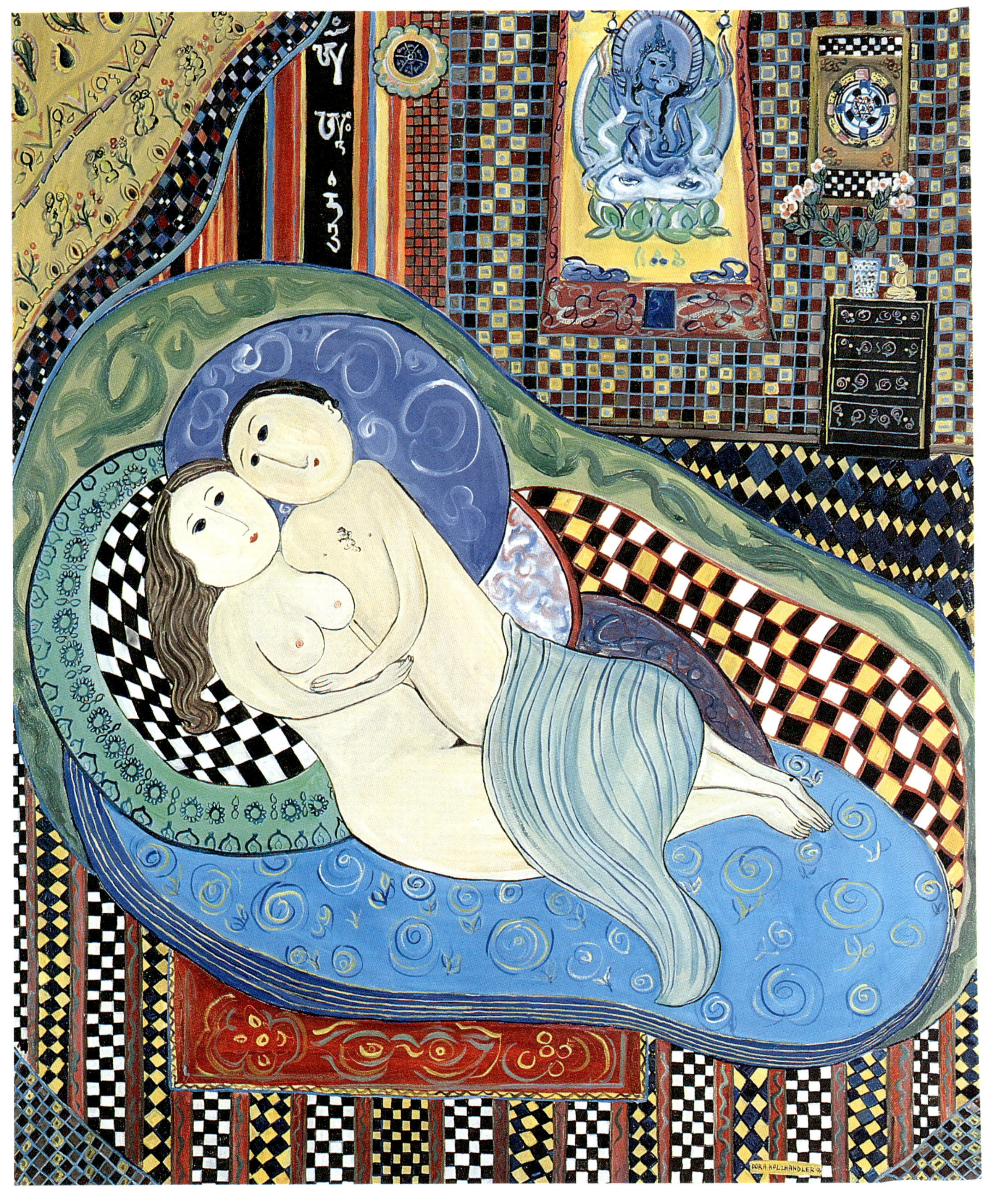

Plate 97
Tantric Lovers   1996   Oil on canvas   99 x 81.3 cm (39 x 32 in)

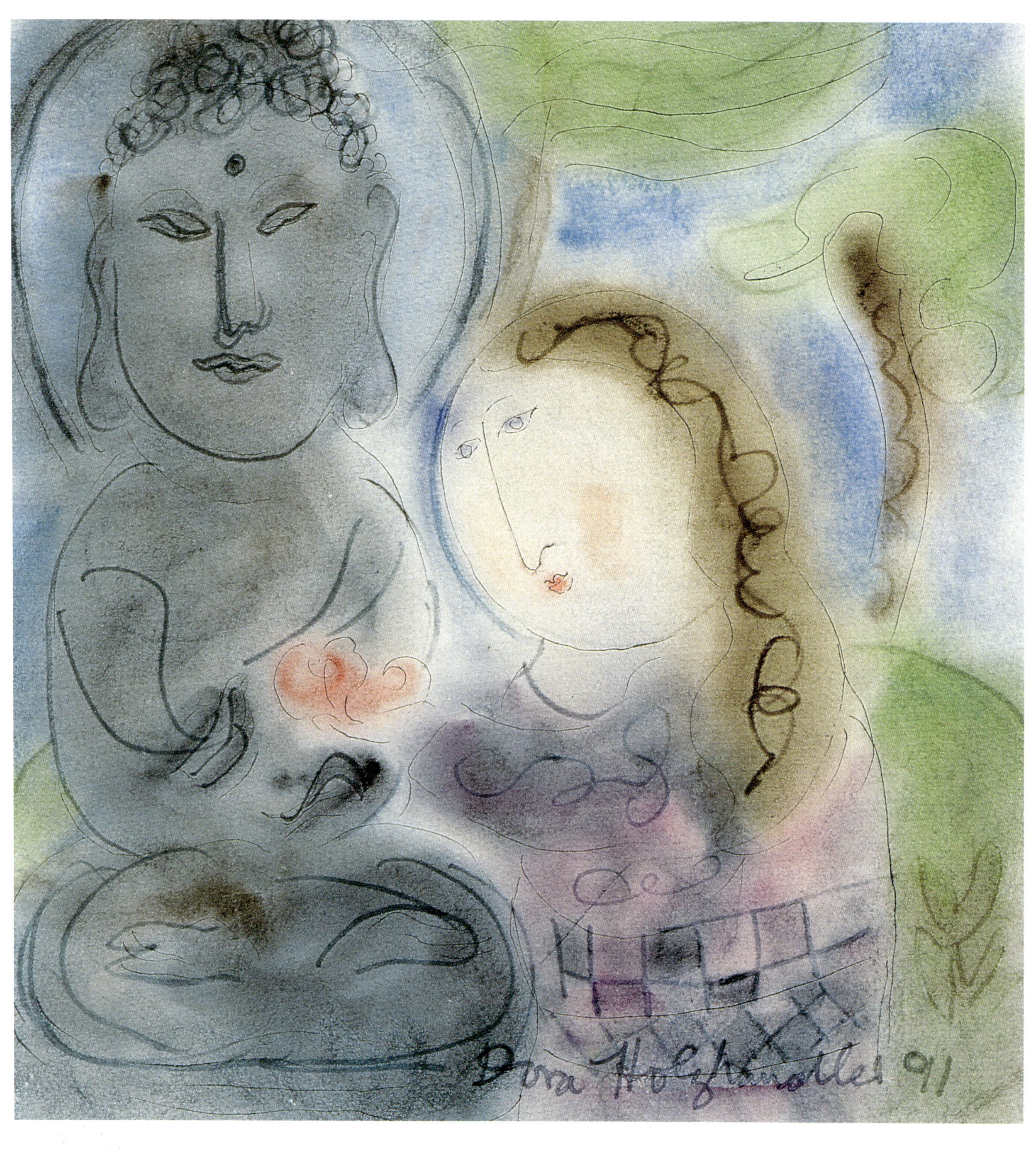

Plate 98
Lady with Statue of the Buddha   1991   Watercolour on paper   33 x 30.5 cm (13 x 12 in)

The Willow Tea Rooms (Plate 94) is inspired by her many visits to Mackintosh's magnificent creation in Sauchiehall Street in Glasgow.

Asked whether on her travels she enjoys visiting religious places or mythological settings, Dora replies swiftly: 'O always! I love religious places of any sort. The minds of people make the atmosphere, make the gods, make the spirits of the place. If it's a Christian place, then the church will contain all the spiritual qualities that the people project. If I come across a synagogue, now that's my home in a strange way; that's the place I was born in, so it has an added meaning.' The synagogue is central in her work but she has also painted Buddhist temples, Christian churches and cathedrals (notably Notre Dame in Paris and onion-domed Russian Orthodox churches as seen once on a three-day trip from Finland to St Petersburg), Rastafarian gatherings, Celtic and Hungarian folk-dances, and scenes inspired by ancient Greek and Roman myth. She makes resonant myth out of seemingly secular, contemporary reality too: rather noble looking Punks observed shopping in London's King's Road, women seated with infinite patience in a National Health ante-natal clinic, a woman hanging out rainbows of washing. 'Art has almost got nothing to do with something visual,' she says. 'It's very strange. You simply have to be it – you have to disappear and your subject appears.'

Dora's art is rooted first and foremost in a love of people – seen simply for who they are in all their radiant, naked reality. In most of her paintings, the human being is uncontrovertibly the figurative centre and symbolical focus. She is also an abstract pattern-maker of the first rank. In her painting of bathers at *Garwood Gorge, Eskdalemuir, Scotland* (Plate 96), her indivisible gifts as both figurative and abstract artist are seen to advantage. Her vision of boulders, rocks and pebbly riverbed is one of grand simplicity. Singled out from the rest of the picture, each mighty boulder can be seen as an almost abstract expressionist inscape, its mossy greens, silvery lights and peaty browns in vigorous flux. Waterfalls – rushing declensions of white light over colours of stone – on left and right are painted with the same pellucid grace as (elsewhere, in other pictures) are diaphanous curtains semi-veiling sun and moon, and bridal veils through which the roses of paradise are glimpsed. Each bather is seen as being utterly at one with their element, each in his or her own perfect place. They are bathing in cosmic spaciousness. Their home is our true human nature.

In an uncertain age in which art has to a large degree lost its centre and its heart, Dora's meditative paintings return us to our origins in the here and now, reawakening in us the compassionate vision that is our birthright. Mothers and children, lovers, solitary contemplatives, family and friends, all the generations are seen with an eye of loving detachment. We are moved by the faces she portrays, by her reverberant colours and patterns, because they reflect the primordial reality of our own minds. Art has more than ever now an integral part to play in our lives – to remind us of who we ultimately are, without masks of illusion. True artists, like the great icon painters, have always known this. Dora Holzhandler has found her own impressively unique way to arrive at this universal truth.

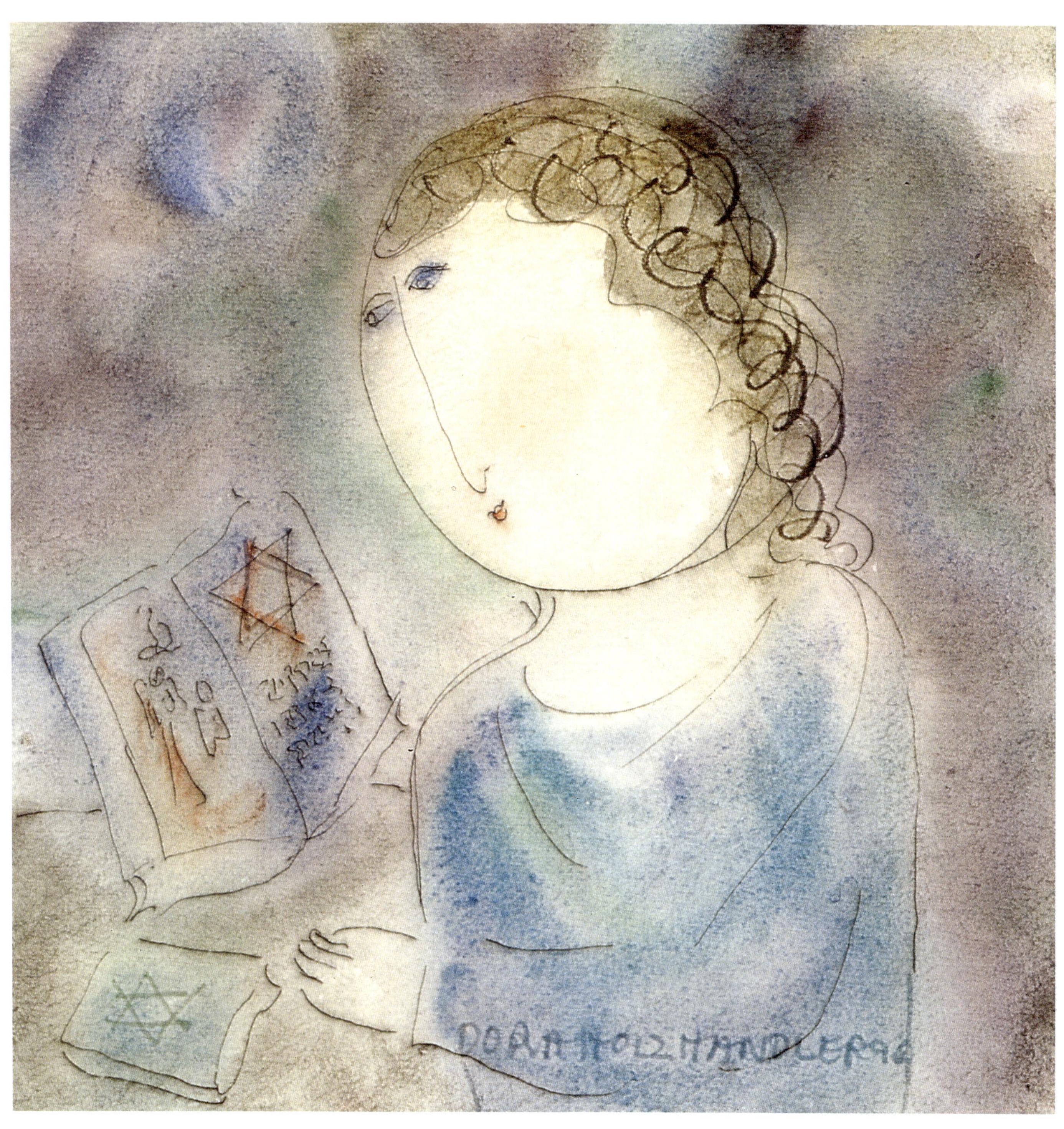

Plate 99
Lady Reading Kabbalah   1996   Watercolour on paper
26.7 x 25.4 cm (10¹/₂ x 10 in)

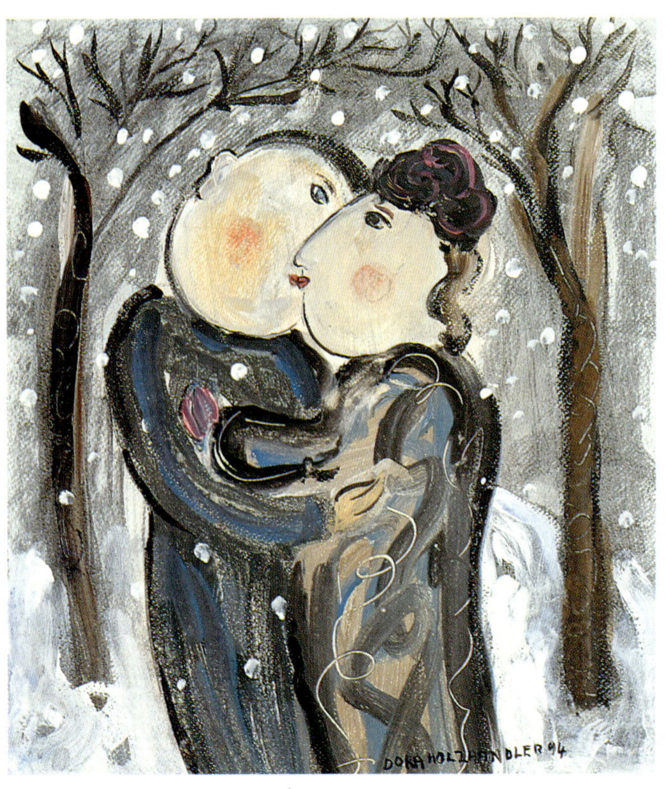

Lovers in Winter   1994
Gouache on paper   41.3 x 34.3 cm (16 $^{1}/_{4}$ x 13 $^{1}/_{2}$ in)

Notes

1 Chögyam Trungpa, *Cutting through Spiritual Materialism*, Shambhala Publications, Boston, and Robinson and Watkins, London, 1973, p.123.

2 Quotations by the artist come from an unpublished autobiography, *My Book*, 1981, or from her conversations with the author.

3 Eric Newton, *The Manchester Guardian*, 6 February 1962.

4 William Blake, 'Ah! Sunflower', in *Songs of Experience*, in *William Blake*, Penguin Books, Harmondsworth, 1976, p.51.

5 Aldous Huxley, *The Doors of Perception*, Chatto & Windus, London, 1954.

6 Allen Ginsberg, 'Big Eats', in *Cosmopolitan Greetings: Poems 1986-1992*, HarperCollins, New York, 1994, p.69.

7 Eric Newton, *The Manchester Guardian*, 6 February 1962.

8 Edna O'Brien, *Foreword* to Graham Modern Gallery catalogue for Dora Holzhandler's one-woman exhibition, New York, 1985.

9 Jack Kerouac, 'Lady', in *Pomes All Sizes*, City Lights Books, San Francisco, 1992, p.103.

10 Aldous Huxley, *Heaven and Hell*, Granada Publishing, London, 1978, pp.137-8.

11 Quoted in William Anderson, *Cecil Collins: The Quest for the Great Happiness*, Barrie and Jenkins, London, 1988, p.138.

12 *The New English Bible*, Genesis, ch.3, v.24, Oxford University Press and Cambridge University Press, 1970, p.2.

13 *The New English Bible*, The Song of Songs, ch.4, v.12, p.802.

14 *The Zohar*, Dr Paul P. Levertoff, Maurice Simon and Harry Sperling (trans.), The Soncino Press, London, Jerusalem, New York, 1978, vol.3, pp.10-11.

15 W.B. Yeats, 'The Rose of Battle', in *W.B. Yeats: The Poems*, Richard J. Finneran (ed.), Macmillan, London, 1983, p.37.

16 Gertrude Stein, 'Sacred Emily', in *Geography and Plays*, Four Seas Company, Boston, 1922, p.187.

17 Letter from Pierre Bonnard to Henri Matisse (winter 1936-7), referring to 'très beaux ciels nuancés' at Deauville, in Richard Howard (trans.), *Bonnard/Matisse: Letters between Friends*, Harry N. Abrams, New York, 1992, p.52.

18 Emily Dickinson, 'A Wind That Rose', in *A Choice of Emily Dickinson's Verse*, Faber and Faber, London, 1969, p.57.

19 William Blake, 'A Dream', in *Songs of Innocence*, in *William Blake*, Penguin Books, Harmondsworth, 1976, p.38.

20 Roman Vishniac, *A Vanished World*, Allen Lane, London, 1983; Roman Vishniac, *To Give Them Light*, Simon & Schuster, New York, 1993, and Viking, London, 1993.

21 *New Frontiers of Naive Art in Europe*, Royal Festival Hall, London, exhibition catalogue, Muller, Blond and White, London, 1984.

22 *The New English Bible*, Isaiah, ch.11, v.6-10, p.824.

23 *The Zohar*, vol.4, p.38.

24 'Rozhinkes mit Mandlen' ('Raisins and Almonds'), part of a song from the operetta *Shulamis* written in 1880 by Abraham Goldfaden (1840-1908), founder of the modern Yiddish theatre. Quoted in *Mir Trogn A Gezang: The New Book of Yiddish Songs*, compiled and translated by Eleanor Gordon Mlotek, The Workman's Circle Education Department, New York, 1989, p.4.

25 *The New English Bible*, Genesis, ch.2, v.3, p.2.

26 *The Zohar*, vol.3, p.380.

27 Jack Kerouac, 'First we buy the meat', in *Pomes All Sizes*, City Lights Books, San Francisco, 1992, p.63.

28 Emily Dickinson, 'I tried to think a lonelier Thing', in *A Choice of Emily Dickinson's Verse*, Faber and Faber, London, 1969, p.36.

29 T.S. Eliot, 'Little Gidding', in *Four Quartets*, Faber and Faber, London, 1979, p.48.

30 *The Zohar*, vol.4, p.38.

31 Allen Ginsberg, 'The Lion for Real', in *Kaddish and Other Poems 1958-1960*, City Lights Books, San Francisco, 1961, p.53.

32 Arthur Rimbaud in a letter to Georges Izambard, 13 May 1871. 'Le poète se fait *voyant* par un long, immense et raisonné *dérèglement* de tous les sens.' ('The poet becomes a seer by a long, vast and reasoned disorientation of all the senses'; translation by P. Vann.) Quoted in C. Chadwick, *Rimbaud*, University of London, The Athlone Press, London 1979, p.20.

33 Quoted in Sarah Whitfield, 'An Outrageous Lyricism', in *Georges Rouault: The Early Years 1903-20*, Royal Academy of Arts and Lund Humphries Publishers, London, 1993, p.11.

34 Colette, in a letter dated April 1911, *Letters from Colette*, Virago Press, London, 1980, p.21.

35 Quoted in Isidore Epstein, *Judaism*, Penguin Books, Harmondsworth, 1990, p.156.

36 Quoted in entry on Morris Hirshfield in Jane Turner (ed.), *The Dictionary of Art*, Macmillan, London, 1996, vol.14, pp.574-5.

37 Dr A. K. Coomaraswamy, *The Transformation of Nature into Art*, cited in Aldous Huxley, *Heaven and Hell*, Granada Publishing, London, 1978, p.99.

38 Quotation from *The Talmud*, cited in Aryeh Kaplan, *Jewish Meditation: A Practical Guide*, Schocken Books, New York, 1985, p.72.

39 Quoted by Painton Cowen, *Rose Windows*, Thames and Hudson, London, 1979, p.7.

40 Quotation from the Buddhist 'Heart Sutra', translated in full in Donald S. Lopex Jnr, *Elaborations on Emptiness: Uses of the Heart Sutra*, Princeton University Press, 1996, p.viii. Partial translation reads: '… form is empty, emptiness is form. Emptiness is not other than form; form is not other than emptiness.'

41 John Milton, *Animadversions*, in *The Complete Prose Works of John Milton*, Yale University Press, New Haven and London, 1982, vol.1, p.690.

42 Jack Kerouac, 'Buddha', in *Pomes All Sizes*, City Lights Books, San Francisco, 1992, p.97.

43 Charles Baudelaire, 'L'Invitation au Voyage', in *Les Fleurs du Mal*, Fleuron, Editions Slatkine, Paris and Geneva, 1995, p.70.

44 *The Zohar*, Maurice Simon and Harry Sperling (trans.), The Soncino Press, London, Jerusalem, New York, vol.1, pp.33-4.

45 *The New English Bible*, The Second Book of Samuel, ch.6, v.4-5, p.345.

46 Baal Shem is Hebrew for 'Master of the Name'.

47 An illustration of mindfulness at all times is seen in this story about Rabbi Levi Yitzhak of Berditchev (d.1809), a disciple of the Baal Shem, cited in Martin Buber, *Tales of the Hasidim: The Early Masters*, Schocken Books, New York, 1947, p.222: 'Once the rabbi of Berditchev saw a drayman arrayed for Morning Service in prayer shawl and phylacteries. He was greasing the wheels of his wagon. "Lord of the world!" he exclaimed delightedly. "Behold this man! Behold the devoutness of your people. Even when they grease the wheels of a wagon, they are mindful of your name!"'

48 Chagall quoted in Aleksandr Kamensky, *Chagall: The Russian Years 1907-1922*, Thames and Hudson, London, 1989, p.74.

49 Jack Kerouac, 'Skid Row Wine', in *Pomes all Sizes*, City Lights Books, San Francisco, p.110.

50 In the Kabbalah, each letter of the Hebrew alphabet is given a distinct symbolic meaning, *aleph* taking on a unique and fundamental role. In the Zohar, God addresses *aleph* personally: '*Aleph, Aleph* … on thee shall be based all calculations and operations of the world, and unity shall not be expressed save by the letter *Aleph*.' (*The Zohar*, Maurice Simon and Harry Sperling (trans.), vol.1, p.13.)

51 Christopher Smart, 'Jubilate Agno', in *Christopher Smart: Selected Poems*, Carcanet Press, Manchester, 1979, p.41.

52 Moses Nachmanides, quoted in Noah benShea, *Jewish Wisdom through Time; The Word: A Spiritual Sourcebook*, Villard, New York, 1995, p.168.

53 Barry Fealdman, *Jewish Chronicle* exhibition review, 30 October 1987: Dora's 'frail, diaphanous watercolours seem to express her innermost emotions'.

54 Isaac Bashevis Singer, 'Joy', in *The Collected Short Stories*, Penguin Books, London, 1984, pp.36-7.

55 Eric Newton, *The Manchester Guardian*, 6 February 1962.

56 The Duchess of St Albans, *Art and Antiques*, May 1972.

57 Sogyal Rinpoche, *The Tibetan Book of Living and Dying*, Harper, San Francisco, 1992, and Rider, London, 1995.

58 Chinese Zen Master Ummon quoted in Shunryu Suzuki, *Zen Mind, Beginner's Mind*, Weatherhill, New York and Tokyo, 1982, p.43.

59 *The Zohar*, vol.3, p.224.

60 *The Zohar*, Maurice Simon and Harry Sperling (trans.), vol.1, p.163.

61 '*Oyfn Pripetshik*' ('At the Fireplace'), originally titled '*Alef-Beyz*', by Mark M. Warshawsky (1840-1907), a discovery of the writer Shalom Aleichem. Quoted in *Mir Trogn A Gezang: The New Book of Yiddish Songs*, compiled and translated by Eleanor Gordon Mlotek, The Workman's Circle Education Department, New York, 1989, p.2.

62 Richard Cork, *David Bomberg*, Yale University Press, New Haven and London, 1987, pp.146-74.

63 Aryeh Kaplan, *Jewish Meditation: A Practical Guide*, Schocken Books, New York, 1985, p.76.

64 John Russell Taylor, *The Times*, 30 March, 1996.

65 Hermann Muthesius writing about Mackintosh and his associates in *Das englische Haus*, Wasmuth, Berlin, 1904-5. English-language abridged edition, Dennis Sharp (ed.), Janet Seligman (trans.), *The English House*, Granada Publishing, 1979, p.51.

Selected Exhibitions

1949   *Young Contemporaries*, RBA Galleries, London

1954   Beaux Arts Gallery, London

1958   John Moores exhibition, Liverpool

1960   Chenil Gallery, London – one-woman exhibition

1962   Portal Gallery, London – one-woman exhibition

1964-80   Crane Arts, London – mixed exhibitions

1967   Grosvenor Gallery, London

1971   Langton Gallery, London – one-woman
exhibition

1972   *Naive Art from the Collection of Dr and Mrs Arthur
H. Sams*, Municipal Art Gallery, Los Angeles

1973   Langton Gallery, London – one-woman
exhibition

1976   Galerie de Beerenburght, Holland

Langton Gallery, London – one-woman
exhibition

1977   London University

Langton Gallery, London – one-woman
exhibition

1979   *Spirit of London*, Royal Festival Hall, London

1978-87   Rona Gallery, London – mixed exhibitions

1980   Crane Arts, London – one-woman exhibition

1984   *New Frontiers of Naive Art in Europe*,
Royal Festival Hall, London

British Naive Painters, Concourse Gallery,
Barbican Arts Centre, London

1985   Crane Kalman Gallery, London – one-woman
exhibition

Beaux Arts, Bath – one-woman exhibition

Ben Uri Art Society, London

*First American Exhibition: Dora Holzhandler –
Paintings and Watercolours*, Graham Modern
Gallery, New York – one-woman exhibition

1986   *Peintres Naïfs Britanniques* – Musée Municipal,
Carcassonne; Galerie Paul Valéry, Sète; Galerie

de Salles, Nîmes; Musée Fabre, Montpellier

1987   Galerie Antoinette, Paris

Dora Holzhandler: Paintings of Jewish Life,
Rona Gallery, London – one-woman exhibition

1989   *Dora Holzhandler: Paintings of a Jewish Childhood
and a Visit to Israel*, Rona Gallery, London –
one-woman exhibition

1990   Beaux Arts, Bath – one-woman exhibition

Rona Gallery, London – one-woman exhibition
Festival of Jewish Culture, part of 'Glasgow '90'
– one-woman exhibition

1991   *Works on Paper*, Holland Gallery, London –
one-woman exhibition

1992   *Dora Holzhandler: Glimpses from a Jewish Life*,
The Sternberg Centre, London – one-woman
exhibition

Dora Holzhandler: Spring in Paris, Rona Gallery,
London – one-woman exhibition

Works on Paper, Bowmoore Gallery, London –
one-woman exhibition

1993   *Naivistit Iittalassa '93*, Finland – Guest Artist

Works on Paper, Holland Gallery, London –
one-woman exhibition

Watercolours and Ceramics, Rebecca Hossack
Gallery – one-woman exhibition

1994   *Paintings in Gouache*, Rona Gallery, London –
one-woman exhibition

*L'Chaim! To Life!: The Jewish Year in the Art of Dora
Holzhandler*, St Mungo Museum of Religious
Life and Art, Glasgow – one-woman exhibition

1995   *L'Chaim! To Life!: The Jewish Year in the Art of Dora
Holzhandler*, Jewish Museum, Manchester –
one-woman exhibition

Rona Gallery, London – one-woman exhibition

1996   Boundary Gallery, London

Beaux Arts, Bath – one-woman exhibition

1997   Rona Gallery, London – one-woman exhibition

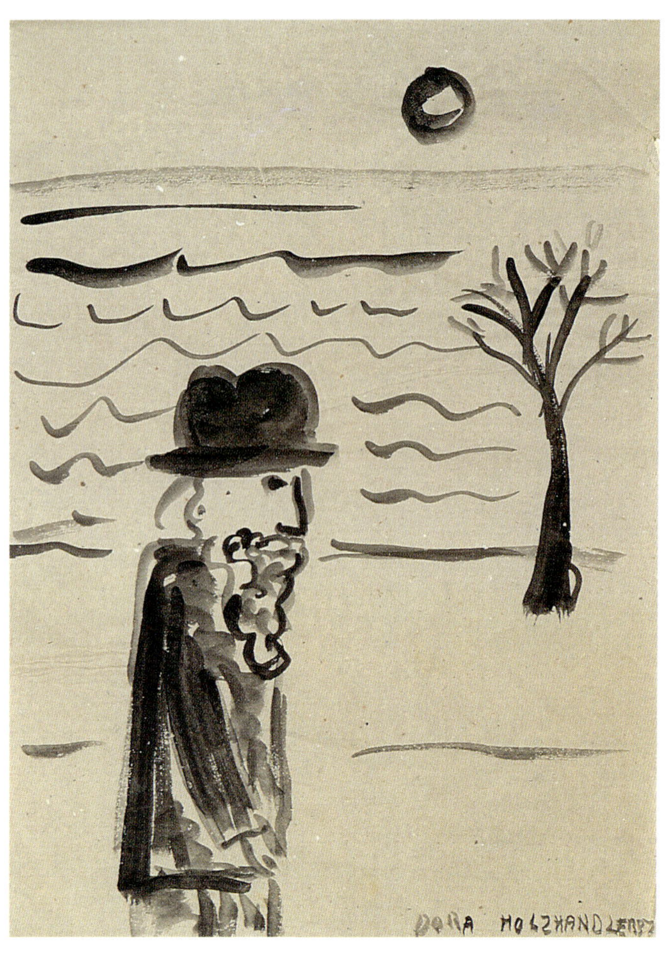

Rabbi by the Sea   1987
Indian ink on paper   40.6 x 31.7 cm (16 x 12½ in)

Bibliography

SELECTED ARTICLES REFERRING TO THE ARTIST

Artley, Alexandra, 'Many Mansions', *The Spectator*, 15 May 1993

Burland, Cottie, 'Dora Holzhandler', *Arts Review*, 28 February 1962

Duchess of St Albans, 'Dora Holzhandler', *Art and Antiques*, May 1972

Dyke, Peter, 'Dora Holzhandler', *Arts Review*, 6 May 1972

Fealdman, Barry, 'Naive Joy', *Jewish Chronicle*, 3 March 1978

Fealdman, Barry, 'The Magical Naivety of Dora Holzhandler's Paintings …', *Jewish Chronicle*, 1 March 1985

Fealdman, Barry, 'An Honest Look at the World', *Jewish Chronicle*, 22 November 1985

Fealdman, Barry, 'Jewish Life by Design', *Jewish Chronicle*, 30 October 1987

Fealdman, Barry, 'In the Folk-art Idiom', *Jewish Chronicle*, 14 April 1989

Fealdman, Barry, *Jewish Chronicle*, 26 April 1991

Fealdman, Barry, 'Childhood Memories of Paris', *Jewish Chronicle*, 15 May 1992

Hale, John, 'The New Naives', *Town Magazine*, November 1964

Hossach, Ian, 'Refreshing Perspective of Her Art', *The Glasgow Herald*, 14 October 1994

Lee Tomkins, Sharman, 'Dora Holzhandler', *Arts Review*, 25 June 1976

Morgan, Kathleen, 'In the Frame', *The List*, 21 October 1994

New Moon (unsigned preview), December 1990

Newton, Eric, *The Manchester Guardian*, 6 February 1962

Russell Taylor, John, 'In the House of Fun', *The Times*, 30 March 1996

Rydon, John, 'The Queen … as You Have Never Seen Her Before', *Daily Express*, 27 March 1971

The Sunday Times, 'Paper Dolls' (unsigned preview), 18 April 1991

Talbot, Linda, 'A Naive Domesticity', *Hampstead and Highgate Express*, 30 October 1987

Talbot, Linda, 'The Mundane Mysticism of Folk', *Hampstead and Highgate Express*, 14 April 1989

Trauts, Trebor, 'Dora Holzhandler', *Arts Review*, 19 May 1973

Vann, Philip, 'Holland Park Transfigured', *The World of Interiors*, February 1985

Vann, Philip, 'In Search of Their Roots', *The Artist*, March 1985

Vann, Philip, 'Dora Holzhandler', *Arts Review*, December 1985

Vann, Philip, 'Marvelling at the Mundane', *Jewish Chronicle Magazine*, 25 September 1987

Vann, Philip, 'Dora Holzhandler', *Galleries*, April 1989

Vann, Philip, 'Dora Holzhandler: A Temperamental Primitive', *Artist's and Illustrator's Magazine*, September 1990

Vann, Philip, 'Magical Mystical *Tour de Force*', *Jewish Chronicle*, 14 October 1994

Vann, Philip, 'The Peaceable Kingdom', *Country Living*, December 1995

Vann, Philip, 'Dora Holzhandler', *Contemporary Art*, Winter 1996

Vincent, Martin, 'Dora Holzhandler', *City Life*, April 1995

Wadia, Bettina, *Arts Review*, 21 March 1964

Wertheimer, Fay, 'Happy Happening Hippy', *Manchester Evening News*, April 1995

Williams, Sheldon, 'Dora Holzhandler', *L'Arte Naive* (Reggio Emilia, Italy), October 1975

SELECTED BOOKS REFERRING TO THE ARTIST

Garland, Madge, 'The Changing Face of Childhood', in John Hadfield (ed.), *The Saturday Book*, Hutchinson, London, 1962

James, Ian, *Inside Israel*, Franklin Watts, London, New York, Sydney, 1990

Korn, Irene, *A Celebration of Judaism in Art*, Todtri Productions, New York, 1996

Langley, Myrtle, *Religion*, Dorling Kindersley, London, New York, Stuttgart, 1996

Lister, Eric, and Williams, Sheldon, *20th Century British Naive and Primitive Artists*, Astragal Books, London, 1977

Rushton, Willie, *Adam and Eve*, Bell and Hyman, London, 1985

Schwab, Walter, and Weiner, Julia (eds), *Jewish Artists: The Ben Uri Collection*, Ben Uri Art Society and Lund Humphries Publishers, London, 1994

Spalding, Julian, *Gallery of Modern Art, Glasgow: The First Years*, Glasgow Museums and Scala Books, London, 1996

Williams, Sheldon, entry in *The World Encyclopaedia of Naive Art*, Frederick Muller, London, 1984

Work in Public Collections

SELECTED CATALOGUES

Vann, Philip (ed.), *New Frontiers of Naive Art in Europe*,
    Royal Festival Hall, London, Muller, Blond and White,
    London, 1984
Dora Holzhandler, Crane Kalman Gallery, London, 1985
*First American Exhibition: Dora Holzhandler – Paintings and
    Watercolours*, Foreword by Edna O'Brien, Graham
    Modern Gallery, New York, 1985
Peintres Naïfs Britanniques, British Council and Rona
    Gallery, London, 1986
Dora Holzhandler, Rona Gallery, London, 1987, 1989
Dora Holzhandler: Glasgow '90: Festival of Jewish Culture,
    Rona Gallery, London, 1990
*L'Chaim! To Life!: The Jewish Year in the Art of Dora
    Holzhandler*, St Mungo Museum of Religious Life and
    Art, Glasgow, and Rona Gallery, London, 1994

Brighton Art Gallery and Museum

Musée d'Art Naïf Anatole Jacovsky, Nice

The Ben Uri Art Collection, London

The Gallery of Modern Art, Glasgow

The Museum of Art, Haifa

The Museum of London

The Nuffield Foundation

The St Mungo Museum of Religious Life and Art, Glasgow

The Sternberg Centre, London

Photographic Credits

All works are private collection unless otherwise stated in
the captions. All transparencies have been lent by Rona
Gallery, except the following:

The artist
Plates 15, 16, 20, 22, 23, 28, 29, 36, 49, 52, 64, 65, 66, 67, 68,
    69, 74, 75, 77, 95, 96, 97, 98, 99, 100

Bridgeman Art Library
Plates 2, 12, 47, 57, 72

Crane Kalman Gallery
Plates 1, 4, 6, 7, 8, 46, 59, 70, 76

Gallery of Modern Art, Glasgow Museums
Plate 61

Holland Gallery
Plates 17, 56, 58, 71, 73

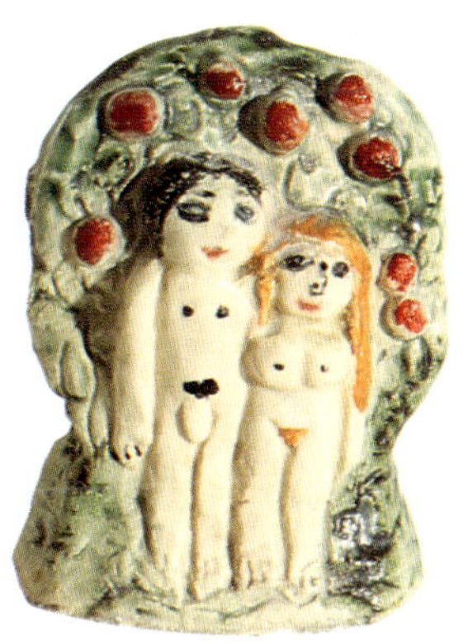

Plate 100
Adam and Eve   1990   Ceramic
7.6 x 5 cm (3 x 2 in)

Index

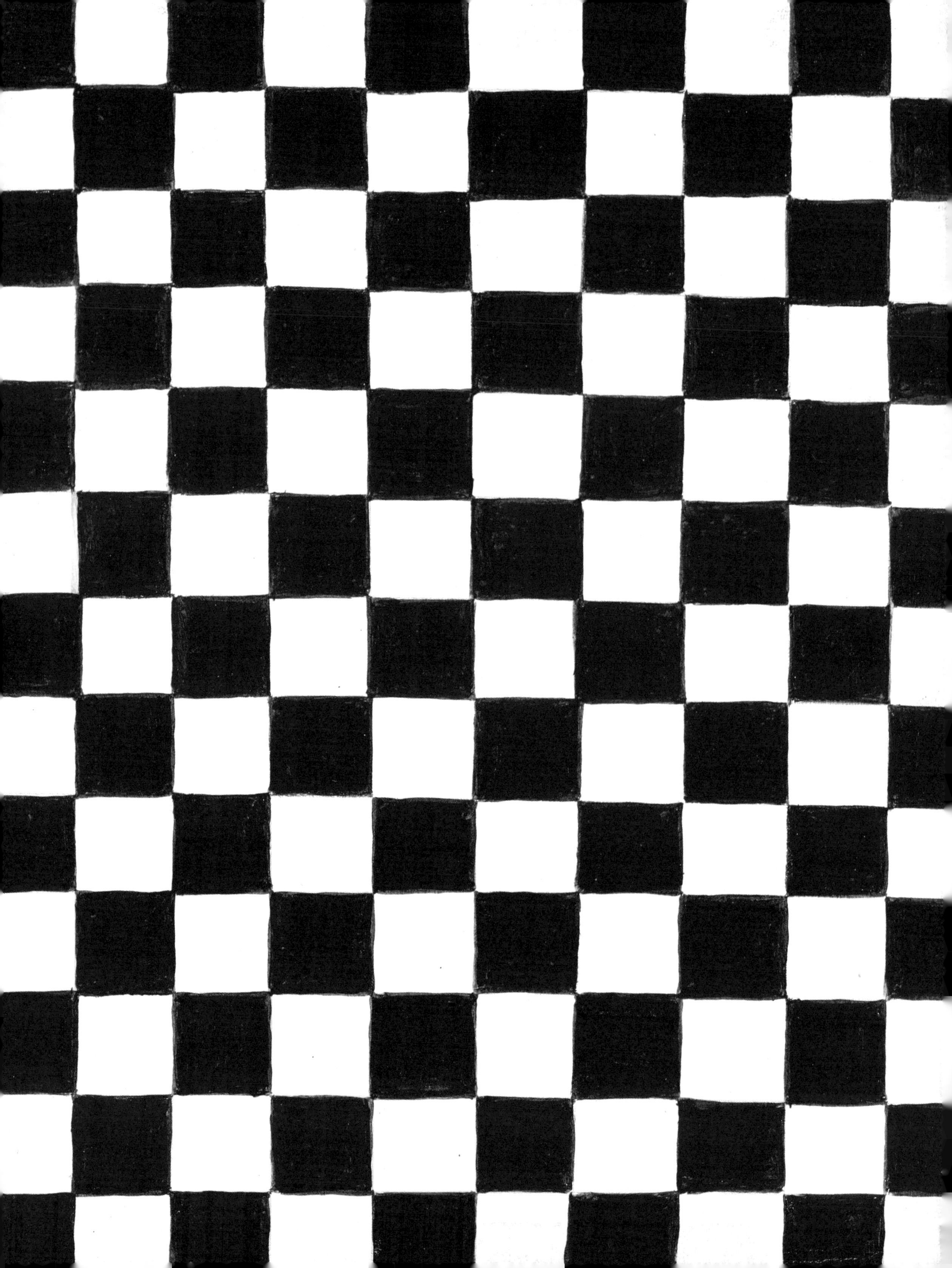